The Silent War

The Silent War

A History of Western Naval Intelligence

RICHARD DEACON

David & Charles
Newton Abbot   London   Vancouver

Hippocrene Books
New York, NY

British Library Cataloguing in Publication Data

Deacon, Richard
  The silent war.
  1. Intelligence service—History   2. Navies—History
  I. Title
  359.3′432′091812   VB230

  ISBN 0-7153-7557-1

Set in 11pt Monotype Baskerville
and printed in Great Britain
by Latimer Trend & Company Ltd Plymouth
for David & Charles (Publishers) Limited
Brunel House Newton Abbot Devon

Published in the United States of America
by Hippocrene Books, Inc.
171 Madison Avenue
New York, NY 10016

Library of Congress Catalog Card Number 78-51955
ISBN 0 88254 466 7

Published in Canada
by Douglas David & Charles Limited
1875 Welch Street North Vancouver BC

Contents

		page
1	From Enmity to Neutralism	9
2	Submarine Influence	29
3	The Beginning of Organized Intelligence	42
4	Planning for War	59
5	Communications Revolution	74
6	Admiral Hall: A Modern Machiavelli	96
7	Intelligence and Submarine Warfare	116
8	Germany Solves British Ciphers	133
9	The Misinformation Game	147
10	Lessons of Pearl Harbor	168
11	The Turning Point	180
12	The Cold War	198
13	Intelligence on the Seabed	215
14	The Spy-Ship as an Aid to Political Strategy	224
15	Chess Under the Oceans	238
16	Ocean Surveillance Above and Below	251
17	Glimpse Into the 1980s	264
	Notes	275
	Bibliography	282
	Acknowledgements	284
	Index	285

List of Illustrations

page

Benjamin Franklin 17

The Bauer U-boat 18

Commander Charles Davis as US Chief Intelligence
    Officer 18

Wilhelm Steinhauser, head of the German spy ring in
    England in 1914 35

Louis Alexander Mountbatten 35

A. E. W. Mason 36

Admiral Grigorovich congratulating Francis Cromie 36

Franz von Kleist Rintelen 53

Felix von Luckner with Sir Reginald Hall and Admiral
    Borrett 54

Lieutenant Joseph Rochefort 71

Rear Admiral Doenitz welcoming a U-boat crew on its
    safe return to base 71

Map of Pearl Harbor discovered by the US Navy in a
    captured Japanese submarine 72

Inside the Admiralty decoding room, February 1941 89

Ian Fleming at the Admiralty 89

Captains L. F. Safford and A. D. Kramer during the
    hearing of the Joint Pearl Harbor Inquiry Committee 90

Admiral Alan Kirk 107

Captain Ellis Zacharias 108

page

Lyndon Johnson awards the National Security Medal to
Frank Rowlett   125

The Purple Machine   125

US Navy low-level photograph of Mariel, Cuba, showing
Russian armaments   126

Artist's impression of *Alvin*   143

Photograph from *Alvin* of the nose of the US thermonuclear weapon that fell into 400 fathoms off the coast
of Spain   143

The deep ocean floor as seen from *Trieste I*   144

The *Hughes Glomar Explorer*   144

I

From Enmity to Neutralism

It was by exploration that naval intelligence first developed, and perhaps the first example of this was when Alexander the Great ordered the building of a glass barrel to explore the depths of the sea 'for obtaining intelligence therein'. Curiously enough, it began in the very area in which today it plays the most vital role of all—beneath the oceans. There was a feeling that probing underwater would produce more results. Thus Bohaddin, an Arabian historian, mentioned a submarine craft which enabled a sailor to get into Ptolemais when that city was under siege during the Crusades; and Sir Nicholas Harris Nicholas, the nineteenth-century historian of the Royal Navy, referred to the fourteenth-century use of 'Kettle Hats', special helmets supplied to those employed in a primitive form of submarine reconnaissance.[1] Leonardo da Vinci, the Florentine Renaissance artist and inventor, developed plans for an underwater warship, but kept them secret. He was afraid that the knowledge gained from such an enterprise would make war even more frightful than it already was.

Western naval intelligence developed somewhat haphazardly from the struggle between Britain, France, Holland and Spain for the mastery of the western seas; it was largely organized by the secret services of those powers and not by their navies. That able and pertinacious Elizabethan statesman, Sir Francis Walsingham, gave Britain an advantage in this respect. He alone, by building up a secret service which he frequently financed out of his own pocket, made it possible for the build-up of the Spanish Armada to be accurately assessed in London. Communications may have been slow, hazardous and often hindered by the arduous task of deciphering messages; yet, through the network which Walsingham established in Spain, France, Italy and Portugal, he was able to send to Queen Elizabeth I purloined copies of the reports of the Grand Admiral of the Spanish Navy, the Marquis of Santa Cruz. These reports provided all the information anyone could wish to know about the Armada—the numbers and types of ships, their armaments, personnel and stores. Walsingham's final document to his Queen was entitled: 'A Copy of the General and Particular Relation which the Marquis and the Secretary, Barnaby de Pedrosa, sent to the King of Spain on 22 March 1587, containing a list of ships in various ports, of sailors, soldiers, stores, details of wages and other expenses.'[2] Walsingham was in fact the father of organized modern espionage, and it was his insistence on giving absolute priority to naval intelligence that saved England from invasion.

The clergy, whether Anglican or Roman, were prominent among the early underwater-craft inventors, and most of them seem to have been impressed with the idea of using such 'boats' as instruments for spying. John Wilkins, Bishop of Chester, wrote a book in the early seventeenth century entitled *Mathematical Magick*, in which he described how 'an ark could be soe framed for submarine navigacion . . . and which can, with a modicum of intelligente imaginacion, be adapted to be bothe the eyes and the ears of the King's Navie'. One can only interpret this as a proposal to use the craft for espionage. The seventeenth-century Abbé Borelli designed another underwater boat, a craft propelled by underwater oars with blades which opened and shut like a fish's fin. A picture of this craft appeared in the *Gentleman's Magazine* in 1749, by which time a prototype had been built by Nathaniel Symons of Devonshire. Again, it was a Jesuit priest, Ciminius by name, who wrote to the French King in 1685 that he had invented a craft that would 'enable men, and even armies, to rise and descend to the bottom of the sea, fully armed, their hands and feet at liberty, to stay there for a whole week'.

Had the submarine, even in its most primitive form, been developed by any single navy in this period it would have given a great fillip to purely naval intelligence, and might even have switched some political power from the armies to the navies.

But, in the seventeenth and eighteenth centuries, naval espionage still largely depended on what was provided by the civilian secret-service chiefs and the military. At that time, control of cryptography, for example, was vested mainly in the military, especially in France. It was John Wilkins, that same Bishop of Chester, who wrote a manual on cryptography stressing again that the Royal Navy had a greater need for developing ciphers than the Army.

The prime interest of most senior naval officers in the field of intelligence in these centuries was for information which would lead them to capture ships and obtain prize money. It was as a result of intelligence passed to him by a Jewish agent in Jamaica that Admiral Blake captured the Spanish Fleet at Teneriffe in the Cromwellian era. Much the same applied to all Western navies of this period. Senior naval officers preferred to keep intelligence to themselves and to exploit it for private gain. Information that should have been passed on was retained for purposes of individual piracy.

Between 1770 and 1800 there was an attempt by the French naval chiefs to develop a more radical intelligence system. No less than four Frenchmen designed submarines, though only one of these—that of Le Sieur Dionis of Bordeaux—got beyond the drawing-board stage. One of these Frenchmen, Beaugenet, aimed to take an underwater craft up the Thames to London Bridge, planning, as he put it, 'to obtain advance intelligence of the enemy's intentions and armament'.

The history of American naval intelligence began with the War of Independence, which revolutionized concepts of naval espionage on both sides of the Atlantic. The American Colonists, starting absolutely from scratch, had to create some formalized espionage service against the most powerful navy in the world, that of the British. At first this was organized by Major Benjamin Talmadge of the Second Regiment, Light Dragoons, nominated for this task by General Washington. Talmadge had been in the same class at Yale University as Robert Townsend, his junior officer, and the close understanding between them was influential in the field of naval intelligence, particularly as Townsend lived in Oyster Bay, New York State, and was therefore in a strategic position to observe the movements of the British fleet which was blockading the coast.

The naval intelligence of the Colonists was a highly specialized and successful operation within the larger network controlled by Talmadge. It was given the code-name of 'Samuel Culper'. Probably to baffle inquisitive allies, Townsend was 'Samuel Culper, Junior', while Abraham Woodhull was 'Samuel Culper, Senior'. Townsend's store, well stocked with goods, was visited by many British customers, all of whom were discreetly quizzed in the hope that they would unconsciously let drop some vital titbit of information. Townsend himself moved between Oyster Bay and New York, while Woodhull, with whom he was in constant contact, remained in Setauket. Communications were primitive. Messages were often passed verbally by horseback riders, while Woodhull's confederate, Caleb Brewster, hoisted a black petticoat on a clothes-line to signal to Woodhull his arrival on the shore of Long Island. It was Brewster, an experienced sailing man who knew every current, every twist and turn around the coasts, who supplied the bulk of the information on British naval movements. Up and down Long Island Sound he sailed, and sometimes some distance out to sea, a diligent, skilled observer who was responsible for a wealth of material that eventually reached Washington himself.

Most of these reports were written in invisible ink between the lines of normally written letters. Many of them are still preserved, notably in the Washington Papers. James Jay, brother of the first Chief Justice of the United States, was the inventor of this invisible ink and he wrote: 'I writ with black ink a short letter to him, his brother and likewise to one or two other persons of the family, none exceeding three or four lines in black ink. The residue of the blank paper I filled up, invisibly, with such intelligence and matters as I thought would be useful to the American cause. All these letters were left open.'[3]

Invisible ink was used because, at that time, the crude codes of the day were being broken all too easily and quickly. This network was, however, dangerously compromized more than once by the insistence that it should undertake counter-espionage as well as espionage. The two functions rarely mix and Townsend was forced to go in fear of his life as a result. He reveals something of his problems in this letter, dated 20 October 1780.

When I conclude to open another route, you shall be informed of it. I do not choose that the person you mention, or any other of his character, should call on me. . . . The army which embarked last week are generally supposed intended to make a diversion in Virginia or Cape Fear in North Carolina, to favour Lord Cornwallis. They take but few horses, but a number of saddles with an intention to mount a number of dismounted dragoons who are going with them. The Cork and English fleets are, I expect, arrived by this. I hope and expect that all my letters are destroyed after they are perused,

Samuel Culper, Junior.[4]

David Bushnell, an American from Maine, was the first to design a submarine which could be armed with a primitive type of torpedo, in 1771. The 'Culper' network was anxious that this craft should be used to spy on enemy shipping, but were overruled by the military who insisted that the craft, *Turtle*, should be employed for action against shipping. In 1776 Bushnell despatched a sergeant, Ezra Lee, in the submarine to attack HMS *Eagle* in the Hudson River. The attempt ended in failure and Lee narrowly missed blowing himself up.

Submarine construction and, indeed, the kind of intelligence for which the craft was intended by many of its early advocates, might have developed much faster in the eighteenth century but for the fact that almost all inventors of underwater craft came up against a great deal of prejudice because the submarine was regarded as a mean, cowardly and inhuman method of warfare. In America, Puritan doctrines not only frowned on the underwater craft as an invention of the Devil, but the hatred of this new weapon was so marked that Bushnell eventually settled in Georgia and changed his name to Dr Bush, solely because he did not wish to be associated with the system of warfare which had been advocated for his craft. And it was not until the Civil War, in the middle of the next century, that the submarine was at last regarded as a legitimate instrument of war.

Naval intelligence directed from America outside her own shores began with the appointment of such naval agents as William Bingham in the West Indies, Oliver Pollock in

Louisiana (then French territory), and Benjamin Franklin, Silas Deane, John Adams and Arthur Lee in Paris. These latter also used assistants in various Dutch, French and Spanish ports. The biographer of John Paul Jones, Samuel Eliot Morison, indicates that Adams and Franklin were responsible for setting up a Navy purchasing and liaison office in Paris and this was the nucleus of an American naval intelligence office in Europe.

The picture of all this is still confused, or confusing, unless one is a fanatical partisan of one side or the other. In no sphere was it more confusing or controversial than in that which concerns Benjamin Franklin, still somewhat of an enigma even to detached modern historians. For Franklin is on record as having stated that the Colonists would never win without having 'first-class intelligence of the activities of the Royal Navy' and the advantage of France as an ally. For much of the war Franklin was, in private, frankly a pessimist, secretly critical of all the Colonists' generals, including Washington, and sometimes almost a defeatist. That he himself supplied a very great deal of naval intelligence is unquestioned; that he could interpret what he learned correctly and pass his interpretation on to others is indisputable.

There is something about Franklin which makes even the most objective of historians bend his head in a reverence which sometimes blinds him to the truth. More than Washington, more than Alexander Hamilton, both of whom are now seen to have had feet of clay, Franklin holds a kind of secular beatitude in the minds of American historians. Yet the question must be asked, shocking though it may sound, was Benjamin Franklin a secret British agent? 'So great is the reputation [of Franklin] that almost no modern writer has undertaken to question the uprightness of his actions, or failed to accept his testimony at face value,' wrote T. P. Abernethy in his account of the often strange relationship of Franklin and Arthur Lee. 'Such historical practice is, of course, not justifiable. A discarding of hero-worship and a careful weighing of all contemporary evidence would produce a conclusion quite different from that which has been reached.'[5]

Some years ago intensive research by various university professors was carried out with the aim of refuting the allegation that Franklin was a member of the notorious Hell-Fire Club, the nickname given to the secret society known as the 'Knights of St. Francis of Wycombe', founded by Sir Francis Dashwood, one-time Chancellor of the Exchequer in Britain. They failed to reach any firm conclusion on the matter. Yet the evidence on the British side of the Atlantic points conclusively to his membership of this strange society under whose cloak of revelry lay a centre of British espionage. Franklin's membership of such a society would seem to be either totally out of character, or else suggest that he was the complete hypocrite. For, by becoming a member of this society, Franklin, the Presbyterian and moralist, became close friends over a number of years with a notorious and dissolute rake.

The Hell-Fire Club originated in London, moved to an island on the Thames between Cookham and Marlow, thence to a disused Cistercian abbey at Medmenham and finally to some caves carved out of the hill on which stood West Wycombe Church. The male members of the club were known as 'monks' and wore habits of various colours; the females were called 'nuns' and wore white habits and masks to preserve their anonymity: a club rule stated that 'the ladies consider themselves as the lawful wives of the Brethren during their stay within monastic walls'. Was it so strange that the sober scholar, Franklin, became a member of such a club? In 1745 he spent a whole year in bawdy revelry in the taverns of Philadelphia and wrote verse such as: 'Fair Venus calls: her voice obey/In beauty's arms spend night and day.' Even in his seventies Franklin was frantically pursuing Madame Brillon, the young wife of an ageing French treasury official. Franklin's correspondence and his papers show that he stayed at West Wycombe House in the summers of 1772/3/4. Significantly, he paid a sixteen-day visit there in July 1772, which was the month each year in which the Chapters of the Franciscan Brotherhood were held, normally lasting two weeks.

The most conclusive evidence of Franklin's membership comes partly from his own writings and partly from independent sources. In a letter he sent to a Mr Acourt of Philadelphia, not quoted by any of the Franklinophiles, he mentioned 'the exquisite sense of classical design, charmingly reproduced by the Lord le Despencer at Wycombe [Dashwood had by then been elevated to the peerage], whimsical and puzzling as it may sometimes be in its imagery, *is as evident below the earth as above it*'. This must surely be a reference to the caves and, as nobody but a member of the club was allowed into them, this alone suggests that Benjamin was a member.[6]

There is also the story, told by the painter Guiseppe Borgnis, that when he went with Franklin to an inn at Marlow the landlord asked: 'Is not that Master Franklin?'

'No,' replied Franklin, 'it is Brother Benjamin of Cookham.'

And in one entry of the society's wine books is the note: 'On the 7th. of July, 1773; Brother Benjamin of Cookham, 1 bottle of claret, 1 of port and 1¾ of calcavello.'

What intrigued the French was the political nature of the society's membership. Apart from Le Despencer and Franklin, members included the Earl of Sandwich (First Lord of the Admiralty), Thomas Potter (Paymaster-General), the Earl of Bute (a former Prime Minister) and John Wilkes, George Selwyn and Bubb Dodington, all Members of Parliament. Another member was a former French spy who had sought refuge in England—the Chevalier d'Eon de Beaumont who had originally been sent to London to discover how best the French could invade that country. Mademoiselle Perrault, of Paris, the descendant of one of the 'nuns' of Wycombe, has testified that the diaries of her ancestor reveal that d'Eon made Franklin's acquaintance in the early 1870s and that 'Franklin used d'Eon, whom he trusted, to advise him of the pitfalls of French political intrigues, and he allowed d'Eon to use him as an informant on French affairs and secret plans to be passed on to the British.'[7]

That Franklin tried, in his own subtle way, to serve two nations—England and the cause of the American colonies—is plain enough up to about 1770. Thereafter there was much double talk and contradictory action. He did not regard this as two-faced, but as working out his own grand design for world politics which he alone among the colonists could perceive. This was not arrogance, but a realization that his intellectual powers were far superior to those of the Colonial leaders. Franklin's grand design was that there was room in the future for a free America and an all-powerful British Empire. One could say that in a devious and somewhat circumlocutory man-

1 Benjamin Franklin (1706–90)

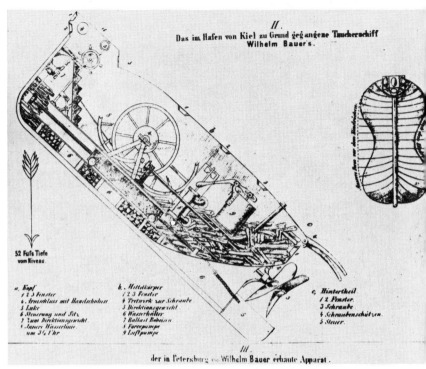

II.

Das im Hafen von Kiel zu Grund gegangene Taucherschiff
Wilhelm Bauer's.

52 Fuſs Tiefe
vom Niveau.

a. Kopf   b. Mittelkörper   c. Hintertheil
1 2 3 Fenster   1 2 3 Fenster   1 2 Fenster.
4 Armschluss mit Handschuhen   4 Tretwerk zur Schraube 3 Schraube
5 Luke   5 Direktionsgewicht   4 Schraubenschützen
6 Steuerung und Sitz   6 Wasserhälter   5 Steuer.
7 Zum Direktionsgewicht   7 Ballast Behälter
1 Innere Wasserlinie   8 Forcepumpe
um 3½ Uhr.   9 Luftpumpe

III.

der in Petersburg von Wilhelm Bauer erbaute Apparat.

2 (*above*) A diagrammatic view from 1855 of the Bauer U-boat, indicating also
how the catastrophe occurred in the Kiel harbour

3 (*below*) Commander Charles Davis seated at his desk while serving as US
Chief Intelligence Officer, 1889–92. Standing to the left is Harry Smith, Chief
Clerk, and seated in the background is Lieutenant G. W. Mente (*US Navy*)

ner Franklin was the first of the prophets of an Atlantic alliance. He liked the English way of life and once told his Scottish friend, Lord Kames, that he had 'long been of opinion that the foundations of the future grandeur and stability of the British Empire lies in America'. True, this view was modified within ten years, but he retained his belief that a powerful British Empire was, in the long term, in the Colonies' as well as England's best interests.

Franklin was far-sighted enough to realize that America needed the Royal Navy as a shield for many years to come, that without this she might well be at the mercy of more predatory powers than Britain. His quest for intelligence, both as a private individual and as a diplomat, was devoted to this end. He feared that if the French were allowed to colonize unclaimed land in America, this might spoil his own chances of new acquisitions of territory. It was for this reason that he acquired lands in Canada and urged the British to colonize in the west to prevent the French from gaining further territory.

His deviousness is partly explained by a curious statement he once made in an essay entitled 'Observations on my Reading History in Library': 'the great affairs of the world, the wars, revolutions etc.,' were, he wrote, 'conducted by those who, while maintaining the public interest, acted from selfish interests whatever they may pretend'.[8] Thus at a time when he was proclaiming that 'America did not aim at independence', he was secretly arranging for the smuggling of arms into the Colonies to achieve that very aim which he disavowed. And later, when he was boldly and openly demanding independence without strings, in equal secrecy he was keeping the British Foreign Office and Secret Service informed not only on every aspect of Colonial policy, but on all manner of information concerning France and Spain.

Franklin fully realized that in Paris he was in a unique situation. If the Colonial forces lost, he could not be blamed and he would be safe from the British. From Paris he might then even be able to switch his allegiance back to Britain. On the other hand, if the Americans won, he could bask in the credit which his position as minister to France would give him. Thus, from his headquarters at Passy, Franklin continued to carry on writing to statesmen, diplomats and business partners in England—Lord Shelburne, Lord Camden, d'Eon de Beaumont, Thomas Walpole, Thomas Wharton and John Williams. Not only that, but many of those who worked in Franklin's headquarters and in his house at Passy were active and confirmed members of the British Secret Service.[9]

Blundering British generals in America had clumsily turned a revolt into a war and thereby precipitated a revolution. The British Secret Service, under the direction of the Hon William Eden, tried to retrieve this situation, pouring the oil of secret diplomacy on troubled waters and spending vast sums of money in bribes to set matters right. Eden (later Lord Auckland) left a large collection of papers which testified to the success of his espionage drive, showing that many who have hitherto been held up as American patriots were in fact agents of the British Secret Service. Perhaps the greatest surprise of all is that the American Navy Office and purchasing mission in Paris was the centre of this infiltration and that Benjamin Franklin himself was a tool of the British.

The Comte de Vergennes, who was so largely responsible for aiding the Colonists, complained that every move by the Americans in Paris was known to the British Ambassador, Lord Stormont. Arthur Lee, one time American representative in London, caustically commented that no precautions were taken in Franklin's Paris embassy to guard secrets, 'that servants, strangers and everyone was at liberty to enter and did constantly enter the room while we were talking . . . and that the papers relating to it lay open in rooms of common and continual resort'.

Inside the American Embassy was a cell of British intelligence organized by Edward Bancroft, Franklin's chief assistant and friend, passing on all information he obtained from his master straight to the British. Not only did Whitehall learn all the American secrets, but many items of French intelligence as well, for the French trusted Franklin and gave him a great deal of information. It might be argued that Franklin was duped by his assistant and was merely incompetent where security was concerned. But any close study of Franklin's character would belie such a suggestion. Franklin was widely travelled, sophisticated, an efficient administrator, worldly wise, cognisant of intrigues, naturally cautious and, above all, constantly warned of leakages of information from his embassy. It is unthinkable that he did not know what was going on. Most of this intelligence and indeed the bulk of the leakages concerned naval matters. What they ensured and what Franklin's undercover dealings with the British underlined was that his standing in London remained high and that, in the event of the Colonies failing to win the war, his influence with the British would still be considerable. This chapter is the story of the slow progress of all Western naval intelligence services from a state of almost permanent enmity to a tolerant neutralism. Franklin was the apostle of neutralism long before it came about.

Edward Bancroft was the key man in the British espionage network in France, yet without Franklin's information Bancroft would have counted for nothing. That he was highly regarded is clear from the fact that the British gave him a pension of £1,000 a year. Bancroft's information was usually passed to Lord Weymouth or Lord Suffolk, but Franklin kept to himself special tit-bits of intelligence which he wished to pass on personally, either direct to the British Ambassador, or by devious routes to the Franciscans at Wycombe.

In the papers of one John Norris, of Hughenden Manor, Buckinghamshire, there is the enigmatic comment: '3 June, 1778. Did this day Heliograph Intelligence from Dr Franklin in Paris to Wycombe.' Norris had built a 100ft tower on a hill at Camberley, Surrey, from the top of which he used to signal and place bets by heliograph with Lord le Despencer at West Wycombe.

Other agents of the British at this time, also specializing in naval affairs, were Paul Wentworth, American-born and a former agent for New Hampshire, and Silas Deane of Connecticut, a close friend of Franklin. Wentworth was head of the British network in France and co-operated with Franklin and Bancroft. Copies of most of Franklin's reports sent from Passy to America during the War of Independence are today in the British archives and many of them must have been sent to London by Bancroft under the code-name of Edward Edwards, with the knowledge of Franklin.[10]

In London it was well known that Franklin was by nature 'a man of property', obsessed by the acquisition of land. With this in mind William Eden, in 1777, authorized Paul Wentworth to pass on to Franklin the news that, without prejudice to past events, any American who could establish an accord between England and the Colonies could expect as his right any reward he desired, either of title, lands or office. Franklin must have received this information with more than a glimmer of interest, for at a later meeting with Wentworth he intimated that he might be prepared to go to London. Wentworth offered him a safe conduct pass and Franklin indicated that he might deal with a properly authorized person.

Had Franklin irrevocably rejected these overtures, it is unlikely that they would have been renewed in 1778, when William Pulteney, an English secret agent, made a further and more positive offer to Franklin to try to win him over. Franklin did not absolutely reject this offer, as his biographers have suggested, but made a copy of it, which he gave to Deane. The following month he wrote to Deane:

The negotiator is gone back, apparently much chagrined at his little success. I have promised him faithfully that since his propositions could not be accepted, they should be buried in oblivion. I therefore earnestly desire that you would put that paper immediately in the fire on receipt of this, without taking or suffering to be taken any copy of it, or communicating its contents.[11]

Franklin, the man who so meticulously preserved his own correspondence and took copies of all letters and papers received, was, in this instance, acting out of character. It is by no means certain that he did not at this very moment make some verbal arrangement with the British. But though he would not commit himself irrevocably to the British cause, Franklin continued to aid London with information. Sometimes this was done by direct diplomatic channel, for, on 11 July 1782, Richard Oswald was writing from Paris to Lord Shelburne in London:

... our conduct towards them [the Colonies] ought to be of a somewhat different nature: they have shewn a desire to treat and to end with us on a separate footing from the other

Powers, and I must say in a liberal way, or at least with greater appearance of feeling for the future interests and connections with Great Britain than I expected. I speak so from the text of the last conversation I had with Mr. Franklin . . . therefore we ought to deal with them tenderly and as supposed conciliated friends.

I really believe the Doctor [Franklin] sincerely wishes for a speedy settlement and that after the loss of dependence we may lose no more, but on the contrary that a cordial reconciliation may take place over all that country.

I was pleased at his shewing me a State of the aids they had received from France, as it looked as if he wanted I should see the amount of their obligations to their Ally, and as if it was the only foundation of the ties France had over them . . . which the Doctor owned in so many words.

In another memorandum Oswald wrote that he had been tipped off 'in the easy way of conversation with the Doctor' of an alliance with Spain. This information, he added, was passed on informally, 'yet, I imagine, with a view to its being properly markt and communicated, *also, and most likely, with the same good intention as on former occasions.*'[12]

This again suggests that Franklin had been passing on information to the British over a lengthy period. Oswald's view was that this 'early notice of a closer union with Spain' was communicated so that 'the consequences of a mistake on our part might be duly attended to, and in that sense perhaps friendly to England'.[13]

The last item of intelligence from Franklin was again indicative of his long-term view that a strong Royal Navy was in the best interests of America, for, however carefully concealed his true motives might be, it will be seen that a good deal of what he passed on to the British was information of special value for Britain's naval policy.

Franklin's mission to France was in part to organize and develop the Naval Office, while at the same time to win the French as allies against the British. And yet in the early years in Paris he expressed doubts about the wisdom of the latter aim in the light of the experience he gained in the Naval Office in Paris. To his old friend and lieutenant of the Philadelphia

Assembly, Joseph Galloway, he wrote in 1777: ' . . . we could maintain the contest, and successfully, too, without any European assistance, and I am satisfied . . . that the less commerce or dependence we have upon Europe the better we should do without any connexion with it.'[14] Franklin did not include Britain as being in Europe!

He may well have sincerely held this view, but it makes nonsense of the claims of so many of his biographers that he determinedly and consistently sought to bring France into the war on America's behalf. It has been said that it was Franklin's loyalty to Bancroft (the British spy in his office) that made him refuse to suspect treachery and that Arthur Lee, the man who railed most against spies in the Paris embassy, was insanely jealous of Franklin. But when Arthur Lee confronted Franklin with the charge that Bancroft was a spy in the services of the British and actually gave proof of this, showing how Bancroft's links with the British Secret Service had been uncovered, and how, when he visited London, he was in touch with the Privy Council, Franklin still stubbornly declined to accept the evidence. He countered by denouncing Lee and insisted that Bancroft's visits to London produced worthwhile intelligence for America.

The truth was that all Bancroft brought back from these trips was false information provided by the British, as Franklin must have known. And it was not only the quarrelsome Arthur Lee who denounced Bancroft, but John Quincy Adams and Jefferson as well. Even King George III spoke in these forthright terms of Bancroft: 'The man is a double-agent. If he came over to sell Franklin's secrets in London, why wouldn't such a fellow return to France with a British cargo for sale?'[15]

There is some evidence, too, that Bancroft often went to London to carry out commissions for Franklin on the Stock Exchange. When Franklin returned to America from France, a Congressional Committee was appointed to examine his accounts which showed a deficit of £100,000. Asked to explain this, Franklin enigmatically replied: 'I was taught as a boy to read the Scriptures and to attend to them, and it is said there, "Muzzle not the ox that treadeth out his master's grain" '?

Was Franklin really a double-agent, or were his leakages of information to London merely devious policy-making, partly personal and partly political? John Vardill, a loyalist clergy-man who was a British spy in London, overheard Joseph Hynson, a seafaring man from Maryland, boast to a girl that he was 'very close to Franklin'. He knew that Hynson was a potential recruit to the British Secret Service and he bribed him to betray American dispatches. Vardill's correspondence with Hynson, which is in the British Museum in London, reveals that Franklin passed on to London information about sailing dates, shipments and supplies to America and details of cargoes. This act of crass stupidity, if not downright treachery, caused great losses in American ships and cargoes.[16]

Lord le Despencer's illegitimate daughter, Rachel Antonina Lee, told Thomas de Quincey that her father, in his last years, used solemnly to toast 'Brother Benjamin of Cookham, who re-mained our friend and secret ally all the time he was in the enemy camp'. She asserted that 'Brother Benjamin' was Franklin and that he 'sent intelligence to London by slow and tortuous routes, sometimes through Ireland, by courier from France and through a number of noble personages in various country houses'.[17]

Nor was 'Brother Benjamin' the only code-name. It was in his use of not one, but many, peculiar code-names that Franklin sought to cover his tracks. In his letters from Passy he sometimes signed himself Jackson, Johnson, Nicholson and Watson. Vardill referred to Franklin as signing himself on one occasion as 'Naval Liaison Officer, Passy' and heading his communica-tion as 'Concerning the Freedom of the Seas'. The British Secret Service referred to Franklin in their dispatches as 'No 72'.

Much depends, in assessing Franklin's role in all these matters, on how one interprets the character of Arthur Lee. To Franklinophiles Lee is 'cantankerous', 'insane', 'obsessed with jealousy and hatred', 'vindictive and unreliable'. But all this is based on Franklin's own assessment of Lee. The former wrote of Lee in 1780, in a letter to Joseph Read, that he was a man to beware of, 'for in sowing suspicions and jealousies, and in cre-ating misunderstandings and quarrels, in malice, subtilty and indefatigable industry, he has I think no equal'. He suggested on other occasions that Lee was 'sick in mind'.

But whatever Lee's shortcomings, he was beyond any iota of

doubt a great American patriot. He deserves greater credit than has been bestowed upon him. He was direct and forceful where Franklin was evasive and acquiescent. Even Bancroft in his correspondence with Paul Wentworth made it abundantly clear that Lee was incorruptible—'impossible to bribe'. It is certain that Lee was just as convinced of Franklin's complicity of intrigues with the British as he was of those of Bancroft. He was sure that Franklin and Silas Deane had used, for their own purposes, funds provided by the Continental Congress and the Lee papers reveal this in Arthur's letter to Richard Henry Lee on 12 September 1778, when he alleged that Franklin was 'concerned in the plunder' and that in due course he would 'collect proofs' of this.[18]

In his relations with France Franklin was more than a match for nimble Gallic minds. Expressing his delight with 'this most civilized country in the world', he played the part of an ambassador of culture and science and almost ostentatiously cultivated a friendship with Voltaire. It was his clever fostering of the legend of Franklin the scholar and wit that made his reputation in France remain so high for years after his death.

A different picture altogether is given by Mathieu Pidauzat de Mairobert. This author revealed in *L'Espion Anglais* that Franklin in private criticized the French aid to America in scathing terms, saying that

> ... not only do they sell their merchandise extremely dear, but they give us their rejects. In regard to arms especially, they have given us only discarded muskets, which have become in our hands more deadly to those who carry them than to our enemie; as for personnel, America has been the sewer of France. In place of the experienced officers we need ... we have received only blackguardly swindlers, men ruined in reputation or head over heels in debt, or conceited fops, insulting our sincerity, our good nature, seeking to debauch our wives and daughters, fitted to infect us with their own corruption, carrying vices until then unknown among us.

Perhaps this bitter assessment of French aid, allegedly passed on to the British, explains Franklin's early doubts about its value. There is no doubt that Franklin not only spied on the French, but used Bancroft in this role when he sent him to Ireland in 1789. In Lecky's *History of England* it is stated that 'no documental evidence exists of a French agent having been in Dublin in 1784, but it is certain that five years later one Bancroft, an American by birth, was sent on a secret mission from France to Ireland'. Now Bancroft would only have gone to Ireland on Franklin's authority and with his knowledge, but the interesting revelation is that he went there as an agent of the French. This much is clear from the researches of Dr Fitzpatrick in the Dublin archives and in the files of the French Foreign Office which contain Bancroft's report to the French.

It is plain from that report that Franklin had authorized Bancroft to make this trip on behalf of the French and that he knew its findings. The French had been interested in finding out whether it might be worth their while to support an Irish rebellion in the same way that they had helped the Americans. Bancroft's report severely discouraged any such project, urging that the Irish had no funds to pay for such aid, and that there was no prospect of any beneficial results for France from this plan.

Franklin seems always to have aimed to have a friend in every camp and somehow to have proved himself right in doing so. At the time of the peace negotiations, John Quincy Adams seems to have been convinced, against the majority, that Franklin was still playing a double game with the British. Adams saw in these negotiations that 'Franklin's cunning will be to divide us; to this end he will provoke, he will insinuate, he will intrigue, he will manoeuvre'. It was the verdict of a man, dismissed by Franklin as 'sometimes being out of his senses', but who, nevertheless, had had the sagacity to propose the appointment of General Washington as Commander-in-Chief. It was Adams who became Washington's vice-president and who finally succeeded him to become the second President of the United States.

Bancroft and Franklin remained friends long after the war and Franklin sought Bancroft's advice when writing his autobiography. After all, perhaps Bancroft was part and parcel of the legend, the vital part which had to be discarded. And who better than Bancroft to suggest which papers should be kept and which destroyed? And in 1787 it was Bancroft who put together some of Franklin's papers and had them published.

There was in Franklin's make-up something of Talleyrand, something of a medieval pope and even, at his worst, the amoral astuteness of Pierre Laval. On the other hand there were some of the virtues of Milton, Isaac Newton and William Blake. Perhaps his problem was that Franklin was a citizen of the world—an Atlantic man, if you like—in an age of imperialist rivalries. This may have given him a greater objectivity than his contemporaries and enabled him to turn treachery into a blessing and to ensure that the end justified the means. Certainly he was the first apostle of an Atlantic alliance: he had a remarkably fine grasp of the realities of naval power, coupled with a knowledge of what the freedom of the seas really meant. He concluded that for the future freedom of the seas America and Britain must pool their naval strengths so that, united, they could stand out against any other combination.

Never was a man so able, so erudite, so apparently idealistic yet so devious a diplomat and administrator, so avid a speculator that he made a fortune on the London Stock Exchange through his banker friend, Thomas Walpole, on the eve of France becoming an ally of America. Has there been, in the whole of history, a man who so effectively masked his worldly cynicism by an outward show of being a shy provincial scholar bent only on doing good deeds and actually publicizing himself as an honest man bewildered at the roguery around him. But, not to put too fine a point on it, probably both America and Britain benefited from Franklin in the sphere of intelligence that was often of a distinctly naval kind, and certainly it was Franklin who laid the foundation stone of America's own naval intelligence.

2

Submarine Influence

As far as naval intelligence was concerned there is no doubt that Britain enjoyed a great superiority over France during the Napoleonic Wars. In this field the British were more aggressive, more enterprising and far more ruthless.

How much first-class intelligence remained in Admiralty pigeon-holes in the light of what we now know of the often inefficient administration in London one cannot tell. But a study of some British coups of this period shows that in very many cases (probably all the successful ones) the Admiralty was by-passed and that the best of naval intelligence was either engineered by non-naval sources or by independently minded flag officers such as Nelson.

One enterprising agent who does seem to have established some contact with the Admiralty, however, was one John Barnett. He claimed that he had the confidence of women who were Napoleon's mistresses and managed to persuade the Admiralty to allow him to go aboard HMS *Lion* when that warship was cruising off the Egyptian coast in the Mediterranean. He proved to be a most assiduous collector of intelligence and organized a whole network of spies inside Egypt, including many low-paid French clerks. Making furtive trips ashore by night, by means of a small boat which took him from HMS *Lion* to Egyptian territory, he sometimes remained in Egypt for days at a time, visiting Cairo and, by bribing Egyptians and French alike, gradually built up a detailed dossier on Napoleon's life in the Egyptian capital.[1]

Another agent who greatly aided the Royal Navy at a

critical moment was James Robertson who had spent most of his life in a Benedictine monastery. Posing as a salesman, Robertson made trips to various islands off the Danish coast where Spanish forces under the Marquis de la Romana were marooned. The British aim was to enable them to escape. Robertson managed to contact de la Romana and he located the Spanish troops, getting a message across Heligoland to inform the British Admiral Keates to be ready to take off the Spaniards within the next few days. As a result the Royal Navy sent ships to Nyborg and took off some 9,000 troops who were taken back to Spain where they later took part in the Duke of Wellington's campaign.[2]

Nelson, as one would expect, organized his own intelligence network, trusting neither the Admiralty nor most other sources. Though he has not often been praised as an intelligence officer, he rated highly as an organizer in this field. He employed his frigate captains to keep watch from their ships on who went in and put out of various neutral ports, insisting on being kept informed on all such movements:

'. . . from Cape St. Vincent to the head of the Adriatic, I have only eight [frigates] which . . . are absolutely not half enough . . . frigates are the eyes of the fleet'. His shrewd assessment of the Baron Thugut, the sinister Chancellor of Austria, was apt. Of this upstart son of a Linz boatman, whose original surname was Thunigutt, meaning 'good for nothing', Nelson told the British Ambassador, Lord Minto: 'For the sake of the civilized world let us work together, and as the best act of our lives manage to hang Thugut . . . as you are with Thugut, your penetrating mind will discover the villain in all his actions . . . Pray keep an eye on the rascal.'[3]

The final confrontation with the French at sea depended to a large extent on accurate naval intelligence on the British side. True, Nelson often had to spend much time checking rumours like that he received from Cadiz that Villeneuve's allied fleets were heading for the Caribbean: 'if I hear nothing [further], I shall proceed to the West Indies'. Here Nelson was acting on a seaman's hunch that the rumour was right. As it happened Nelson soon had confirmation that Villeneuve was heading for the Caribbean from so reliable a source as Rear-admiral Donald Campbell, the British-born flag officer of the Portuguese Navy. Campbell was later sacked from his command for giving information to Nelson.

Occasionally Nelson received faulty intelligence. There was the occasion when General Brereton, commanding the British forces in St Lucia, informed him that 'it was apparently clear that the enemy had gone south' to attack Trinidad and Tobago. Nelson should have suspected the always dangerous qualification 'apparently'. Instead, he set off in pursuit only to find that Villeneuve's fleet had headed in another direction three days before. 'But for false information I should have been off Fort Royal as they were putting to sea,' wrote Nelson afterwards. 'Our battle, most probably, would have been fought on the spot where brave Rodney beat de Grasse.'[4]

It was not until 1800 that a practical submarine was actually floated in French waters and so revived the idea of an underwater method of gathering intelligence. This was the *Nautilus*, built after a design by the American engineer, Robert Fulton. But Fulton's craft failed on various attempts to damage British shipping and Rear-admiral Decrés rejected the invention on the grounds that it was 'fit only for Algerines and pirates'. Again, there was the prejudice: 'an immoral weapon', he called it. Even Napoleon I decided that Fulton was a rascally adventurer and became acutely suspicious when the inventor suggested that, if France would not use it as a weapon of attack, surely she could honourably employ it as 'a vital adjunct of intelligence'. So Fulton, not surprisingly, took his invention to the enemy, Britain, arriving in London in 1804 to offer his services.

The British seemed favourably disposed towards Fulton at first, despite the fact that he had already dealt with the French. Later Fulton wrote: 'Lord Sidmouth invited me to England and Mr. Pitt adopted my plan in part. I knew if it succeeded against the Boulogne flotilla, the ingenuity of the French engineers would be exerted: they would soon get possession of the engines with the mode of using them, and the invention would recoil on England to the destruction of her maine.'[5]

Quite what he meant by 'engines' is not altogether clear: certainly at this time there could be no question of engines, in the modern sense of the word, being used in a craft. But it would seem that Fulton, probably as a patriotic American, was so anti-British that he was prepared, despite a rebuff from the French, to double-cross the British authorities with whom he was dealing. Maybe he was attempting a one-man effort in counterespionage. But his statement suggests Napoleon I was perhaps not far wrong in his summing up of Fulton, who proved to be both rascally and perfidious. Documents show that he received as much as £1,653 18s 3d from the British Government 'in satisfaction of all claims'.

Lord St Vincent, First Lord of the Admiralty at the time, would have nothing further to do with Fulton and went so far as to assert that 'Pitt is the greatest fool who ever existed to encourage a mode of war such as this'. This damning statement finished Fulton as far as Britain was concerned and he returned to America. But the French had not altogether ignored the very experiments they professed to despise. They went ahead with their own research into the subject of underwater craft—not for the purpose of attack, but for gathering intelligence.

Just how disorganized naval intelligence was in the Napoleonic Wars is exemplified by this item of correspondence by William Pitt:

> The King consented that the correspondence with the naval officers, usually in the Board of Admiralty, should be given to Mr. Pitt . . . the rule or custom being, the Secretary of State sends all the orders respecting the Navy, which have been agreed to in the Cabinet, to the Admiralty, while the Secretary to that Board writes those orders out again in the form of instructions from the Admiralty to the Admiral or Captain of the fleet or expedition for whom they are designed. But during Mr. Pitt's administration he wrote the instructions himself and sent them to their Lordships to be signed, always ordering his Secretary to put a sheet of white paper over the writing. Thus they were kept in perfect ignorance of what they signed.[6]

This is perhaps the most notorious example in history of a navy being kept more or less in total ignorance of what it was doing, or being asked to do.

Possibly because, in Europe at least, it was the military who dominated both signalling systems and the development of cryptography, no strikingly original changes in intelligence methods came from the leading navies of Napoleonic times. Every flag officer was not a Nelson—himself an anti-Admiralty man—assiduously making his own arrangements to be kept informed, and for the most part such intelligence was passed laboriously by letter and only rarely by the most primitive forms of signalling. As late as 1800 the Admiralty still lagged behind even the private signalling system operated by John Norris of Hughenden Manor twenty years earlier. Yet in France it was the 'lightning telegraph' of M Chappe which enabled the simplest messages to be passed across land relatively swiftly. This system was the forerunner of the semaphore signal organization, comprising a network of posts with moveable arms which were set up along all the main roads radiating from Paris to the frontiers of France. The first comprehensive, instructional, naval signal book had been introduced in 1780, but it was not until 1817 that Captain Frederick Marryat of the Royal Navy adapted the French signalling system into a British model in which coloured flags represented the numbers of words listed in a 9,000-item signal book. Marryat, who served under Admiral Lord Cochrane, became a novelist when he retired from the Navy and found greater fame as the author of *Mr Midshipman Easy* and *Children of the New Forest*. Not until the first half of the nineteenth century came the revolution in communications of S. F. B. Morse—with the code that bears his name. It was this substitution cipher, with dots and dashes replacing letters, which forced the Western navies to take cryptography seriously and to develop new codes and ciphers, consequently improving intelligence systems which had varied from the brilliantly haphazard to the virtually non-existent.

In the 1850s, however, the subject of the submarine once again appeared on the distant horizon of advanced naval thinking as a potential instrument for intelligence-gathering. Since the War of Independence the Americans had become more acutely aware of the need for naval intelligence. It was because of superior naval intelligence prior to the battle of Lake Erie in the war of 1812 that, on 10 September 1813, the tiny 55-gun flotilla of Captain Oliver Hazard Perry USN, was able to

33

defeat the 65-gun British detachment under Captain Robert Barclay RN. It is probable that James Fenimore Cooper, author of *The Last of the Mohicans*, who was then serving as a midshipman in the US Navy on patrol vessels on the Great Lakes, was engaged in some kind of intelligence work, possibly leading up to the first spy-fiction novel, *The Spy* (1821), though the background for this book was the War of Independence.

The advent of steam and more powerful armaments meant that the navies of the world required specialized information on engineering and technical details and the US Navy was ahead of the Royal Navy in realizing the need to obtain this from trained observers. In 1827, the Secretary of the Navy, Southard, wrote to the American minister to the United Kingdom requesting his assistance in gaining

> ... accurate information of everything connected with the naval forces of other nations ... to communicate to me such information respecting the naval force of Great Britain, or other nations, as you may be able to procure ... especially respecting the number, situation, use and employment of their naval vessels, the number, character, etc. of their navy and dock yards; the number and mode of furnishing their seamen; the means of educating their officers; the amount and character of the expenditures; and, generally, anything which will enable this department completely to comprehend the extent and character of the naval means of the nation. Copies of the annual detailed estimates for the service would be useful.

Similar letters went out to ministers and representatives in thirteen other countries and the intelligence so gathered was added to that obtained by ships' officers regarding local conditions on their stations.

This could be called the beginning of the 'naval attaché system', one in which the United States Navy stole a march by demanding rather more positive information from its own attachés than did the British Admiralty.

The system gradually paid off and the Americans soon became aware of most new experiments being attempted on the continent of Europe as and when these affected naval matters.

4 (*right*) Wilhelm
Steinhauer, ex-Pinkerton
detective and bodyguard to
the Kaiser, was head of the
German spy ring in
England in 1914

5 (*below*) Louis Alexander
Mountbatten (1854–1921)

6 (*above*) The English author Alfred Edward Woodley Mason (1865–1948)

7 (*below*) Admiral Grigorovich, Russian Minister of the Navy, congratulating Francis Cromie RN, commander of the E19, which penetrated the Baltic from Britain

For example, Captain Matthew C. Perry, then commanding the steam sloop USS *Fulton*, was ordered to go to Europe in 1838 'for the purpose of collecting . . . information in reference to armed steamers . . . so far as permitted by the proper authorities'.[7]

According to the Soviet Ministry of Defence, the first Russian rocket-firing submarine was designed and built by General K. A. Shilder, a naval engineer, in 1834. This claim may be somewhat suspect, but independent sources in America and Germany suggest that it is none the less based on established facts. The craft was said to be 20ft long, with a displacement of 18 tons and able to descend to a depth of 40ft. The actual rocket was in the shape of a small barrel filled with powder and was exploded by an electric charge passing through a cable linked with electric batteries inside the submarine. These latter details would appear somewhat improbable to the expert, and independent reports state that when, on 24 June 1838, the submarine operated off Kronstadt, two rockets exploded before reaching their target and, when a further five rockets were fired, water filled the tubes and caused the craft to founder.

In 1846 the United States learned of the experiments being carried out by Dr Payerne when he built an 'underwater worker' for use in the construction of the huge breakwater at Cherbourg. The Americans sent an engineer over to France to obtain full details of this invention for their own naval authorities. It was partly as a result of this that an American shoemaker, Lodner Philips, built a cigar-shaped submarine boat a few years later. This had an underwater gun and was highly successful when it was launched in Lake Michigan.

Then, in 1850, Wilhelm Bauer built the first German submarine, a project that was taken up by the German Army! But when the craft made diving trials, Bauer narrowly escaped with his life. Having failed to impress the Germans or the Austrians, Bauer was then tempted by a British spy. A young naval lieutenant, on leave in Germany, agreed to pass on details of Bauer's craft to the British Admiralty. In the random and inconsequential fashion in which so much naval intelligence was conducted in that era, fate played a curious part in furthering Bauer's invention. The young lieutenant's message was supposed to be passed by a senior naval officer to the

Admiralty, but the former decided this was a Consular matter and sent the report to the British Consul in Hamburg. The latter had a friend who knew the Prince Consort and he decided to by-pass the British Foreign Office and let his friend have the information. Finally the story of Bauer's submarine landed on the desk of Prince Albert, Queen Victoria's husband.

The Prince Consort seems to have been interested in Bauer's plan, for the report was minuted by him for the attention of Lord Palmerston, the Foreign Secretary. Unfortunately, when Bauer was asked to come to Britain he was beset with ill luck. His new craft sank during trials and the crew went with her. However, he refused to admit defeat and took himself off to Russia. By this time he had remedied many of the defects of the craft and realized the need for showmanship. He made a surprise and triumphal entry into harbour in Russia to display his latest vessel. But despite this initial success, failure once again marred Bauer's experiments and the Russians tired of him, though they may well have utilized his plans in modifying their own submarine designs.

US Navy Engineer-in-Chief Daniel B. Martin was sent overseas in 1854, charged with obtaining all technical details of screw propellers. The Civil War saw agents from the USA extensively employed abroad on naval intelligence, reporting on the construction of warships in private yards in Britain as well as utilizing agents at home to gather information on the employment of naval personnel in Confederate-held territory. The two agents in Britain reporting on warship construction were William H. Aspinall and John M. Forbes, neither of whom was a naval officer. It was during the American Civil War that great advances were made in submarine development. The Americans were then the only power in the world which had attempted to set up espionage operations devoted solely to obtaining information on submarine construction.

They had followed very closely the experiments carried out in France and Russia and were not unmindful of their own discarded experiments through Bushnell in the War of Independence. In the USA, if not in Europe, the submarine was at last regarded as a vital and legitimate weapon and an accessory for intelligence. In 1866 the first self-propelling torpedo was invented by Robert Whitehead. The first submarine which actually sank another enemy vessel under combat conditions was the Confederate *Huntley*, built during the Civil War, the Union frigate *Housaatonic* being the victim.

It was in the 1870s that there occurred a bizarre episode in the history of the submarine which possessed all the elements of a melodramatic film—the beautiful Russian spy, the eccentric German inventor, Irish Republican plotters and a lone British agent who steals the plans of the submarine. The story began more or less where Wilhelm Bauer left off. A senior Russian naval officer who had been associated with Bauer's experiments had obtained plans of the craft and, when he died, they came into possession of his mistress, one Anna Popova.

Now Madame Popova was a member of what was jokingly referred to in European capitals as the Tsar's *corps d'élite'*, a carefully selected team of Russian ladies, specially noted for their good looks, charm and social qualities, who were used unofficially as emissaries and spies in various parts of the world. Anna Popova was sent to Washington and was in the American capital between 1876 and 1880, when relations between Russia and Britain were somewhat strained. Madame Popova's mission, apart of course from some discreet spying, was to exacerbate relations between the United States and Britain.[8]

One suggestion as to how Madame Popova should stir up trouble between the Americans and the British was that she should plead the cause of the Fenians, or Irish-American rebels, with leading senators and congressmen. It was an idea that horrified the Russian diplomats, but appealed to General Loris Melikoff, head of the Russian Secret Police. He instructed Anna Popova to make contact with the Fenians and report back to him. She had already made the acquaintance of such Fenian leaders as Colonel Clingen and O'Donovan Rossa and was able to report back to St Petersburg that the Fenian organization totalled more than 11,000, that its members were well disciplined and had their own codes and passwords, and that they were sworn on solemn oaths 'to prepare unceasingly for an armed insurrection against the British'.

Having made friends with Senator Jones of Florida, Anna Popova used him as an intermediary with the Fenians, discussing the possibility of Irish-American intervention on the side of Russia should war break out in Europe involving Britain.

Then, doubtless greedy for more money to sustain her lavish entertaining, Popova sold the plans of Bauer's submarine to the Fenians for a sum of $500.

The idea of acquiring a weapon which would enable them to attack the then supposedly invincible Royal Navy was seized on with imaginative alacrity by the Irishmen. They at once set up a small committee to study the plans and to examine the feasibility of developing the craft. But much technological progress had been made since Bauer first launched his submarine in 1850 and, while his plans were undoubtedly a help, they tended to show what to avoid when building a submarine rather than how to build one. Madame Popova's former lover had attached to the plans his own criticisms of the craft.

Nevertheless, the Fenians set about building a submarine and among the experts they consulted was John Philip Holland, a native of Liscannor, County Clare, Ireland, who had emigrated to New Jersey in 1872, where he took up a teaching post. Holland had begun sketching his own ideas of a 'submarine boat' while still at school. In New Jersey he not only maintained an interest in this subject, but actually built a submarine soon after his arrival in America. It was rather like a giant cigar in shape, some 16ft long and 2ft wide, operated by a one-man crew lying amidships and pedalling as on a bicycle, the pedals turning a propeller at the stern. After one of his designs was rejected by the US Navy, he linked up with the Fenians who not only gave him help, but asked for a design.

Eventually the Fenians built a submarine torpedo-boat on the Jersey side of the North River at a cost of some $37,000. This much was discovered by a British secret agent whose real name was Thomas Beach, but who had infiltrated the ranks of the Fenians under the name of Major Henri Le Caron. Beach had come into the British Secret Service by accident. As a young man he had left his home in Colchester for America and served in the US cavalry in the Civil War. Then he had discovered a strange-looking $20 bond with the words 'The Irish Republic' stamped across it. He made discreet inquiries and learned that these bonds were being used by the Fenians to raise funds in the USA, and that they were given in exchange for ready cash to any gullible Irish immigrant in America who could be persuaded that an Irish Republic was an imminent possibility. Beach's information was passed on to London and it was then that he was invited to spy on the Fenians.[9]

Beach's discovery of the Fenian submarine was perhaps his most important piece of intelligence and yet the one item that was so ineptly handled by the authorities in London. He obtained plans of the craft, together with sketches, and his report stated that 'nothing ever came of it, for it was apparently completed only to be towed to New Haven where it lay', presumably without ever having been put to any use. Maybe the cost of maintaining and developing such a craft was too great a drain on Fenian funds. Beach's report was eventually passed to the British Admiralty, but at that time there was no adequate intelligence organization to assess its value. The report lay in the Admiralty files, totally neglected for years.

It was not until the turn of the century that the major powers began to realize the significance of the submarine. Meanwhile Holland continued his experiments. His *Fenian Ram* was built in 1881, a 30ft, three-man craft, driven by a 17hp double-acting pil engine which gave her a speed of 7 knots on the surface. She had been armed with a tube in the bow from which dynamite could be forced under water. This was a great improvement on Holland's first craft, but he soon realized that it was very difficult to steer a submarine under water without some means of seeing where one was going! He persevered and, in 1887, when the United States Government—thanks mainly to advice from the newly created Office of Naval Intelligence—actually invited people to send in ideas about the best methods of building such craft, Holland submitted his seventh design and won a contract to build the first real US submarine—the *Plunger*. Later he improved this with further designs and the first active service submarine of the US Navy was named after him on 13 October 1913, one year ahead of the British.

Yet the British had had the chance to establish a lead of many years in submarine technology had they heeded Beach's report. Towards the end of the century a naval engineer found Beach's report in the archives and, as a result, Britain produced her first experimental submarine in 1901. But they could have had it a quarter of a century before, for as early as 1875 Holland's offer of a design to the US Navy had been rejected as 'a fantastic scheme of a civilian landsman'.

3
The Beginning of Organized
Intelligence

It was not until the late 1870s that the British Admiralty even considered the need for setting up a department for collecting and analysing intelligence on foreign navies and defence works and even then it was a timorous attempt which did not take effect for some years. Other navies were not much better, though the Americans and Germans showed some signs of developing proper intelligence systems.

Admiral Sir William James best summed up the complacent attitude inside the Royal Navy in this period when he stated:

> Apart from assisting the Army, the main duty of the Navy during those hundred years was policing the seas and 'showing the flag', and, as there was no prospect of a maritime war, the efforts of the officers and men were devoted to achieving a high standard of seamanship, discipline and smartness, and little attention was paid to fighting efficiency. . . . The tranquil life disappeared almost overnight. A rival had appeared and the time had come to concentrate on fighting efficiency, metallurgy, engineering and oil-power to increase the battle-power of all men-of-war.[1]

The rival was, of course, Germany. One of the reasons for the tardy realization by the world's navies of the need for systematized intelligence had been that, on the naval side, there had been so much less secrecy and more willingness among the powers to reveal each other's developments in the nineteenth century. While the armies had retained their mistrust of one another, the navies had been more anxious to exchange ideas. Throughout the middle years of the nineteenth century it had been the custom for European powers in periods of peace to throw open their dockyards and naval establishments, as well as their armament factories, to foreign inspection. There was, therefore, no particular impediment to obtaining intelligence in this sphere: it was something fairly simply obtained by any diligent naval attaché.

But by the late 1860s this situation had begun to change. The United States had already become somewhat more than disenchanted with the naval attaché system. It was felt that this method of obtaining intelligence was slow, limited and in many cases positively deficient. When the Civil War ended in 1865 the USA sent various technical missions to Europe with instructions that particular attention was to be paid to naval matters. From 1870–2 an ordnance mission was maintained overseas under the direction of Commander Edward Simpson USN, while Commodore C. R. P. Rodgers, whose son and grandson later joined Naval Intelligence, played a co-ordinating role. In 1882 the Office of Naval Intelligence was established by General Order 292, signed by William H. Hunt as Secretary of the Navy. This read:

23 March, 1882.

An 'Office of Intelligence' is hereby established in the Bureau of Navigation for the purpose of collecting and recording such naval information as may be useful to the Department in time of war, as well as in peace. To facilitate this work, the Department Library will be combined with the 'Office of Intelligence' and placed under the direction of the Chief of the Bureau of Navigation. Commanding and all other officers are directed to avail themselves of all opportunities which may arise to collect and forward to the 'Office of Intelligence' professional matter likely to serve the object in vew.

The main difference in this new development was that naval officers on active service as well as attachés could from then on contribute to naval intelligence. The ONI thus became the first real Government intelligence agency to function in Washington, and it is interesting to note that this body had a five years' start on the British whose Naval Intelligence Division (NID) was not created until 1887. The first US Chief Intelligence Officer was Lieutenant Theodorus Bailey Myers Mason and one of the first things he did was to publish a report which he had compiled on the Pacific war waged between Bolivia and Peru on the one hand, and Chile on the other.

Mason was a natural choice for this job. He had travelled widely in Europe and South America and had long since appreciated the need for some centralized organization which could evaluate intelligence reports. He had pressed this plan upon the Secretary for the Navy and, though surprised that one of such junior rank should be chosen for the post when it was created, vigorously set about organizing the Office. He was fortunate in having, in Secretary Hunt, an ardent reformer, but this was offset by Hunt being replaced by William E. Chandler a month after the Office was set up. Chandler, according to his biographer, Leon Burr Richardson, had had no experience of the Navy other than a brief stint as a solicitor attached to the Navy Office at the end of the Civil War and he had no knowledge whatsoever of foreign affairs.

A stickler for secrecy, Mason would brook no interference from outside in the affairs of the ONI. He only had three assistants to conduct the work of the Office which, in the early days, was only a tiny annexe of the Bureau of Navigation. They were A. G. Berry (later Rear-admiral Berry), Templin Potts (who later became Chief Intelligence Officer) and M. Fisher Wright. No special secretarial or clerical staff were allotted to the ONI and when such labour was required requests to borrow personnel from the Bureau of Navigation had to be made. The briefing given to Mason stated that 'in order that the [Naval] Department be supplied with . . . information as to the progress of naval science in this and other countries, and the condition and resources of foreign navies, an Office of Naval Intelligence has been established for the collection and classification of such information and for its publication as far as may be suitable.'[2]

The ONI was authorized to publish a monthly bulletin and to support the US Naval Institute. Bulletins were issued, but it is fairly certain that Mason kept a great deal of information for the eyes of very senior officers only. It was laid down that intelligence staff officers were to be recruited from those who showed proficiency in languages and 'drawing and sketching'.

Pressure for the creation of a properly organized naval intelligence came not from within the British Admiralty, but from naval attachés overseas. They could see for themselves that there was no adequate system of co-ordinating naval intelligence in Whitehall. Commander Hubert Grenfell, the British naval attaché in Rome, complained that there was a wealth of information that could be provided and much of it came to consular agents, but that they were loath to forward this to Whitehall because 'there is no well-known head of department on whose discretion they can rely'.[3]

Complaints from other centres were even more caustic. Naval attachés in France and Russia sent back reports that the organizations, of those countries as far as naval intelligence was concerned, were, in the 1870s, far superior to that of Britain. Some of this criticism filtered through eventually to the First Lord of the Admiralty, who was then W. H. Smith, founder of the well known chain of bookshops. It was Smith who recommended the creation of a naval intelligence division. Even then the admirals who had desks in Whitehall derided the idea of using naval officers in such a cause and fatuously suggested that an extra Civil Service clerk could do the work.

Thus the situation in Britain was almost the reverse of what it had been in the USA. In the former it was the naval attachés who were clamouring for a centralized system of intelligence and meeting resistance at the Admiralty. In the USA it was because of the lack of productiveness among the US naval attachés that a demand came from the Navy Department itself for setting up an Intelligence Office.

Little was achieved in Britain until the Admiralty received a most unwelcome prod from the Army, the underlying motive of which seemed to be to 'take over' naval intelligence. The man who stirred things up was Colonel Charles Gordon (later General Gordon), who was to be murdered by the Mahdi's forces at Khartoum. Writing from Mauritius, Gordon informed Lord Northbrook, the new First Lord, that it was 'owing to a want of knowledge that we have come to grief in many places; we have a great inclination to drift along till things come to a crisis . . . next to having no information is the having information and keeping it shut up.'

Gordon, who had had experience in the Far East as well as in Africa and the Indian Ocean, wanted naval intelligence to be passed to the War Office and assessed there. He blamed the Admiralty for not doing anything about the intelligence they received and failing to pass it back either to the Fleet or anyone else.

Following these complaints, Admiral Sir George Tryon agreed in principle, in 1882, to the setting up of a foreign intelligence bureau at the Admiralty, but dilatorily did no more than appoint a foreign intelligence committee with a naval officer as chairman to assist the Admiralty. The first Director of Naval Intelligence was Captain William Henry Hall, who, with a tiny staff, made what was in effect a dummy run of a naval intelligence organization. His preliminary work was followed up by Admiral Tryon in 1887 when the NID proper was brought into existence.

In the early stages of this Admiralty re-appraisal of the question of intelligence, fortunately, if somewhat fortuitously, attention was paid to ciphers as well and it was in this field alone that for some years any real progress was made. Admiral Sir Francis Beaufort, one of the more enlightened and literate minds of a relatively ill-educated officer class in the Royal Navy, created what was known as the Beaufort System which gave Britain a considerable lead over France and Germany in cryptography. Even Beaufort had to rely to some extent on a detailed memorandum compiled more than a quarter of a century earlier by a Lieutenant R. P. Cator who had devised a cipher system of his own and had even been in correspondence with Edgar Allan Poe on the subject. Cator had adapted the French Vigenère cipher by placing the index letters on the right instead of the left, completely reversing the Frenchman's encipherment process. But the papers Cator wrote had lain for years unread in an Admiralty pigeon-hole, suffering the same fate as Thomas Beach's report on the Fenian submarine. There is a record of a note from Admiral Beaufort to Cator, stating:

Poe has been of more help to British Intelligence than the whole pack of informers we employ. He has thrown an entirely new light on ciphers both from the point of view of creating new ones and of deciphering those of the enemy. Without a safe and accurate cipher system intelligence is almost useless. I find Poe of more use in this respect than Balzac, who has even managed to fox his French readers by his ciphers.[4]

This was obviously a reference to Balzac's *La Physiologie du Mariage*.

There was little for the new planners of intelligence to work on. Nearly all the worthwhile material had been obtained more than half a century previously and the early individualist enthusiasts had disappeared. For the most part the latter were either dedicated officers like Cator, or eccentric characters such as Commander Richard James Morrison, who appears to have combined a passion for intelligence with a devotion to astrology. Morrison, despite the fact that he joined the Navy at the age of eleven the year after Trafalgar, was also much better educated than most naval officers. He retired on half pay as a lieutenant in 1829, but somehow retained a mysterious part-time association with the Admiralty, as much later he was given the rank of Commander.

Morrison had specialized in navigation while in the Navy and this had led him to study astronomy, which, he later admitted, first aroused his interest in the subject of astrology. He was full of ideas which ranged from organizing a boys' force for the Royal Navy to utilizing astrology for intelligence purposes, and, in 1827, proposing a plan for 'propelling ships of war in a calm'.[5] Keenly interested in cryptography, Morrison developed a theory that astrology could be an aid to breaking down ciphers of other powers. His erudition led to his publishing, in 1860, the lengthy treatise on *Astronomy in a Nutshell, or the Leading Problems of the Solar System solved by Single Proportion only, on the Theory of Magnetic Attraction* and, two years later, the two volumes of his *Handbook of Astrology*. While one knows a great deal about Morrison's activities as an enthusiastic astrologer (under the *nom de plume* of Zadkiel Tao-sze he owned, edited and published *The Herald of Astrology*, later changing its title to *Zadkiel's*

Almanack), very little is to be gleaned about his intelligence work. He seems to have had a number of enemies in the Admiralty, even suing for libel one Rear-admiral, Sir Edward Belcher, and winning his case. Most probably many of his reports were either discarded or lost and their lordships looked upon him as either a crank or a mountebank. Yet he seems to have had the ear of the Prince Consort and had correspondence with Captain R. P. Cator, both men being members of an occult society called the Mercurii which, declared Morrison, was concerned with 'scientific intelligence . . . and was one reason why our meeting-place must remain secret'.[6] He took considerable pains to conceal his identity on occasions, not merely by employing the pseudonym of Zadkiel, but by calling himself 'Mr Samuel Smith' and addresses for him in the name of this fictitious person can be found between 1840 and 1860 in Paddington, Clapham, Cloth Fair in the City of London, Reading and various poste restante numbers.

Eccentric though he may have been, Morrison was highly regarded by the French Commandant Bazeries of the Army Cryptographical Department, one of the world's greatest authorities on ciphers. The latter said of him: 'He is a prophet neglected in his own country and would make an excellent director of espionage.'

Captain William Hall had to work almost single-handed to develop his intelligence network, having only a civilian clerk as assistant. His main contribution was to insist on a detailed analysis of foreign armaments production so that comparisons could be made with Britain's own firms. But Hall had to contend with fierce criticism. Lord Charles Beresford, who had been appointed a Junior Lord of the Admiralty, foolishly exposed the weaknesses of naval intelligence in a report which he leaked to the press. He stated that there was 'no staff to prepare for war' and that there should be a much larger intelligence department, divided into two sections, under the command of a flag officer. The *Pall Mall Gazette*, one of the most influential newspapers of the day, published Beresford's report and launched an attack on Hall, describing him as 'a mere compiler of information, a contemporary gazetteer in breeches'.[7]

This was grossly unfair to Hall who had himself provided Beresford with the information about the deplorable unpreparedness of Britain as regards naval intelligence. All Hall could do at this time was to point out the deficiencies of a service for which he was given neither funds nor staff to remedy. The Germans were not slow in picking up the report in the *Pall Mall Gazette* and there is a message, dated 3 November 1886, from Kapitan Moller to the German naval attaché in London, stating:

It is doubtful whether there is much worth while information in the archives of the British Admiralty and that which exists must be probably outdated. What is clear from the Beresford Report is that there is as yet no proper liaison between the British Admiralty and the armament firms in England. That is to say, as yet there is no attempt by the Intelligence Department of the Admiralty to conceal the vital work being done in various naval armament factories. It is quite clear that it is in this area that Germany must concentrate because the English in their quest for information have failed to realize that it is more important to protect the information they have on their own doorstep.

It was about this time that the German Navy called for a major effort by their own intelligence to obtain details of construction in British dockyards and armament factories.

In 1887 the post of Director of Naval Intelligence at the British Admiralty was handed over to Captain Bridge, but Admiral Sir Lewis Beaumont, who was at that time supervising the intelligence work, paid this tribute to Hall:

What I can and do congratulate you most truly and sincerely is having done six years of most valuable work under circumstances of great difficulty and discouragement . . . and it will be more and more known throughout the Service that, but for you, the Department, which is admitted by all to be essential, would have languished and died in the early years and might not have been recreated for many years.[8]

This period was the era of the cryptographers' battle: in the field of naval intelligence it was the one thing above all others that mattered vitally. It slowly dawned on the great naval powers of Europe that two things were essential in this sphere: first, that one kept changing one's own codes and ciphers to avoid discovery by a potential enemy; secondly, that one sought constantly to discover the systems being used by that same enemy. What had pushed cryptography into the foreground had been the development of telegraphic and wireless systems. France, which had been in the lead in cryptography, now lagged behind owing to a complacency about the Vigenère system. The Germans made considerable strides with elaborate double and triple transposition systems, but tripped up on their own ingenuity. Their cipher requirements failed to meet two cardinal requirements, that error should be minimized through ease of operation, and that it must not require special apparatus which, if it fell into the hands of the enemy, would reveal the secret of the cipher. Britain went ahead by producing the Playfair Cipher, one of the simplest then designed and therefore the most practical.[9]

This cipher was named after Lyon Playfair, a noted scientist of his day, but was actually invented by his friend, Charles Wheatstone. These two men are said to have amused themselves by deciphering coded messages which were at that time a feature of the London newspapers and out of this hobby grew a desire to improve cryptology. The British Admiralty was the first to realize, however, that good as the Playfair Cipher was, it was far from being safe from detection. It could not be broken down quickly, but once a decipherer had collected enough material in the way of messages he could break it by the use of the bigram frequency tables and the reconstruction of the ciphering square.

The armaments race, promoted mainly by the greed of the various groups of armament manufacturers which sprang up all over the world in the latter part of the nineteenth century, gave the naval intelligence services the task of keeping a constant watch on what the major arms firms were producing and to whom they were selling their goods. For it was to foment competition between swiftly growing navies that the arms magnates combined their productive zeal with political cunning. The boom in the arms industry resulted in a whole series of mergers, extending all over the world. Orders flowed in so fast that small firms could not carry them out. So Skoda in Austria bought out several rival firms, Hiram Maxim merged with Torsten Nordenfelt in 1888, and Krupps in Germany and Putiloff in Russia extended their industrial empires by taking over smaller rivals.

It was fortunate for the US Navy that the ONI was already established by the time the Spanish-American War broke out in 1898. Mason, during his term of office as Chief of Intelligence, had been greatly assisted by Commodore John G. Walker, Chief of the Bureau of Navigation, without whose co-operation the development of the ONI would have been very much slower. Mason, who was succeeded by Lieutenant R. P. Rodgers, son of the Superintendent of the Naval Academy, during his relatively short term of office, compiled a whole series of reports for the ONI ranging from a study of the French operations against Tunis, British operations in Egypt, and his own first-hand account of the Pacific War to the development overseas of modern torpedo craft, marine boilers, docking and repair facilities and liquid fuel. This produced some useful results, for example, the creation of the Port Directory and a comprehensive survey of merchant ships with a view to suggesting possible uses for them in the event of war. This last-named report was invaluable when the Spanish-American War occurred.

In 1894 the operations of the Spanish Government had caused a rebellion in Cuba and the sympathy of the vast majority of United States subjects was on the side of the Cubans. In January 1898, the US Navy sent their warship, *Maine*, on a goodwill visit to Cuba and, while in harbour at Havana, the ship was destroyed in a mysterious explosion, 266 of the crew losing their lives. This was the incident which provoked the war, though there had long been a demand by many Americans for action against the Spanish Governor-general of Cuba, the Marquis of Teneriffe, who had the reputation of being a harsh oppressor of the Cuban people. On the other hand, the Spaniards were certainly not anxious to be drawn into any war with the USA. An uneasy peace had prevailed for several months prior to the explosion aboard the *Maine*.

An official inquiry into the *Maine* disaster was held by the US Government and the Navy conducted their own investigation. Evidence showed that the explosion was caused by a submarine mine and the superficial judgements of both the American Consul-general in Havana and the commanding officer of the *Maine*, Captain Charles D. Sigsbee, were that this was the work of Spanish officials. Indeed, it was hinted, without any evidence to support the theory, that the Spanish naval attaché, Lieutenant Ramon Carranza, had planned the whole operation. Whereupon the attaché challenged both the Consul-general and Captain Sigsbee to a duel. This was coldly declined on the grounds that duelling was illegal in the USA, but Carranza continued to taunt his adversaries with cowardice for some weeks. Eventually he left Cuba, not to return directly to Spain, but to visit Montreal and Toronto.

By this time the ONI were making their own investigations into the affair of the *Maine*. They were greatly assisted by the reorganization of the naval attaché system, by which it was arranged to keep naval officers at various key centres abroad as permanent representatives. Chief among these was Lieutenant-commander F. E. Chadwick, who had been posted to London in 1882 and had helped to organize intelligence networks in Russia, Sweden, Norway, Denmark, Germany, Holland, Belgium and Spain. But the really vital appointment in this period was when Lieutenant W. S. Sims (later Admiral Sims) went to Paris as Intelligence Officer. Sims was a go-getter, tremendously ambitious, with ideas of his own as to how intelligence should be organized. From 1897 onwards he bombarded the ONI with lengthy reports from across the Atlantic, all of them invaluable when war came. Sims had been told in Washington that he need not worry about Spanish intelligence because this would be provided by agents in Spain, most of whom were Spaniards. Sims' language on hearing this news was unprintable and his tongue lashed the mentality of the bureaucrats who relied on agents of the nationality of a potential enemy. He set out to organize his own network in Spain and, for good measure, Russia too. It was from Russia that he learned for the first time of the machinations of a sinister arms salesman of Maxim-Nordenfelt by the name of Basil Zaharoff.

Sims reported to Washington during the war that Zaharoff not only had friends at the Russian Imperial Court, but in high social circles at Madrid as well. Meanwhile a Cuban, who was suspected of being implicated in the *Maine* affair, had been

8 A postwar photograph of von Rintelen, a leading German spy, especially on naval matters, during World War I

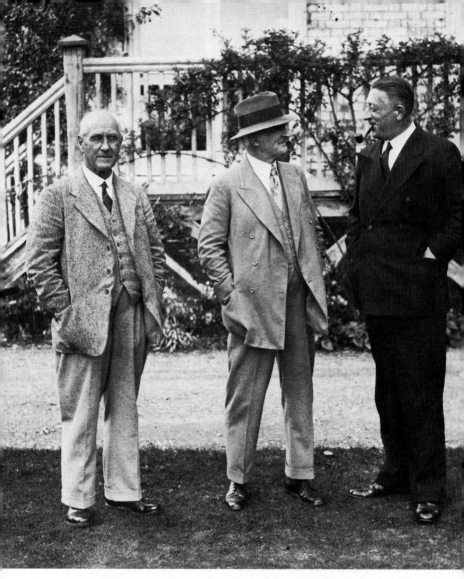

9 The German 'Sea Devil' Count Felix von Luckner (*right*) after lunch with his old enemy Admiral Sir Reginald Hall, wartime Director of Naval Intelligence (*centre*), in 1935. To the left is Admiral Borrett (*Radio Times Hulton Picture Library*)

questioned by US naval intelligence officers. The Cuban reported that a Spaniard, who had confided in him when seeking details of the layout of the harbour at Havana, had said that 'the Maxim-Nordenfelt Company wishes to see Spain at war with the USA so that it can increase its sales of arms'.

Hiram Maxim was well enough known to the Americans and, to a lesser extent, so was Nordenfelt, but the name of Basil Zaharoff was an unknown quantity until the report came from Lieutenant Sims. The young naval officer delegated to make inquiries into the Maxim-Nordenfelt firm was sent to Washington on another inquiry at the US Treasury which then had its own highly effective intelligence branch. And, in going through Treasury files, the young officer came across a dossier on Basil Zaharoff which confirmed a great deal of what Sims had already reported. Four years earlier Zaharoff had gone to South America where the Chaco War was being waged between Bolivia and Paraguay. He had persuaded the Bolivians that they were not yet strong enough to wage war effectively. 'Make peace,' he told them. 'Buy time to prepare for war in a few months. I will then send you all the arms you want.' Bolivia took his advice.

Over the next quarter of a century the ONI built up a lengthy dossier on Zaharoff. They learned that he had a secret friend at the Spanish Court, the Duchess of Villafranca, whom, years later, he married. According to the *Internationale Biographische* archives of Berlin, Zaharoff had acquired '£30 millions worth of orders in Spain two months after his meeting with the Duchess of Villafranca'. Though nothing was ever proved about his having been involved in the sabotage of the *Maine*, the evidence of the Cuban was significant. To step up his sales of arms to Spain, Zaharoff helped to precipitate a war in which the Spanish Fleet was totally destroyed in Manila Bay, Spain lost her Far Eastern colonies, Cuba was declared free and Porto Rico and the islands of Guam in the Ladrones were surrendered to the United States.

This war gave the ONI its first chance to operate in conditions of active service. They decided to keep a watch on the buccaneering Spanish naval attaché, Ramon Carranza, when he went to Canada. He had installed himself in a house in Tupper Street, Montreal, where he had various mysterious callers. One of these was a naturalized American of British birth named George Downing who aroused some curiosity because of his use of aliases. Downing was shadowed from Montreal to Washington where he adopted the name of Alexander Cree and visited the Navy Department. Those keeping watch on Downing were about to call off the shadowing on the grounds that he must be one of their own spies when one of the 'shadows' reported Downing had posted a letter. 'Forget all about it,' he was brusquely told, 'and forget you have ever heard the names of Downing or Cree.'

'Nevertheless,' replied the enthusiastic 'shadow', 'we have not absolutely established the identity of Downing. The fact that he got into the Navy Department does not necessarily mean that he works for them. I suggest we should at least have this letter intercepted, if only to be sure whether he is one of our own men.'

It was a sensible point to make, though it is not often that a junior intelligence officer will argue with his senior. Espionage was still regarded as a very dirty word in the United States in those days and the officer in charge of the case agreed very reluctantly to have the letter intercepted. When it was brought to his desk, however, he must have had a cold sweat at the thought of how very nearly he missed unmasking an enemy spy.

The letter was dated 7 May 1898 and written in ordinary language to one 'Frederick W. Dickson, 1248, Dorchester Street, Montreal'. It stated that a cipher message had that day been sent from the Navy Department in Washington to the commander of the US cruiser *Charleston* at San Francisco, ordering him to sail to Manila with 500 men and machinery and stores for making repairs for ships under the command of Commodore George Dewey.[10]

How vitally important this intelligence could have been to Spain was realized at once. Only six days earlier Dewey had won a naval victory off Manila, but, having suffered considerable damage and being in need of repairs to various ships in his squadron, he desperately needed aid as the Spaniards were still in control of shore defences. How Downing had managed to elicit this item of information on a brief visit to the Naval Department remained a mystery, but it certainly revealed the need for a tightening up of security inside the Department itself. Downing was arrested and, though it was wartime and, as a naturalized American citizen, he had been guilty of treason, he would probably have got away with a prison sentence of a few years. However, while awaiting trial, he hanged himself in his cell.

Carranza, protected by the neutrality of Canada, continued to build up his anti-American espionage network undisturbed for several months. One of his methods of recruiting agents was to persuade them to volunteer for the US Army or Navy and then, when they reached Cuba or some other theatre of war, to desert and supply as much information as they had gathered to the Spaniards. So that they could identify themselves to the Spanish commander in the area in which they deserted, they were given a plain ring on the inside of which were engraved the words *Confianza Augustina*. It was a foolishly insecure system of identification as, once the Americans discovered one agent, they were able to warn the Army and Navy to keep a watch for new recruits wearing rings. The network created was mainly inside the US Navy and it was the ONI which tackled the problem.

Altogether some 600 people inside the USA were denounced as spies during the Spanish-American War and most of the intelligence concerning these came from naval sources. A Texan of Spanish descent and a graduate of West Point, the US military academy, was employed as an agent and sent to Madrid where he adopted the name of Fernandez del Campo, posing as a wealthy Mexican of Spanish sympathies. This was one of the first moves of the ONI in response to Sims' plea that Spanish agents should be replaced by US citizens. The Texan posed as one who was hostile to the USA and he was given quite a lot of information in consequence. At this time a rumour had swept the whole of the USA to the effect that a Spanish fleet was about to set sail to menace the whole eastern seaboard of America. What the Texan learned was at least reassuring: the destination of the 'punitive fleet' was not the USA, but the Philippines and the aim was the destruction of Dewey's cruiser squadron. This was vital information for the US Navy and the Texan agent speedily left Spain for Tangier and from that city passed on his information to the US Navy. It was worth 'a whole squadron of ships', according to one naval authority, for the Texan not only gave the destination of the

57

Spanish Fleet, but the quantity of coal in the bunkers. It was to the credit of the ONI that the identity of this agent was kept secret throughout a long and often hazardous operation.

Captain John R. Bartlett was CIO during the war with Spain and he made strong representations about the depletion of his staff because of their recall to active service: 'By successive detachments of officers to sea duty the entire work of the Office devolved on myself and one ensign, retired. In time of war the routine business of the Office is greatly increased. During the past five months the amount of information furnished to the Naval War Board alone was equal to that furnished to all the Bureaux of the Department combined.'[11]

The Secretary of the Navy congratulated the ONI on the 'valuable and accurate information in regard to the defences of Cuba, Porto Rico and the Philippines, as well as . . . the location of vessels of the Spanish Fleet' on the outbreak of war. Photography had played a useful role for the first time in supplying intelligence and this work had been specially developed years before by Lieutenant Rodgers. Where the ONI showed a weakness was in their inability to provide a running plot of the location of enemy warships. It was this weakness which created nagging anxiety in the Navy Department that the Spanish Fleet might launch surprise attacks on the eastern seaboard.

An effort to eradicate this lack of information was made by the War Board rather than the ONI itself. They sought two volunteers in Ensign William Buck and Ensign Henry H. Ward to masquerade as British yachtsmen and to follow the Spanish Fleet. Buck tailed Admiral Camara's Spanish squadron in the Mediterranean and Ward kept watch on Admiral Cervera's squadron when it sailed from Cadiz to Porto Rico. It was Sims in Paris, however, who earned himself the title of the 'first spymaster of the US Navy'. The network he had set up in Spain before the war now paid dividends. He received valuable assistance from the French in obtaining intelligence on Spain and his biographer, Morison, tells how one of his agents was provided by the great Georges Clemenceau himself. The standard of Sims' reports was of such excellence and meticulous accuracy that not one word or comma was ever altered in them before they were transmitted to the fleet commanders.

4

Planning for War

Admiral Sir Lewis Beaumont, who was head of NID in 1894, managed to persuade the authorities to expand the Division so that when Rear-admiral Custance took over as DNI, in 1899, he inherited what was then the best intelligence service of all Britain's armed forces.

It was an astonishing metamorphosis in a matter of little more than ten years. By this time the NID had retrieved from the forgotten files the report of the agent Thomas Beach and his plan of the Fenian submarine. They were able to point out how this had already been adapted by the US Navy. Yet when, after strong pressure from the NID, the Royal Navy launched its first submarine at Barrow in 1901, Admiral Lord Charles Beresford, then second-in-command in the Mediterranean, declared that the craft was 'no more than a play-thing and thus unworthy of serious attention as a ship of war'.

Rear-admiral Reginald Custance was sufficiently farsighted to realize that, with all the leading navies of the world engaged in an arms race, a still stronger NID was needed. He organized a special section devoted to trade intelligence. This was, however, somewhat unimaginatively developed and some of the British armament firms claimed that this branch of the NID was always 'two years out of date, if not much more'. The Germans had begun to systematize intelligence long before the British, though, curiously, they too had been prodded into action by the military rather than by their own Navy. The genius who inspired the German Navy to build up their own intelligence system was Count Helmuth Karl Bernhard von

Moltke who had been Chief of Staff to the Prussian Army. Von Moltke had such a passion for organization, which, he insisted, should reach down to the lowest levels with the same efficiency and precision it had on high, that he urged similar organizational developments for Army and Navy alike. His ideas on formulating a plan for systematic intelligence overseas was adopted by the German Admiralty who, by the turn of the century, already had an extremely professional and well organized Naval Intelligence Bureau.

Their methods were to rely mainly on civilian spies, in stark contrast to the British NID who still believed that naval intelligence was something which could only be gathered by naval officers and assessed by Admiralty clerks! The Germans concentrated their spy network mainly against Britain where many German nationals then lived, and after that against France and Russia. By far their greatest effort was devoted to gathering detailed information from the dockyards and armament factories of the British Isles. An important sub-section of German naval intelligence was devoted to North Africa, for the German General Staff had long visualized a struggle for power, centred on North Africa, between Britain, France and Germany. The German Navy was anxious to see Germany acquire at least a foothold, if not a dominating position, in Morocco where Britain and France were both seeking to strengthen their influence. A grave international crisis was created by the arrival of a German gunboat off Agadir on 1 July 1911, sent as a warning to the French against the annexation of Morocco. The repercussions of this crisis were sufficient to bring about a further reorganization of the NID.

Prior to this, Admiral Custance had been succeeded as DNI, in 1902, by Admiral Prince Louis of Battenberg, an able and devoted patriot who was later to be treated so shabbily by the politicians who supinely succumbed to the hysterical demand that anyone with German connections and a German name must automatically be an enemy of Britain. Battenberg understood the Germans only too well and he urged that some of von Moltke's ideas should be adopted in Britain and that the NID should be given higher status, demanding that 'preparation for war, in every particular, should be in his [the DNI's] charge, but it must be applied in a comprehensive manner'. Perhaps it was his German upbringing and Teutonic zest for organization which gave Prince Louis this conception of the NID's role. Certainly this was not what was envisaged for the NID by anyone else at the Admiralty and, indeed, to have given the NID responsibility for planning for war in 1902 would have been even more dangerous than to have delegated the same authority to the CIA in the Vietnam War. An intelligence department's function is to inform and advise; when such a body actually assigns itself the right to interfere in politics and take political decisions—as the NID was to do in certain periods of World War I—then the dangers increase, for it means that the intelligence department acquires executive action without accountability. What Prince Louis managed to achieve, however, was in the long run more important; he ensured that, from then onwards, on all questions of naval policy, the NID was closely consulted.

The Russo-Japanese War, in the early years of the century, alerted both the British and the Germans to the vital new role which naval intelligence played. The Japanese code of *bushido* laid down that spying was an honourable and highly patriotic duty and, prior to the war with Russia, they set out to obtain information on the Russian Fleet. Two Japanese naval officers volunteered as spies and, having effectively buried their identities, turned up in St Petersburg as clerks working for commercial firms. One of them not only married a Russian woman, but joined the Russian Orthodox Church. These two men sent back masses of vital information to Japan. Colonel Immanuel, in a report to the German General Staff in 1908, commented on the activities of these two spies and even attributed the swiftness of the Japanese victory over Russia to 'superior intelligence—especially on the naval side'.

It is doubtful if any of the western naval intelligence services, except possibly that of the United States, had any real conception of how the war of the armament manufacturers was being waged, not only above their heads, but in such a manner that vital decisions in the political sphere were often being taken by armament firms rather than their governments. The armament kings had, in a remarkably short time, made themselves the richest men in Europe; by takeover bids, by amalgamations and mergers, by cunningly concealed cartel arrangements with other firms in other countries (sometimes countries who were the enemies of their own), they had also acquired power that put them almost beyond reach of control by their own governments. Their tentacles extended to such subsidiary activities as newspaper ownership, through which channels they sought to pump out not merely propaganda, but deliberate lies to foster wars and promote ill-will between nations. Only one naval intelligence bureau decided that this was the time to investigate the machinations of the armaments manufacturers and this was the ONI. The lessons of the Spanish-American War had made the US Navy increase both the appropriations and the number of personnel for that Office. Captain Sigsbee, who had been in command of the USS *Maine* at the time of the explosion, took over the post of CIO in 1900 and was strongly in favour of keeping a close watch on the machinations of the armament firms. Yet the probability is that the leading armaments firms such as Krupp, Vickers and Scheider-Creusot, had better intelligence systems than either the armies or navies of that era. The reason for this is not difficult to seek: they all had a vested interest in war, their trade was worldwide and their agents everywhere had easier access to government departments than the average spy. There were easy profits to be made by many firms simply by selling arms to both sides, which happened as much in the Boer War as in the Russo-Japanese War.

At a vital period in the development of the British NID, when the need was for one man to be at the helm for several years, there were no fewer than eight directors in twelve years. Battenberg was followed by Ottley (1905), King-Hall and Slade (1907), Bethell (1909), Jackson (1912) and Oliver (1913). At the same time, inside the German Admiralty there were much abler assessors of intelligence than in Whitehall, but the Germans do not seem to have benefited greatly thereby. The German Admiralty relied heavily on the German Secret Service and a single spymaster, Gustav Steinhauer, who regarded the whole field of naval intelligence as his own. A great deal of money was spent in developing a spy network that covered the whole of Britain and this worked splendidly until war broke out. Then the whole system broke down.

Perhaps the Germans became too complacent. Their cardinal error was not to revise a system that had been working efficiently for all of fourteen years. All espionage systems, however successful, need to be changed every few years. Another factor which may have contributed to German complacency was the knowledge that the laws of Britain were so lax and ineffectual in the face of the growing threat of espionage that the catching of spies was greatly impeded. It was not until just before World War I that this legislative handicap was remedied. Gustav Steinhauer, who was mainly responsible for naval intelligence, had been a private detective in the famous Pinkerton Agency of America. He was, nevertheless, an amateur in the spy game and though he planted many spies inside Britain, he cared nothing for their safety and took no steps to give them worthwhile protection in the event of war.

In 1907 the German Naval Intelligence Bureau was guilty of great indiscretion during the visit to Britain of Kaiser Wilhelm. British detectives were detailed to guard his party. Among the Kaiser's entourage was the Acting Chief of Naval Intelligence and the detectives following the party thought it odd that this German officer should go to the unfashionable Caledonian Road to call at a barber's shop. They were even more puzzled when he left and it became obvious that he had neither had his hair cut, nor been shaved. The bright young detective who noted these things had the good sense to report them to his superiors. The barber's name was Karl Gustav Ernst who was of German descent but had been born in England and was therefore a British subject. He was a key figure in the German spy network in Britain and his barber's shop was the 'post-office' for the organization. It was more than two years after this that any action was taken to investigate the case of Ernst. The NID seems to have disregarded the whole affair, for it was the newly formed MI5 (or British counterespionage) which eventually tracked down this agent working for the German Admiralty.

The truth was that, despite the fact that it had grown and developed, the NID still lagged behind its German counterpart. The brief originally given to the DNI when the division was formed still stood: 'to collect, classify and record, with a complete index, all information which bears a naval character, or which may be of value during naval operations, to keep up our knowledge of progress made by foreign countries in naval matters and to preserve the information in a form readily available for reference'. The frequent changes of directors at the NID had weakened its authority in the immediate pre-war years. The trade division was abolished—a foolish decision—the section concerned with preparations for war was disbanded and a Naval Mobilization Department set up in its stead. Thus at a vital moment the NID was actually reduced in strength by about 50 per cent.

It was a son of Captain William Hall, the first DNI, who made his own unofficial probe into reports of the enormous construction programme being carried out in German naval dockyards. This was Captain Reginald Hall who at that time had command of the cadet training-ship, HMS *Cornwall*, which was visiting German ports. Hall soon found that the Germans were much more vigilant in guarding their own secrets and dockyards than the British. One item of information he required was the number of building-slips at Kiel, but this was difficult to obtain because the slips were close to the dockyard which was heavily guarded on the shore side and far away from where the *Cornwall* was berthed. Visiting Kiel at that time was the Duke of Westminster in his small, but powerful, motor-boat, and Hall persuaded the Duke to let him borrow the boat so that he could race up the harbour at high speed and get within reach of the slips to photograph them.

During this visit to Kiel, Hall gave encouragement to two of his officers, Lieutenant Brandon RN, and Captain Trench, of the Royal Marines, to go ashore and find out what was going on in the dockyard. Later these young officers volunteered for other intelligence work of this nature and Hall not only supported their request, but made the strongest representations to the Admiralty about the need for more intelligence on German naval installations, declaring that the existing Admiralty charts of this area of the German coast were out of date and that the only accurate data about the Frisian Islands was to be obtained in Erskine Childers' book, *The Riddle of the Sands*.[1] In May 1910, Brandon and Trench were given permission to make a tour of the Frisian Islands and German coastal defences generally. It was given in a somewhat mean and grudging spirit, the strict understanding being that it would be an unpaid holiday jaunt, with the implication that their lordships at the Admiralty would be delighted if the pair succeeded, but that they could expect no help if they failed and were caught.

Captain Regnart of the NID, after consultation with the new director, Captain Bethell, gave these orders to Brandon and Trench who, somewhat amateurishly armed with cameras and notebooks, set off on their mission with boyish glee, but great determination. Dutifully, they took numerous photographs of gun emplacements and sea-defences generally, made sketches and notes all under cover of a walking holiday. Then, at Borkum, they were caught spying at night by a vigilant sentry and arrested. The Germans soon established their identity and both men were sentenced to four years' imprisonment. It was not until May 1913, some seventeen months before the expiry of their sentence that Brandon and Trench were pardoned by the Kaiser on the occasion of King George V's visit to Berlin. Even then they were disgracefully treated by the Admiralty who declined to have anything to do with the whole business and even refused to meet some of the heavy financial loss these officers had incurred through their wholly patriotic initiative while legitimately on leave. They had volunteered for the work and clearly had the go-ahead from the NID. But the DNI lied in the most blatant fashion about the mission, declaring that the officers had been taking a pleasure trip while on leave and that whatever happened to them was their own fault. He had no knowledge of any mission having been assigned to them.

It was a squalid story of cheeseparing indifference by the Admiralty. Both Brandon and Trench suffered financially through their spying. The expenses of their trial had amounted to £380 each (a large sum in those days) and they had also been charged by the Germans for food, fuel and lighting during their imprisonment while awaiting trial.

Meanwhile the US Office of Naval Intelligence had made great strides in obtaining technical intelligence over a wide area of the world; its staff now included five clerks, a translator, a draughtsman and security guards, yet the appropriation was only slightly more than $9,000 a year. The ONI's evidence on the imbroglios of the international armament firms convinced the US Navy that the arms firms were actively sponsoring warmongering. They regarded Zaharoff even then as a sinister agent of British imperialism. In case this should be regarded as a highly xenophobic attitude, perhaps this statement by Zaharffo himself years later will justify their suspicions:

> my associations in Germany were really an attempt to establish an intelligence organization in that country. This way I was able to tell the Allies far more about the enemy than could their own espionage services. . . . I would not, and I did not, hesitate to sell arms to Germany's potential allies, or to make deals with German firms, despite the fact that Germany was the potential enemy. I maintain that this knowledge we acquired of the enemy's potential was of the utmost importance to the Allies when war came.[3]

Thus Britain became increasingly dependent on the goodwill of a cosmopolitan arms salesman whose office was in Paris and, when war came, Zaharoff was probably worth at least two battleships to the Royal Navy.

In one respect the Americans were wiser than the British in the appointments of the Chief Naval Intelligence Officer. A number of their CIOs served two periods, Mason, Captain Seaton Schroeder and Captain Rodgers among them. Rodgers held the record of a total of seven years as CIO on two separate terms of office. In 1910 the ONI was reorganized, some seven years after it had been moved to the Mills Building, 1816 N Street, NW. It was in this period that the Japanese Navy, fresh from its triumphs over the Russian Navy, became a prime target for American Naval Intelligence. In the course of inquiries the ONI learned that, over a long period, there had been systematic attempts by the British firm of Vickers to obtain large contracts from the Japanese Navy and to bribe senior naval officers to achieve this. Long before 1914 the US Navy's dossiers on arms deals with Japan were exceptionally detailed and accurate. Yet it was not until 27 April 1914, that *The Times* of London reported that

> . . . three directors of the Mitsui Bussan Kaisha, the agents of Messrs. Vickers (Ltd.) in Japan, are accused of bribing Vice-Admiral Matsuo. Herr Hermann, the Tokyo manager of the Berlin firm of Messrs. Siemen-Schuckert, is charged with having given an indirect bribe of £1,100 in connection with

the wireless contract obtained by the German firm, and with the destruction by burning in the German Consulate at Yokohama of evidence in the shape of documents which it was notorious had been stolen.

US Naval Intelligence carried out their own inquiry into the allegations against Vickers and their agents in Japan. One report, dated 29 March 1911, stated that

> ... what is most disturbing about the dealings both direct and indirect of the firms which the agent Basile Zacharoff [sic] represents is that inquiries into the nature of the contracts they obtain often show that several countries are involved. M. Zacharoff is the accredited representative of Vickers, but it would appear that he also has links with Japanese, French, Russian and German arms firms and does not seem to be unduly worried that some of these arrangements should cut across one another. It is advisable that any purchases by the US Navy of armaments and spares from sources outside of Zacharoff's private empire should be a closely guarded secret from the many spies M. Zacharoff seems to have.

The substance of this somewhat vague and ill-defined report was used in 1934 when there was an inquiry by a Senate Committee of the USA into the operations of US armament firms. But if the report of 1911 may have seemed vague, the inquiry into the allegations against Vickers after the Siemens-Schuckert relevations was much more precise. The *Japan Weekly Chronicle* in reporting this inquiry stated that:

> ... in the evidence of Admiral Fuji it is explicitly stated that the Vickers Company remitted to Admiral Fuji on various occasions in 1911 and 1912 sums reaching the great total of 210,000 yen. ... Whether the money was accepted by Fuji legally, or illegally, its payment by Vickers was totally illegal and contrary to the Corrupt Practices Act of 1906 (English law).

Subsequent court proceedings showed that £115,000 was paid out as commissions on the battle-cruiser *Kongo*, which was purchased from Vickers and that Vickers were aware of this bribery and had increased the commission to make it possible. The more US Naval Intelligence learned of Zaharoff, the more unpleasant and corrupt the whole European scene seemed to be. While Mr Arthur Raffalowitch, financial attaché in the Russian Embassy in Paris, was writing a report that 'Zaharoff thinks it will take three or four years to build armoured cruisers on the Black Sea in sufficient strength to overawe Turkey . . .', Zaharoff's own firm, Vickers, had been using the threat of Russian rearmament to co-operate with Turkey in the re-organization of their dockyards, forming the Imperial Ottoman Company, with a majority of British directors, for this purpose.

'One of these days', wrote the US naval attaché covering Turkey, 'the United Kingdom will rue the day she ever allowed Zaharoff such a free rein. Whatever the pious hopes of the British Radicals, Turkey is still committed to the Central Powers and one day the arms which Britain is helping Turkey to make will be turned on the British in the Middle East.' It was an accurate forecast. Years later a shocked British public learned that the Turkish guns served by German artillerymen at the Dardanelles in World War I were of British manufacture and delivered to the Germans and Turks by Zaharoff.

In the immediate pre-war years the Germans did not always take the trouble to conceal their espionage operations inside Britain. They even asked a Plymouth solicitor, Samuel Hugh Duff, to find correspondents in Britain to work for the German News Agency, not only arousing suspicions by offering salaries of £1,000 a year, big money then, but stressing that they only wanted naval and shipping news. Soon the German Admiralty had a complete picture of Royal Navy installations from Plymouth and Portsmouth to Chatham and the Firth of Forth; they knew all about the gunnery range-finding systems used by the British, how the latest submarines were being fitted with guns, which ships had wireless telegraphy and information on dockyard supplies. Surprisingly, however, they had neglected Scapa Flow, the retreat for the Grand Fleet which had been developed in the Orkneys.

It is often suggested that the whole credit for the reorganiza-tion of the NID at this time was due to Captain Reginald Hall. This, however, was far from being the case. Links between the

NID and the newly formed MI5, which were to prove of vital importance in rounding up German spies, had been forged between 1911 and 1914, and before Hall was appointed DNI in November 1914. The man who really made his mark at the NID, and who has never had the credit he deserves, was Rear-admiral Sir Henry F. Oliver. It was he who established a special section of the NID to intercept German naval wireless signals and decipher them.

Oliver had foreseen that, when war broke out, the most essential intelligence as far as the British Admiralty was concerned would be news of German Fleet movements and to keep a constant tab on the whole of the enemy's wireless telegraphy. Diplomatic codes and ciphers had largely been broken down by all the great powers early on in the twentieth century as the diplomatic services had foolishly convinced themselves that their codes were so safe that there was never any need to change them. Oliver ordered an all-out attempt to intercept and decipher all German naval signals and had wisely insisted that the work of this section should be kept so secret that many of the personnel of the NID knew nothing about it. He had selected Sir Alfred Ewing, the Director of Naval Education, to take charge of this section, and this former Professor of Mechanical Engineering at Cambridge proved the ideal man for the job. He was scientifically minded as well as having a keen brain and a flair for talent-spotting. One advantage of applying a ciphering method to the groups in naval and diplomatic code-books was that the cipher key could be changed frequently to baffle the enemy, whereas issuing new code-books posed problems. It took several weeks for a new code-book to reach distant men-of-war.

In their great deciphering venture the British Admiralty was starting from scratch as Britain was the only one of the great powers which had not established in peacetime an organization for the deciphering of foreign military and naval codes. The French and Russians were ahead of the Germans in this respect. However, under Ewing's coaching, the British section soon made remarkable strides, encouraged at every step by Oliver. The year 1911 marked closer co-operation between the British and French in naval matters and there was a high-level conference in London between representatives of both countries to arrange for communications in the event of war. It was then decided to produce an Anglo-French code-book.

Ewing, much of whose previous experience had been purely scientific, concerned with studying such diverse subjects as Japanese earthquakes, magnetism and hysteresis, approached the prodigious task he had set himself with caution and humility. He spent long hours in the British Museum studying ciphers, as well as acquainting himself with code structures of commercial organizations. Luckily, he had at one time taken an interest in cryptography as a hobby and, when it came to choosing a small team of decipherers, his wide circle of acquaintances in this field proved useful. One was a barrister named Russell-Clarke who was a wireless enthusiast: he informed Ewing that he could get German messages on his receiving set and that he thought he could probably intercept messages on a lower wavelength than those being handled at the Admiralty. So Clarke was brought into the section and allowed to set up his own wireless station at Hunstanton in Norfolk. As a result of his success Oliver gave orders for other similar stations to be set up in other parts of Britain. During his cable-testing experiences off the coast of Uruguay as far back as 1875, Ewing had experimented with codes. In 1904, having patented a wave detector, he had read a paper to the Royal Society on his new method of detecting oscillations such as occur in wireless telegraphy. He had also discussed with Admiral Oliver the possibility of novel methods of constructing ciphers.

Ewing recruited to his section four teachers at the naval colleges of Dartmouth and Osborne, all of whom had a good knowledge of German. Of these the ablest was undoubtedly Alexander Guthrie Denniston, who had been educated in Bonn and at the Sorbonne in Paris and who, for more than a quarter of a century, was to be the Royal Navy's mastermind in the field of ciphers.

The German Admiralty belatedly began to question their dependence on Steinhauer and to blame him for having failed to appreciate the importance of Scapa Flow. Under pressure from his naval paymasters, Steinhauer committed a blunder in a panic effort to please. He employed in Scotland a highly inefficient, talkative rascal named Dr Armgaard Graves who was easily caught and sent to prison in 1912. Graves made the nature

10 (*above*) From a photograph in his service jacket, a snapshot of Lieutenant Joseph Rochefort, USN (*US Navy*)

11 (*below*) Rear Admiral Doenitz, Officer commanding a U-boat flotilla, gives a few words of welcome to a submarine crew on its safe return to base in Germany in November 1939

12 A map of Pearl Harbor discovered by the US Navy in a captured Japanese submarine. According to the US Navy, 'Japanese symbols drawn on the chart indicate the anchorage of ships and details of military establishments around the inner harbor of Pearl Harbor' (*Associated Press*)

of his enquiries so obvious that he was introduced into a club in Scotland as 'my very good friend, the German spy'.

How lacking the German Admiralty was in information on Scapa Flow as late as June 1914, may perhaps be gathered from the fact that, even at that date, they were desperately anxious to know the answer to so elementary a question as to whether the largest battleships of the Royal Navy could anchor there. Steinhauer did not have a single agent in the area whom he could trust to find this out, so he actually went to Scapa Flow himself (according to his own version of events) and, pretending to be fishing in company with a local Scottish angler, surreptitiously took soundings with a knotted line. The British have always denied this story, not surprisingly, for it reveals their own total lack of security in the vicinity of Scapa Flow. On the other hand this extraordinarily amateurish manner of obtaining accurate soundings reflects little credit on the German Admiralty. They could much more easily have carried out their own soundings years before from one of their own fishing vessels, either openly, or disguised.

5

Communications Revolution

They sat around the table in his official room and proceeded
to inspect the material without a notion of its contents, or
how to set about what for each of them was a wholly novel
task. . . . They began to grope their way into a jungle without
experience or guide, labouring hard to decipher the messages,
but finding it rather like hammering on an iron safe with the
object of knowing what was inside.[1]

Thus Sir Alfred Ewing's son, A. W. Ewing, described the
beginning of the deciphering work. It was a long time before
Ewing, who had set to work in the office which was later to
become famous as 'Room 40', was able to take even a single day
off duty. It was a test of character really, this bringing of order
out of chaos and heralding the dawn of a revolution in the field
of communications. But Ewing was helped by two unexpected
bonuses. First, a German signal-book was captured from a
German merchantman off Australia in the early weeks of
World War I. This was immediately sent to the Admiralty.
Then, on 20 August 1914, the German light cruiser *Magdeburg*
went aground during a fog while raiding the Russian coast. By
the time the fog started to clear, the *Magdeburg*'s captain saw
that Russian ships were steaming towards her from the Gulf of
Finland. He immediately ordered an officer to take the secret
naval code-books, bound in lead, put them in a boat and pull
away from the grounded ship so that they could be dropped in
deep water. At that moment the Russians opened fire on the
ship and in the confusion which followed the German officer

in charge of the code-books seems to have fallen overboard, but whether from the ship or the sea-boat is not clear.

Later, the Russians, having captured the German ship, not only ordered that all bodies washed ashore or seen floating should be recovered and given the traditional naval burial, but that nets should be put out to dredge for other bodies. It has been suggested that this was a purely chivalrous action on the part of the Russians. Maybe, but the fact that they ordered dredging for other bodies suggests they were also looking for the secret code-books which had not been found in the ship. First they found the body of the officer who had been given the books: in his arms were the lead bindings of code-books. A further dredging of the sea was ordered and eventually all the books were recovered.

The Russians who, at that time, were co-operating closely with the Royal Navy, lost no time in sending the books to Britain in one of their own destroyers. As Ewing and Oliver had kept their new section such a close secret, they might not have been so lucky as to receive this bonus, but such was the Russian regard for British naval efficiency that they automatically instructed their Embassy in London to pass the books on to the 'head of the Allied Fleet'. Yet it was nearly eight weeks after the *Magdeburg* went aground that the books arrived in Ewing's office, and then only after he and Oliver had gone round to the Embassy to ask that the books should be given to them and not to the Fleet.

The code-books proved of the utmost value to the NID. 'Thanks to this unexpected prize, those in Room 40, from an early date in November, were able to overhear a host of German naval orders and reports and to interpret them as fast as they came in,' declared Ewing's son.[2] Not only did the code-books supply the code then in use, but the key to the whole system on which the German naval codes were formulated. They were dictionary codes, comprising a series of parallel columns, arranged so that the right-hand columns gave a list of code-signs and the left-hand columns a list of words in dictionary order. The work involved for the deciphering team was arduous indeed, but they soon found that if a single code-sign could be identified with a clear word, after keys had been changed, all the code-signs in that column could be identified simply by putting down opposite the other signs in the column German words in alphabetical order. The result was that once Ewing's team had mastered this technique, however much the Germans might change their keys, their wireless signals for the next two years could fairly easily be deciphered.

It was a brilliant feat by a team of amateurs who had evolved their own systems for deciphering and it helped to turn the tide against the Central Powers in the first bleak year of the war. Twice, for example, German destroyers attempted to attack British troop convoys across the English Channel. On each occasion the deciphering section of the NID had intercepted their signals, enabling British cruisers to be sent to check the destroyers. Once this led directly to the sinking of four German destroyers.

Thus when Captain Reginald Hall was appointed DNI in November 1914, he inherited a vastly improved NID and was able to reap the benefits of the deciphering system which Oliver had built up. He also learned for the first time the importance of civilians being employed in naval intelligence and from that moment set out to recruit them from a wide range of professions. Hall asked Claud Serocold, a London stockbroker, to be his personal assistant, and among others he brought into the NID were Thomas Inskip (later to be Lord Chancellor), Sir Philip Baker Wilbraham, a Fellow of All Souls, A. J. Alan, the short-storywriter, and James Randall, a City wine merchant. The new DNI also established the closest links with MI5 and the Special Branch at Scotland Yard, for he realized that the round-up of almost the entire German naval espionage network in Britain had been carried out by these two organizations within hours of war being declared. Between 4 and 5 August 1914, twenty-one enemy agents were caught, thus forcing the Germans to build an entirely new network.

Hall was perhaps the Walsingham of his age. He felt personally responsible for the security of the Royal Navy and for obtaining intelligence on the enemy's moves; this motivation made him cunning as well as ruthless, something of a diplomat and a politician as well as a sailor and intelligence officer. He was not an innovator in the same way that Oliver had been, but he used his contacts and his powers of persuasion to raise the status of the NID so that eventually it became one of the dominant factors in winning the war.

Meanwhile the German Admiralty decided to organize their own network of spies in Britain and not to rely exclusively on outside agencies as they had done for so long. They acted with commendable speed—as early as September 1914—but perhaps with erratic judgement. For the man they selected as their key spy to go to Britain, Lieutenant Carl Hans Lody, of the German Naval Reserve, was lacking in discretion, careless and altogether out of his depth in such a role.

Though totally inexperienced in espionage, Lody had certain qualifications for the mission: he spoke English fluently, but with an American accent, and he knew Britain well as he had been a tourist guide for the Hamburg-America Shipping Line. He was therefore given a forged passport in the name of an American tourist, Charles A. Inglis, and told to go to Edinburgh. From the moment he arrived in that city Lody committed almost every mistake about which an agent on his first mission should have been warned. He aroused suspicion by the persistent questions he asked about the naval station at Rosyth and by sending intelligence reports in the form of letters to one Adolf Burchard in Stockholm. Some of the material he gleaned was useful and accurate, but perhaps the most farcical of all his items of 'intelligence' was to pass back the totally untrue rumour that had been sweeping Britain for weeks, to the effect that the Russian Army had landed in Scotland! Lody was soon marked down as a possible enemy agent and in due course his correspondence was intercepted and read. The authorities' first reaction was that no genuine spy would behave in such a gauche manner and with such incompetence, but, to make sure, Lody was shadowed from Edinburgh to London and to Liverpool, Holyhead and Dublin. As he was literally the only German agent in Britain at that time, the British had only one man to watch. What finally clinched the case against Lody was the enclosure in correspondence to his contact in Stockholm of a letter to Captain Karl Stammer in Berlin. Stammer, a staff officer in the German Admiralty Intelligence Division, was perhaps one of its ablest members, being confidential secretary to the Chief of Naval Intelligence and one of the principal briefers of spies being sent on missions. It must have been galling for Stammer that his briefings were so often disregarded. Eventually Lody was arrested by the Royal Irish Constabulary in Ireland on the instructions of Scotland Yard. He was tried, found guilty and sentenced to death, being shot at the Tower of London on 6 November 1916. To execute such a spy was really like taking a sledge-hammer to kill a fly.

Lody's replacement in Britain was Horst von der Goltz and once again a forged American passport was used, this time in the name of Bridgman Taylor. His tactics on arriving in London were to try to ingratiate himself with the authorities. He went to the Foreign Office and offered information about the German raider *Emden* and details of projected air raids on Britain. But, as in the case of Lody, von der Goltz was suspected from the outset and called in for questioning at Scotland Yard. They were sure he was a spy, but had no evidence on which to base a charge. The best they could do was to charge him for failing to register with the police and for this offence von der Goltz was sentenced to six months' imprisonment and recommended for deportation.

While von der Goltz (under his false name of Bridgman Taylor) was in prison in Britain, Colonel Franz von Papen and Captain Karl Boy-Ed, the military and naval attachés at the German Embassy in Washington, were recalled at the request of the US Government for having abused their diplomatic immunity. They were given a safe-conduct by the Allies for their Atlantic crossing, but this applied to their persons and not their papers, with the result that, when their ship arrived at Falmouth on 2 January 1916, these papers were examined by the British. Among them was a cheque, dated 1 September 1914, for $200, made out to 'Mr Bridgman Taylor'. This was enough to justify recalling von der Goltz for further interrogation, and this time he admitted everything, even giving the authorities the names of his fellow-agents in the USA. When this information reached Captain Hall in the NID, he rubbed his hands with glee. 'We shall now see if this changes the United States' views about remaining neutral,' he commented. 'We must see that they are informed about the saboteurs in their midst.' For one of von der Goltz's contacts was planning dynamite outrages in American arms factories.

As a result of Ewing's prompting, Hall had set up the Code and Cipher School which was invaluable in coping with the enormous back-log of undeciphered messages. So important did this organization become that eventually there was a strong demand from the Foreign Office that it should have control over the School. While Hall was DNI, he was powerful enough successfully to resist such pressures, insisting that it should remain under the Admiralty. But during Lloyd George's premiership there was a marked hostility between him and Hall and eventually the Admiralty had to give way. On 1 April 1922, the Code and Cipher School was transferred to the Foreign Office. It retained a naval head, however; Commander Denniston, who had been in the NID since Ewing recruited him, brought with him a staff of ninety-one and he remained head of the department until the outbreak of war in 1939.

If the Germans were caught napping in the affair of the *Magdeburg*, they, too, had their successes in cryptography. Long before June 1915, they had broken down the British Playfair and other ciphers, as well as some used by the French, and they were well on the way to deciphering the Russians' messages. Once they broke the Russian ciphers they exploited this by playing a trick on the Russian Fleet. In the vicinity of the Black Sea and Turkey the German Navy was outnumbered by the Russian Navy and for this reason was unable to take the offensive. But the possession of the Russian cipher key gave them a chance to rectify this. Germany had two ships, *Breslau* and *Goben*, attached to the Turkish Navy, based at Constantinople. When the Russian Fleet put to sea the Germans ordered the light cruiser *Breslau* to interpose herself between the Russians and their base. At the same time the Germans tapped out in the Russian naval code a message, purporting to come from the Russian admiral, ordering their fleet to proceed to Trebizond at the eastern end of the Black Sea. Dutifully, the Russian ships obeyed the bogus order and, as soon as they had gone, the *Breslau*, joined by the *Goben*, raided the Russian shore establishments and played havoc with their coastal merchant shipping.

The German Admiralty took the view in 1914 that, while Germany was fighting a war on two fronts, it was absolutely essential to try to ensure that the United States remained neutral. A good deal of political planning went into this concept and German Naval Intelligence in the USA did everything possible to encourage isolationism and discredit the Allies.

Among some senior officers of the US Navy, as can easily be conjectured from the Intelligence Office's interest in the ramifications of the international armaments set-up in Europe and Asia, and the attachment of Japan to the Allied cause, there was deep suspicion of what they regarded as the 'imperialism of the Allies', providing scope for German naval attachés to sow dissension. Thus the two rival navies found that their intelligence services were drawn closely into political planning as the war continued. On the whole German Naval Intelligence saw eye to eye with its own government much more than the British NID did either with the Asquith or Lloyd George administrations.

In the early months of the war the Germans were more successful in the naval-political field, due mainly to the enterprise of Captain Karl Boy-Ed, their naval attaché in Washington. He had not only established friendly relations with certain sections of the American press, but had also exploited the anti-British element among the Irish in the USA. Very early in the war when Sir Roger Casement, the former British diplomat, had visited New York, the German naval attaché had met him and become fully aware of Casement's devotion to the cause of a liberated Ireland, suggesting to Casement that he should go to Germany and encouraging the idea of an Irish Legion linked with the Germans.

Franz von Kleist Rintelen, an officer of the German Naval Reserve with the rank of captain, was sent to the USA with the ambitious project of organizing sabotage, including the fomenting of strikes, the holding up of ships and planting bombs aboard them. Von Rintelen was a patriotic, courageous, highly intelligent officer, never one to shirk a challenge and he also spoke perfect English. He had had some unusual experiences in naval intelligence prior to going to the USA, involving the dispatch of funds by circuitous routes to German warships in foreign waters. In his book, *The Dark Invader*, von Rintelen told how:

> I managed with great trouble to deposit stocks of foreign currency for our cruisers throughout the whole world, from New York to New Orleans, from Venezuela to Uruguay, from Tierra del Fuego to Seattle . . . we transmitted very large sums to confidential agents in these ports who had been appointed in peacetime.[3]

While conducting these confidential transactions a Berlin bank was instructed by the German Admiralty to send half a million dollars to the New York agent for chartering a collier. The honest bank official who had to carry out the instruction innocently took up his pen and, as though we were still at peace, wrote in the letter which was sent to New York: 'On the instruction and for the account of the German Imperial Navy we transmit to you herewith five hundred thousand dollars.' 'When I received a copy of this document next day,' wrote von Rintelen, 'I nearly fainted. Our agent in New York was, of course, compromised.'

Von Rintelen, who knew Britain well, had also had the task of surveying London and Liverpool

> ... with a view to drafting plans, based on photographic enlargements, for effective raids from zeppelins. ... Large-scale maps were printed for us in the Admiralty's own presses and our immediate business was to mark on them with large red circles the so-called 'vulnerable spots'. To our astonishment, however, we learned ... that no guarantee could be given as to where projectiles launched from airships might land.[4]

Although the German Navy suffered from nothing like the constant irritations which the British Foreign Office inflicted on the NID throughout the war, there was friction early in 1915 between the German Naval Staff and von Bethmann Hollweg, the German Chancellor. The former wanted intensified submarine warfare, while Bethmann Hollweg opposed this plan. Von Rintelen became personally involved in all this and, from the beginning of his stay in the USA, he was frustrated by German diplomats on the spot and seems particularly to have incurred the dislike of Colonel von Papen.

Count Bernstorff, the German Ambassador in Washington, even went to the extent of asking the German Admiralty to recall von Rintelen on the grounds that there was not the slightest chance of his being able to fulfil his mission. But they reckoned without the resourcefulness of the naval intelligence officer. Von Rintelen lost no time in recruiting a team of saboteurs, astonishing them by his technical knowledge. With sulphuric acid, chlorate of potash and sugar and lengths of lead piping he was able to show how a whole series of fires could be started in ships at sea. If the ships were not put out of action, at least their cargoes would be damaged.

The cargoes which were his targets were, of course, those in ships carrying ammunition and armaments to the Allied Powers. When, as a result of his sabotage plans, a fire was started in a US merchant ship taking arms to European ports, the captain's duty was immediately to flood the overheated holds, thus damaging the munitions. But, such was the urgent demand for munitions at this period of the war when the shell shortage was acutest that, if and when these cargoes arrived on the other side of the Atlantic, they were retrieved, dried and sent to the Forces. The tragedy was that American shells most unfairly gained a bad reputation because a fair percentage of them had been baked and dried before being delivered to the Allied troops, often causing premature explosions with loss of human life, or were duds that failed to explode when fired at the enemy.

As the war continued so von Rintelen developed other techniques for sabotage. His first inclination had been to concentrate on devices which merely started fires in the holds of merchant ships so that there was no tell-tale explosion, but merely damage done to the cargoes through a fire which might appear to have been an accident. But once these fires increased it was obvious that sabotage would be suspected and von Rintelen decided that greater subtlety would have to be adopted to counteract searches of the ships before they sailed. Together with his aide, Lieutenant Fay, he constructed incendiary devices concealed in children's toys, tinned food and even lumps of coal. Finally, he developed what became known as the rudder bomb by which he aimed to destroy ships' steering gear. In order to satisfy himself that this project was feasible, von Rintelen spent a good deal of his own money, as well as funds provided by the German Admiralty, in building a model ship in a remote part of the American countryside. He attached a detonator to the rudder of this ship and an iron pin at the tip of the detonator was linked to the rudder shaft so that when the shaft was turned the pin turned with it, ultimately causing an explosion which would destroy the rudder.

Lieutenant Fay was given the task of trying out this rudder bomb and went to New York to seek out munitions transports on which he might experiment. Using a motor-boat, which he hired without any difficulty, he was able to fix his devices onto the rudders of two ships without being detected. Both ships sailed and each lost its rudder, one having to be towed back to harbour, the other being abandoned. But from then on von Rintelen and Fay decided not to risk a repetition of their swashbuckling attempts to plant bombs from a high-speed motor-boat: slack as the port authorities seemed to be in the USA, the saboteurs' tactics must force them to take some counter-measures eventually. Yet it was only very slowly that the US Navy recognized that sabotage was being planned around its own dockyards and the nation's ports.

The ONI was still a very small office as late as 1915, having eight officers and as many clerks and only seven naval attachés with two assistants covering eleven capitals. It did not dawn on the authorities that while a small organization could achieve such brilliant results in a small war like that with Spain, it was not capable of tackling the problems posed even by America's neutrality in the midst of a global war. The main need for the ONI was counterintelligence to cope with the security problems, but this was not something for which the ONI was then fitted to cope. This may be judged from the fact that, in 1913, the Navy Department had asked the Burns Detective Agency, not the ONI, to investigate the theft of plans from the USS battleship, *Pennsylvania*.[5]

Nevertheless, by this time Naval Intelligence was responsible for the security of American ships, but it was not until America entered the war that ships' inspections were carried out in a positive fashion. During the uneasy period of neutrality the British had the difficult task of planning their own counter-espionage measures in the USA, directed against Boy-Ed, von Rintelen and their gangs. And it was the NID which spearheaded the effort to break up the sabotage ring in the USA.

The phrase NID was hardly ever used by those in the know: it was always 'Room 40', or '40 OB'. The 'OB' referred to the Old Building of the Admiralty. There has been some confusion over the phrase 'Room 40' which has been taken by some to refer to the NID as a whole. This was not so. Hugh Cleland

Hoy, who was private secretary to the DNI, declared that he 'never entered the room known as "40 OB", nor did I ask to be allowed to see it'. He added that 'in a quiet wing of the Old Building of the Admiralty a home was found for this most secret of all war work, and there in Room 40, Sir Alfred Ewing and his staff installed themselves. 40 OB was of the Intelligence Division, but not in it. It was, in fact, situated nowhere near the offices allotted to the NID and very few knew of its existence at all.'[6]

In the NID there was an incongruous assortment of individuals in this period—Fellows of Oxford and Cambridge, a Director of the Bank of England, a famous music critic, a well-known actor, a publisher, an art expert, a world-famous dress designer and a Roman Catholic priest. There were close links for the first time between the British, Russian, French and Italian Admiralties and Hall even sent out a team of decipherers to help the Italians when they were having problems over Austrian naval signals. After the incident of the *Magdeburg* the NID insisted that whenever any German vessel sank in relatively shallow waters, dredging should be carried out to see if signal- and code-books could be located. Fishing trawlers were also encouraged to enter into this operation and one of them brought up in its net a whole collection of German code-books and other documents. It was several weeks later that the NID realized these contained the key for reading messages between the German Admiralty and their naval attachés overseas. In due course Hall was able to analyse some of the messages going to these attachés and to learn of sabotage plans.

Von Rintelen declared that 'my most fanatical helpers were the Irish. They swarmed about the various ports with detonators in their pockets and lost no opportunity of having a smack at an English ship. They still did not know who I was, for they had been told I was connected with Irish Home Rule organizations. I soon, however, had to refrain from employing them, for, in their blind hatred of England, they had begun to use their bombs in a way we had not intended.[7]

The German naval attaché was horrified to learn that one of his Irish agents had just boasted that he had put two of the explosive devices into the mail room of the *Ancona*, a British ship carrying passengers and not shells or armaments. Realizing that if the devices went off while the ship was at sea an international incident could be caused, von Rintelen sent his aide to recover the 'cigars' (as the devices were called) from the *Ancona* before she sailed.

> Luckily . . . we knew that the 'cigars' were in a cardboard box, made up as a postal package. Weiser knew the address that was on it, and after a long talk with the postal official on the *Ancona* and the exchange of some dollar bills of large denomination, he returned out of breath but happy, with the dangerous parcel in his pocket.[8]

Hall ordered the British naval attaché in Washington, Commodore Guy Gaunt (later Admiral Sir Guy Gaunt) to organize a counterespionage effort against von Rintelen. Gaunt, a rogue sea-dog somewhat in the Elizabethan tradition, had no inhibitions about how to tackle this assignment. He had a hearty contempt for diplomatic niceties and a real appetite for the business of espionage. Gaunt recruited some Czech agents, hostile to the Central Powers, and by devious means and considerable enterprise managed to get them jobs inside the Austrian Consulate-General in New York. As a direct result of this he secured copies of documents being sent to Berlin and Vienna.

One of the most interesting of these documents was a message from Count Constantin Dumba, the Austrian Ambassador, which stated: 'We can disorganize and hold up for months, if not entirely prevent, the manufacture of munitions which, in the opinion of the German military attaché, is of great importance, and amply outweighs the small expenditure of money involved.'

By this time Hall had acquired that rare quality in a naval officer—an astute political sense. He felt sure that, in the propaganda battle being waged in the USA between the Central Powers and the Allies, the revelation of these documents could help turn the tide in favour of the Allies. But the Foreign Office in London was obstructive and wanted to delay a decision. Hall, who had decided long before that the NID needed allies independent of the Foreign Office, had established a close relationship with the US Embassy in London. He showed a copy of the documents to Edward Bell, the secretary at the Embassy in charge of intelligence, who promptly sent it to the US Government. It was this move on Hall's part which paved the way to the US Government declaring von Papen and Boy-Ed to be *persona non grata* and having them recalled to Berlin.

In the meantime von Rintelen and Gaunt led each other a gay fandango of impudent enterprise. As both men were liable to make the most of an exploit and embellish it with many imaginative details, it is not easy to establish from their respective narratives who was the bigger romancer. Von Rintelen told an extraordinary story of how, knowing that Gaunt was on his track, he ingratiated himself with a young American girl in order to be invited to a dance which Gaunt was attending. Posing as 'Commander Brannon' of the Royal Navy, von Rintelen got himself introduced to Gaunt and learned that 'there is a gang working in New York Harbour under the direction of a German officer. He is called Rintelen and has been mentioned a number of times in wireless messages by the German Embassy.'[9]

Years later Gaunt admitted that von Rintelen had fooled him on more than one occasion, but denied that he had been hood-winked to the extent of giving away vital information, including movements of ships, to a bogus British officer whose credentials he had not checked. Eventually, harried by Gaunt's agents and frustrated by hostile colleagues in his own Embassy, von Rintelen was ordered to return to Germany. The message telling him to do so was intercepted by Room 40 and Hall gave orders for a close watch to be kept on all ships calling at British ports. Von Rintelen returned in a Holland-America Line ship, posing as E. V. Gache, a Swiss national. Hoy, Hall's private secretary, stated that when von Rintelen's ship reached South-ampton 'a Scotland Yard detective appeared on the scene, found von Rintelen in his state-room with a well-known West End actress with whom he had become very friendly on the voyage and arrested him'. Admiral James, however, insisted that it was at Ramsgate where von Rintelen's ship was boarded by an armed naval party and that the naval attaché 'tried to bluff them into believing he was a Swiss attached to the Legation in Berlin, but the officer in charge was not satisfied and took him ashore'.

Von Rintelen's own version of events is that he was detained at Ramsgate and he makes it clear that he stubbornly maintained he was E. V. Gache until he learned that a check was to be made with the Swiss authorities in Berne. Then he admitted to Hall, who had insisted on interviewing him at the first opportunity, that he was indeed the German naval attaché from Washington. There seems to have been mutual admiration between Hall and von Rintelen. The latter revealed little in cross-examination by the NID about which he was generous in his comments in his memoirs: 'they never did things by halves. Our people in New York were careless in regard to the code . . . I suspected already that they [the British] were in possession of the German Secret Code.'[10]

Von Rintelen escaped one day from Donnington Hall where he had been interned. Hall ordered that all trains were to be examined at their next stopping points and all outgoing ships to be stopped until given the word of release. It says much for Hall's influence that he could arrange for this promptly to be carried out. Von Rintelen was recaptured in Leicester and the trains were allowed to resume their journeys unhindered, but Hall forgot to send a similar signal about the ships. Two days later there came a message from Scapa Flow asking how much longer neutral ships were to be prevented from sailing as they were congesting British ports. 'This was almost the only instance of forgetfulness on the part of the DNI that I ever noticed,' wrote his secretary, Hoy.[11]

World War I was the first of the 'wireless wars' and both sides had much to learn about the disadvantages as well as the advantages of this new line of communications. Navies depended almost entirely on wireless telegraphy for intelligence as the aeroplane was not yet capable of keeping a watch on an enemy's fleet. The vast bulk of intelligence data sifted by the warring navies came from intercepted wireless messages. German diplomatic coded messages were so carelessly processed that they were picked up and read by the British with the greatest of ease. Perhaps the best illustration of this is from von Rintelen's own observations: ' "Do you know", he [Admiral Hall] asked, "how many routes were used to send telegrams to America?" '

Von Rintelen did not know and found it extraordinary that Hall, now promoted to the rank of Admiral, was able to tell him there were five such routes. Apart from the direct route to New York, there was the Stockholm route which

> . . . had not been safe either, for the British possessed the key to the Secret Code of the Swedish Foreign Office as well. The third way, via Holland and Spain, was no better than the other two, since England had agents in her pay in the post offices of those countries who passed the German wires on to the Naval Intelligence; and they were in the code that Admiral Hall was able to read. A telegram handed in by the German naval attaché at Madrid led eventually to Mata Hari being shot at Vincennes! Even the fourth route, through the American Embassy in Berlin, was accessible to Admiral Hall, for I now learnt that Mr. Gerard, even when the United States were completely neutral, sent our telegrams by cable to the chief telegraph office in London for transmission to America. Since the English were in possession of the key, and Gerard let them know which wires came from the German Government, they had no difficulty in reading them. Thus none of the five routes was secret and they all led to Admiral Hall.[12]

Almost certainly never again in history will there be any Chief of Naval Intelligence who will acquire such influence and authority as Hall did in World War I. Impatience and love of efficiency for its own sake caused him to cut corners and by-pass the politicians. 'Hall is one genius that the war has developed,' wrote Dr Page, the American Ambassador in London, to President Wilson. 'Neither in fiction, nor in fact, can you find any such man to match him. Of the wonderful things I know he has done, there are several that it would take an exciting volume to tell. The man is a genius. . . . All other secret service men are amateurs by comparison.'[13]

Hall often had the advantage of being better informed than the Foreign Office. No Intelligence Officer on the German side wielded anything like his power. The nearest approach to Hall among the Germans was a man who was very much in the shadows and did not acquire comparable authority until long after the war was over. While Hall was at the zenith of his powers, Wilhelm Canaris was still serving with the German

13 (*right*) Inside the Admiralty decoding room, February 1941

14 (*below*) Ian Fleming at the Admiralty

15 Captain L. F. Safford (*right*) talks with Captain A. D. Kramer during an interval in the hearing before the Joint Pearl Harbor Inquiry Committee on 6 February 1946. At the hearing Captain Safford admitted that he broke naval regulations by writing to Captain Kramer in an effort to clear Rear Admiral H. E. Kimmel of the blame for Pearl Harbor (*Associated Press*)

Fleet. Nevertheless, in the story of twentieth-century naval intelligence, the careers of Hall and Canaris are in some ways parallel, at others in stark contrast. Canaris, the son of a Westphalian industrialist with Italian ancestry, was most un-Teutonic in his manner, habits and tastes. In later life he would often call himself 'a Mediterranean by temperament' and on occasions was heard to claim that he had Greek blood in his veins. He served in U-boats in the early part of the war and was then given the task of arranging refuelling and refits for German U-boats in foreign ports. He was highly successful in this work, revealing a talent for diplomacy in his negotiations with port officials and consuls and displaying a remarkable skill in effectively disseminating false information on the movements of German submarines.

Very soon Canaris was marked out for a career as an intelligence officer and could have had a high rank in the German Admiralty Intelligence Service, had he wished. But he preferred to work as a loner. There was about Canaris a baffling quality which contrasted strangely to the forthright Hall. He was a dreamer and it was in his daydreaming that his best ideas for intelligence came. As a young officer, his curiosity about all manner of things and his constant questioning in search of knowledge had caused him to be nicknamed *Kieker* (the peeper). Efficient, quietly spoken, often pensive, courteous, but secretive, he was suspected of being somewhat of a conspirator. Such qualities do not win many friends in a service such as the Navy and Canaris made enemies among those who were jealous of his superior brain power. Intellectually, Canaris was vastly superior to Hall, but it is doubtful if he had the same capacity for swift and vigorous action.

The Royal Navy was indirectly responsible for Canaris getting his first chance to play a lone game as a naval intelligence officer. When the cruiser *Dresden* was halted by the Royal Navy in March 1915, Canaris was interned in Chile. Thereafter his resourcefulness and cunning were tested to the full. Coolly and impudently he escaped from internment, leaving Chile in a British ship with a forged Chilean passport in the name of Mr Reed-Rosas. Arriving in Spain, he set himself up to wage an almost one-man intelligence war against the Allies. Richard Protze, who was later to become Canaris' chief of counterespionage, said that from his base in Spain Canaris 'blew up nine British ships'. He also helped to foment trouble among the tribesmen of Morocco and to create a diversion to occupy the French who had a protectorate there. Canaris' bribes to some of the Moorish tribes and his active incitement to revolt came to the ears of Admiral Hall who immediately alerted one of his ablest overseas agents, the novelist, A. E. W. Mason, whose area of operations was Gibraltar, Spain and Morocco.

Mason, who had sailed in a yacht around the Spanish and Moroccan ports, had obtained much valuable information about German ships and submarines which made use of Spanish facilities by surreptitiously refuelling in Spanish ports. He had learned that the mysterious Mr Reed-Rosas was connected with this. But the latter's identity was still kept secret from the British. It can be seriously doubted whether Mason was able to thwart Canaris' plans to any marked extent, for the German had a remarkable understanding of the Arab character and his influence with the North African tribes from Morocco to Tunis remained strong even during World War II.

The French got on the track of Canaris long before the British and he had a narrow escape from being captured by them on his way back to Germany aboard submarine U-35. Then for a while he returned to submarines. This seems to have been a foolish decision by the German Admiralty, for he would have made an admirable head of Naval Intelligence.

One of the earliest decisions with political implications which Hall had to take was that concerning the former Liberal Member of Parliament, Trebitsch Lincoln. By birth a Hungarian Jew, Lincoln, otherwise known as Ignaz Trevich, had become a Presbyterian in Hamburg, married a German woman, then emigrated to Canada where he was ordained a deacon of the Church of England by the Archbishop of Montreal. In 1903 he came to Britain as a curate at Appledore in Kent, was naturalized as a British subject and, in a sensational by-election, had been elected MP for Darlington. However, his success was short-lived; he lost so much in speculation in the Galician oilfields that he was unable to raise funds to stand for Parliament at the next election. When war came, Lincoln, who was then desperately short of money, secured a job in the censorship of mail department in the Hungarian and Rumanian section. Then suddenly he offered his services to the NID.

'Lincoln's extraordinary idea', wrote Hugh Hoy, who handled this case, 'was that on a certain day a part of the British Fleet should be lured into a selected area of the North Sea and that the High Seas Fleet should be within easy distance. To this officer [one under whom he had worked at the censorship department] he cunningly proposed just the reverse of this snare, and he laid before him a carefully arranged schedule, which proved, ostensibly, the practicability of decoying and destroying part of the German Navy. All his schedule lacked for the complete success of the plan was the insertion of the battle stations of our Fleet. But the imperative secrecy of these stations made any disclosure of them to Lincoln impossible, and his scheme was promptly rejected.'[14]

Lincoln was brusquely dismissed by Hall at the first interview, though the DNI did not finally slam the door on the daringly bizarre project. If Hall erred at all, it was in all probability that he might have played along with Lincoln rather more subtly, if only to find out more. Lincoln was highly sensitive to atmosphere and he detected at once a deep mistrust of his motives. But audacity was one of the main weapons of Lincoln's repertoire as a spy. He went to Rotterdam, ostensibly to obtain information which he thought would finally impress the NID. Hall had, however, ordered that a close watch was to be kept on all Lincoln's movements. He soon learned that Lincoln had visited the German Consul in Rotterdam, a man named Gneist who was notorious as an active spy. Gneist, it was presumed, gave him some valueless information to take back to London as a snare for the NID.

The ex-MP's downfall proved to be the elaborate system of codes he had devised for communicating with the Germans and these were swiftly broken. Hoy cites these examples of Lincoln's codes:

1 ' "Weber, Rotterdam. Best love to Mary, love to Alice and fondest love to aunts in Rosendaal. Do write . . ."

'This meant "Weber, Rotterdam. Two *Lord Nelson* class battleships, two super-dreadnoughts". It was what Lincoln called his "family code" and would seem to be so patently a coded message that even a censor could hardly fail to refer it back for further examination.

2 ' "Sherensky, Rotterdam. Cable prices five consignments vaseline, eight paraffin." This was Lincoln's "oil code" which was slightly less obvious. Translated, it meant that stationed at Dover were five first-class cruisers and eight destroyers.

3 ' "92–02 70–019 140–07 217–033 124–026 91–13 93–15." This was Lincoln's "dictionary code" made out in numbers and meant "Four divisions new troops leaving for France". The first figure referred to the number of a page in a dictionary, the second and third to the column and number of words in the column. Dummy words with no meaning would be added to give plausibility to the figures.'[15]

When Lincoln returned from Rotterdam he claimed he was in possession of the code by which the movements of the British Fleet were being reported to Germany, the code used by German spies in Britain and addresses to which the latter were sending letters and telegrams. Once again he saw Hall who told him that nothing had been done as yet, but that a message had been sent to the German Consul in Rotterdam pretending to come from Lincoln and telling him to be patient as 'things were going very well'. This aroused Lincoln's suspicions and he made immediate plans to leave the country. The extraordinary feature of this case was not so much Lincoln's treachery as the handling of it by the British. Neither Hoy, nor Hall's biographer explain this and indeed dismiss it somewhat cursorily. James simply says that Hall 'frightened Lincoln out of his wits and he fled to New York', while all Hoy says is that 'his quick brain must have been busy even while he talked with Admiral Hall, in forming plans for a hasty departure from the country'.

Why was Lincoln not arrested then? He was already wanted for forging the signature of his former employer on a money draft and this could have been used as a pretext for his arrest. To let Lincoln go was almost certainly a deliberate 'political' decision on Hall's part, and there is some evidence that Lincoln's escape was actually facilitated by the NID. It might be that Hall believed Lincoln could lead his own agents in the USA to another German spy network, if he was allowed to go free. But there is some evidence that people in high places in the Government were liable to be blackmailed by Lincoln and that they had pressed for no action to be taken against him. Both theories were to some extent upheld by Lincoln himself. Later he wrote: 'That night I took a train to Liverpool and two days later I was on the Atlantic, laughing at the discomfiture of Scotland Yard and of Admiral Hall. . . . In America I flattered myself I could work for Germany against England, for I held papers concerning naval and military matters that would have condemned me if discovered. I knew the addresses of scores of agents in the United States.'[16]

In his autobiography, published while he was in the USA, Lincoln hinted that a British Cabinet minister had, both before the war and since, been secretly in league with the Germans and pursued a pro-German policy. This revelation, coupled with Lincoln's journalistic tirades against the British in some American papers, probably did far more harm to the Allied cause than any of his espionage work. Eventually Britain made an application for his extradition and he was arrested and sent back to London, where he was tried on a charge of forging a cheque. He was sentenced to three years' penal servitude, after which he was deported to Hungary.

6

Admiral Hall: A Modern Machiavelli

Admiral Hall's political instincts were tested to the full during the period of planning for the Dardanelles operation, which, enthusiastically backed by Winston Churchill, then at the Admiralty, aimed to shorten the war by making an expedition to the Middle East to knock out the Turks.

The tragedy for Churchill was that his bold initiative was hampered by obstructiveness first from Kitchener, Secretary of State for War, and later by Admiral Fisher, the First Sea Lord. Fisher's actions were not far short of sabotage. Yet, had naval intelligence been acted upon soon enough, it is possible that Turkey could have been detached from the Central Powers without any expeditions being necessary, or at least nothing more than token landings. Unfortunately there was in the Admiralty a coterie which actually despised the NID. In his early days as DNI Hall learned this to his cost. George Aston (later Sir George), who had switched from Military Intelligence to the NID in 1913, found constant pin-pricks in his dealings with those in the Admiralty outside his own department. The Admiralty were totally opposed to using carrier pigeons for intelligence messages, despite Aston's warning that 'pigeon post' might well be effective when wireless broke down, or in areas not covered by wireless. One of the ablest intelligence officers of his generation, Aston was a specialist in Middle Eastern affairs, on which he had provided many reports for the NID even before the war. His information on Turkey was particularly sound, and he believed that Turkey could be detached from the German alliance. Diplomacy in this area was timorous and Hall decided to embark on some political adventuring on his own account. At this stage of the war Germany, being fully engaged on the Western Front, had very much left Turkey to fend for herself and indicated that not much help could be expected from Berlin. Hall sensed that Turkish morale was affected by this attitude and gave top priority to naval intelligence from the Middle East. One of his best agents was Gerald Fitzmaurice, who had for some years been attached to the British Embassy in Constantinople and had been recalled before the war because some appeasing mentor in the British Foreign Office had urged that his activities were not conducive to good Anglo-German relations.

Hall's aim was to try, through his agents, to persuade the Turks to break with Germany and promote revolution against Enver Pasha and the 'Young Turk' Party then in power, or to encourage the more moderate members of the Party to make peace with Britain. If this could be achieved, even partially, then Hall was convinced that it would be possible for British ships to be given a peaceful passage through the Dardanelles. A message came through to Room 40 from an agent in Turkey stating that prayers were being offered up in the mosques for the arrival of the British. Acting on his own initiative and without telling the Cabinet, Hall sent negotiators a letter guaranteeing three million pounds for the success of a plan for reconciliation with Britain. Further, Hall was prepared to pay £500,000 for the complete surrender of the Dardanelles and the removal of all mines. It was a wild gamble and, even if the Turks had agreed, the Admiralty and the War Cabinet might have vetoed payment. But Hall was convinced the daring risk was justified.

Typical of the lack of liaison between the Admiralty and the NID was this memorandum from Admiral Lord Fisher to his naval secretary, Captain Crease, in this period: 'Tell W. R. Hall to find out from the Foreign Office by 11 a.m. where Fitzmaurice is—he was last in Sofia—and what his orders are. He is now the most important person in the Eastern theatre of the war, but unfortunately this is not realized.' Hall was able to assure the First Sea Lord that Fitzmaurice had for some time past been working for the NID.

The relationship between Hall and Fisher is somewhat

obscured by contemporary observers. In the early days Fisher was a strong supporter of Hall and had given him great encouragement. But many of those closely associated with Fisher —or 'in the Fish Pond', as was the naval colloquialism for such men—were hostile to the NID. Hall, believing that his judgement in political matters was superior to that of his seniors at the Admiralty, had cautiously gone his own way, and, had kept quiet as to his own plans. Probably Hall had already begun to question Fisher's judgement and to see signs of that megalomania which in the end was to destroy the First Sea Lord. For a few weeks there was a chance that, unknown to Fisher, unknown even to the British Cabinet, Hall would bring off the greatest coup of the war, for that, and no less, is what it would have been. The Turks were short of ammunition, Turko-German relations were at a low ebb and the chances of a successful coup were in the realms of possibility.

From the intelligence reports before him, Hall knew that the forcing of the narrows would be a hazardous task for the Royal Navy and that disaster might confront the Fleet if all possible precautions were not taken. At the last moment more news came from Turkey, indicating that the shortage of ammunition was dire. Hall confronted Fisher with this information and proceeded, somewhat unwisely as it transpired, to show his own hand. He indicated to the First Sea Lord his plan for establishing an understanding with the Turks. Fisher then, quixotically and quite irrationally, decided to go through with the Dardanelles project which he had hitherto regarded as an operation fraught with hazards. At the same time he ruined all chances of its success by forbidding Hall to go ahead with his negotiations.

Meanwhile some of the NID agents in the field had actually started secret talks with the Turks and achieved a measure of success. Yet, by Fisher's decision, a chance of shortening the war was lost for ever.

It was, however, in the field of Anglo-American relations that Hall was supreme. There could not have been an abler, if often devious and sometimes downright mischievous, public relations officer for the Allied cause. He wielded considerably more political influence in the USA, even if indirectly, than any Allied statesman, not excluding Lord Balfour himself. He was always conscious of the need to give the United States the picture of a compassionate Britain. There was the case of an American youth named Mahan, arrested in 1915 on suspicion of espionage. Mahan had been engaged as a wireless operator aboard a British ship on the east coast. Proof was obtained that he was aiming to spy against the Allies. The son of respectable parents in the USA, the latter made a personal plea to the US President to intervene on their behalf. Hall decided that, as no actual harm had yet been done, and as American goodwill was of paramount importance, he would urge that Mahan be released and returned to America.

In handling Anglo-American relations Hall was much more adroit than the politicians. He achieved this on a personal basis, sometimes by making such people as Dr Page, the US Ambassador, and Edward Bell privy to his secrets. Yet the US Navy was often kept in the dark on vital matters, even after America entered the war. Hugh Hoy declared that Admiral Sims USN, was

... ignorant of the existence of 40 OB, could never understand how our department came to be so accurately informed about the enemy agents who were working from America. It frequently happened that Admiral Hall found it necessary to mention to the American admiral or his staff some suspect, or admittedly dangerous person on the other side of the Atlantic. Oftener than not the suspect had never been heard of by the USA officers and when they pursued inquiries and found our Intelligence Division to be correct in every detail, they spoke with some respect of what they considered to be our mysterious channels of information.[1]

In the controversial case of the *Lusitania*, the Atlantic passenger liner which was torpedoed by the Germans off the south coast of Ireland on 7 May 1915, Admiral Hall's more Machiavellian role in wooing American support requires closer scrutiny. He quite deliberately exploited this incident to stir up anti-German feeling in the United States and to draw the US Government away from its strictly neutral position. The sinking of this ship greatly helped to bring America nearer to entering the war.

Count von Bernstorff said afterwards that German plans had even gone so far as to put on paper a scheme for seizing New York by surprise, but that the sinking of the *Lusitania* had split the German-Americans into rival camps. Until then, so Bernstorff insisted, even the American Secret Service was filled with pro-Germans and in the American establishment there were some of German origin who would have supported an insurrection. If this statement was correct, then Hall's exploitation tactics had greater justification.

' In the torpedoing of the *Lusitania* many Americans lost their lives. The coroner's verdict on the sinking of this ship off Kinsale recorded that 'this appalling crime was contrary to international law and the conventions of all civilised nations, and we therefore charge the owners of the submarine, the German Emperor and the Government of Germany, under whose orders they acted, with the crime of wilful and wholesale murder'. Hall had a *Lusitania* medal commemorating the 'dastardly deed' specially struck as 'a lasting monument to the atrocities of a race steeped in savagery, and whose lust for blood knows no bounds'. British Foreign Office records show that some 300,000 of these medals were struck on the instructions of Hall. They were made by Gordon Selfridge, the department-store owner.

But Hall's propaganda campaign on the *Lusitania*, which was, of course, strictly outside the duties of his office, while winning many allies, was also counterproductive. Whispers arose—and they did not come solely from German sources—that the sinking of the *Lusitania* was actually manipulated by British Naval Intelligence. These whispers have grown into substantial rumours over the years, largely fanned by the British Admiralty's notorious record of not only hiding the truth, but in some instances deliberately suppressing and distorting it.

One single point, however, seems to destroy the arguments of the extremists on both sides of this trans-Atlantic controversy. This is the fact that *Jane's Fighting Ships* of 1914 and *The Naval Annual* of the same year both listed the *Lusitania* as being armed and, in the designation of the former, 'an auxiliary cruiser' and of the latter, 'an armed merchantman'. Thus it was abundantly clear, when war broke out, that this vessel should be regarded as a potential warship and neutrals taking passage in her did so at their own peril. In short, neutrals had been warned and so indeed had the enemy. But, as the details given in these nautical publications were not exactly helpful to the propaganda Hall wished to put over, they were suppressed at the time of the sinking of the *Lusitania*, which means that at least a degree of hypocrisy was being indulged in by the NID. What, however, this argument does not dispose of is the fact that, unknown to the passengers, the ship carried a cargo of munitions destined to be delivered to Germany's enemies, and that there is substantial evidence that the cargo manifests were falsified to disguise this. It was also the opinion of the US Government's Solicitor's Department that, in terms of international law, as reported to Robert M. Lansing, Counsellor to the US State Department, 'the owners and operators of the *Lusitania* appeared to have committed a breach of Section 8 of the Passenger Act of the Navigation Laws of the United States'.

It was this revelation, carefully concealed from the public by the US State Department, which made it difficult for the US Government to do much more than send a protest against the loss of American lives in the sinking of the *Lusitania*. There were certainly some curious features leading up to the *Lusitania* disaster. The ship had inadequate fuel supplies before leaving the USA. When the captain was informed that a U-boat was in the vicinity, as he approached the coast of Ireland, he failed to carry out the normal drill for such an eventuality, that is, to zig-zag at regular intervals. There was also the fact that the cruiser *Juno*, which was to have made a rendezvous with the *Lusitania* off Ireland, was signalled to abandon her escort mission and return to Queenstown. Yet it was known at the time that the U-20 was in the area. Commander Joseph Kenworthy, a member of the NID (Political Section), had been summoned to a meeting in the Admiralty that day by Winston Churchill. There can be little doubt that he was consulted because, at Churchill's request, he had submitted a paper on the political results of an ocean liner being sunk with American passengers aboard. What transpired at this meeting one does not know, but years later Kenworthy, in his book, *The Freedom of the Seas*, wrote that 'the *Lusitania* was sent at considerably reduced speed into an area where a U-boat was known to be waiting and with her escorts withdrawn'. It is not without significance that the Admiralty insisted on censoring this sentence in Kenworthy's book: he had originally written '*deliberately* sent' and that adverb was cut out.

Kenworthy went on to say that 'their Lordships had obviously decided to let the international legality and success of the German U-boat offensive be tested in the court of public opinion'. Whatever this might or might not mean, it snidely suggests that a somewhat cynical decision to leave the *Lusitania* to her fate was taken at the Admiralty that morning. As to the final disaster, the question remains as to whether the extent of the explosions aboard the ship after the torpedo hit her was caused by the highly dangerous cargo the ship was carrying under a falsified manifest. That Hall was aware of the *Lusitania*'s cargo does not seem in doubt, especially as the British naval attaché in Washington, Guy Gaunt, had arranged for the transfer of a cargo of ammunition from the ss *Queen Margaret* to the *Lusitania*. A Cunard receipt for 2,000 cases of ·303 ammunition, marked with the serial NE 101 and with the name *Queen Margaret* cancelled, had *Lusitania* written across it.

There were occasions when Hall, autocrat that he so often was, blithely neglected to inform his colleagues, whether those inside or outside the Admiralty, what moves he was making. Sometimes this secretiveness boomeranged badly. There was the occasion when he arranged with his friend, Tom Marlowe, editor of the *Daily Mail*, to print a special edition of a mere twenty-four copies, six of which had a particular paragraph blacked out. The all-important paragraph read: 'Everything here indicates the imminence of great events. . . . I am able to say that very large forces are concentrated near the coast . . . I was struck by the number of large flat-bottomed boats lying in certain harbours. . . .'

This paper was dated 12 September 1916, when the situation on the Western Front was grave. Hall's plan was to lure German troops away from the main front by spreading rumours of an imminent invasion of the north Belgian coast by the British. The copies of the special edition were smuggled into Holland where they fell into the hands of German agents. Foolishly, Hall did not inform the War Office, with the result that British Military Intelligence in France reported back to London that the Germans' moves towards the coast were probably in preparation for an invasion of Britain. The NID, of course, were certain that it was a natural German reaction to Hall's planted story, but the War Office made plans for the evacuation of towns and villages in south-east England.

It was this impish and Machiavellian desire to fight a private war of his own, often outside the naval sphere, which formed the one weak link in an otherwise extremely able intelligence chief. It was for this reason that Lloyd George, who was Prime Minister when the war ended, neither gave Hall any honours, nor allowed him to attend the Peace Conference where his advice in the background might have been invaluable. In the field of intelligence it is easily possible to be too clever and, while power may or may not tend to corrupt, it can in time overreach itself. Filson Young in his book, *With the Battle Cruisers*, makes the comment that

> . . . in the little parish magazine of *Secret Intelligence* that was served out to Commanding Officers afloat the Admiralty continued to report the *Audacious* as being with the Second Battle Squadron, although everyone in the fleet knew she had been sunk in November, and the fact had been published in the American press. It was a good example of the somewhat childish point of view of Intelligence, in which it seemed to be held a clever thing to tell a lie, in the general hope that someone might be deceived. It was one of the more innocent ways in which we tried to imitate the Germans. When they told lies it was with a definite purpose: we told them without any purpose at all.

May and June 1916, proved to be a severe testing time for the communications systems of both Germans and British. While, initially, the British had a slight advantage, the Germans, first by recognition of weaknesses in the British communications system which they quickly exploited, and then through an appalling blunder by the NID, made the honours just about even. The first major test came with the battle of Jutland, the last large-scale naval battle to be fought in either of the two world wars. The principal signals intercepted by the British before and during the battle were from the same cipher books as had been retrieved from the *Magdeburg*. Room 40 was fully informed as to what the German High Seas Fleet was planning and had a detailed picture of the movements and aims of the German C-in-C. This information was passed on to Admiral Sir John Jellicoe, the British C-in-C. But Jellicoe, who was mistrustful of nearly all innovations and especially suspicious of anything that smacked of 'cleverness', cast doubts on the information he was getting. This mistrust was also shared by Admiral Sir David Beatty, owing to a signal sent by the Admiralty shortly after noon on 31 May. The Operations Division had inquired where the directional stations placed call sign DK. They were given an answer, but nobody saw fit to ask why they wanted this information. This was most unfortunate as DK was the German C-in-C's harbour call signs, but when the latter put to sea he took a different call sign and transferred DK to the W/T station at Wilhelmshaven. This procedure was adopted to conceal the fact that his Fleet was at sea. Room 40 knew all about this, but they were not replying to the signal inquiry. Thus Beatty met the whole German Fleet at sea only a few hours after having been told that it was still in harbour.

Jutland revealed that many officers not only had inadequate training in communications generally, but that they lacked the ability of checking back on signals which failed to make sense. The truth was that Room 40 had grown too swiftly for the Navy either to handle its traffic, or properly assess its importance. Also, while Room 40 knew exactly where the German Fleet was during the night of the battle when Jellicoe's force was hunting for it, the weakness of British naval communications was shown up by the failure of the Royal Navy to pick up the messages which the NID sent them. Jutland pinpointed the weakness of a system by which the NID passed signals, without comment or guidance, to the Operations Division where it could easily happen that the officer on duty at any given moment might be inexperienced. It was evident that what was needed between Room 40 and Operations was an Intelligence Advisory Centre which could interpret the material it was getting from its decipherers, but this proposal met with opposition from the Admiralty staff and it was not for several months that Hall could get this idea accepted.

The German Fleet was swift to detect confusion and misunderstanding among the British ships at Jutland. During the long twilight they detected the recognition signals flashed by one British ship to another for identification. As soon as night fell they flashed those same signals, thus gaining valuable time for their gunnery teams to line up on British destroyers and blow them to pieces. It was not until after Jutland that Germany realized that the British had solved the whole of her naval code system and that changes were made immediately. But the Germans had been no laggards in breaking down Allied ciphers and they had also been the first to make use of high speed transmission to baffle opponents in the communications game. The German, naval-controlled radio station at Nauen followed its evening broadcast of the daily communiqué with signals sent out at such speed that they provided no clue as to whether they were intended as messages, or if they were merely testing signals. One day, in the wardroom of a British warship, the officers had played the entire repertoire of the ship's gramophone records. One of the officers insisted that they should wind up with a record that had been made of what was known as 'Nauen's ragtime gibberish'. Perhaps he had had a little too much to drink, but, in putting on the record, he forgot to wind up the gramophone and the result was that instead of the meaningless radio gibberish there came a series of deliberate cipher groups. Luckily, a cipher officer was among those present and, impressed by this discovery, he checked with the records and found that this was a message from German GHQ to the GOC in German East Africa.

In the cipher war, as soon as one side discovered the ciphers of the other, so each fed false information to the other. But it was the British who perpetrated one of the biggest blunders of the war by such methods and so paved the way to the sinking of the cruiser *Hampshire* with Lord Kitchener, the Secretary of State for War, aboard her on his way to Russia. This is perhaps the classic example of the mistrust between Operations and Intelligence. The sinking of the cruiser *Hampshire* occurred just after the battle of Jutland. The NID had for some time been busy feeding false information to the Germans. A signal book had been recovered from a salvaged German submarine and after this, according to Admiral James, 'Hall and Preston [then Captain Preston, head of the minesweeping service, later Admiral Sir Lionel Preston] followed up this success by printing a fake swept-channels pamphlet which Hall sold for a large sum to the Germans through an agent'.[2]

This statement by Admiral James is vitally important in following up the somewhat complicated story of the sinking of the *Hampshire*, about which the British Admiralty is still reticent more than half a century afterwards. In the spring of 1916 there was a Norwegian named Lange, employed in the deciphering staff of the Marine Section of Colonel Nicolai's Secret Service listening post at Neuminster. He had originally been recruited because of his experience as a wireless operator and his knowledge of British shipping routes. He had also shown an exceptional talent at deciphering. On 26 May 1916, only a few days before the battle of Jutland, Lange made what proved to be the most remarkable coup of his career. He intercepted a message which seemed to be relatively unimportant, but which struck Lange as being unusual. It was a message from a British destroyer to the Admiralty saying that a channel west of Orkney had been swept free of mines. Lange thought it was strange that the destroyer should report direct to the Admiralty and not to the shore station. In consequence he waited to see if the message was repeated. When he heard it repeated four times in an hour he was convinced there was some urgency about it. If somebody wanted the Admiralty to know that this area had been swept free of mines, it could only be because the information was of vital importance to London. He suspected that the answer was that an important ship was to take this route and that the Admiralty had to be advised it was clear of mines.

Colonel Nicolai regarded Lange's action in drawing special attention to the message as being fully justified. He knew that this particular route was never normally used by shipping, and he had also heard of Lord Kitchener's impending visit to Russia. On the strength of all this information instructions were sent to the submarine mine-layer U-75, commanded by Ober-Leutnant Kurt Beitzen, to proceed at full speed to the west coast of Orkney to lay mines on the specified route. It was one of the mines laid by U-75 which sunk the *Hampshire*. Now Admiral James stated in his biography of Hall that

Amberger, who laid the mines that sank the ship in which Kitchener was going to Russia, mistook Marwick Head for

16 Admiral Alan Kirk, USN (*Press Association*)

17 Photograph taken in May 1945 of Captain Ellis Zacharias, USN (*US Navy*)

Hoo, and laid them in the wrong position. But it was not Amberger who laid these mines. Admiral Sir Lionel Preston wrote to me as follows: 'When I became Director of Mine-sweeping at the Admiralty I was permitted to follow all movements of mine-laying submarines in the Very Secret Room, where they were plotted. I thus got to know each German submarine commander by name and the ship he commanded. How far these names were accurate I cannot say, but Amberger was allotted to U-80 and his area of operation was in the Minches. I understand, however, at a later date that a young submarine commander, whose first trip it was, as a commanding officer, was for some reason or other allotted the job of dropping his mines off the Hoo, and that there is no doubt whoever laid them, they were erroneously dropped off Marwick Head. This was Ober-Leutnant Kurt Beitzen and not Amberger. I can say this, the mysterious Amberger was never captured under this name, nor could he have had any part in the laying of mines off Marwick.'[3]

Lists of German submarine commanders show that between 1915 and 1918 the U-80 had three commanding officers—Korvetten-Kapitan von Glasenapp, Korvetten-Kapitan Gustav Amberger and Korvetten-Kapitan Scherp. Glasenapp and Scherp are both dead, but some twenty years ago Herr Max Scherp, a distant relative, confirmed that Korvetten-Kapitan Scherp was the last commander of the U-80 and said this submarine was used 'primarily for secret missions and very special mine-laying assignments'. As to Amberger, he was not in command of U-80 until August 1917. One of the pieces of 'evidence' upon which the rumourmongers based their claim that the Germans knew the route the *Hampshire* was to take was the report that some of the mines recovered off Marwick Head bore the inscription 'Death to Kitchener'. This 'evidence' is a complete distortion of the facts. About a month after the cruiser sank, Admiral Preston personally dismantled a mine found ashore near Cape Wrath. This was inscribed with the words *Kurfels Kitchener* and was believed by the admiral to have been laid by Amberger in U-80.[4]

To the British Mine-sweeping Department Amberger was well known and regarded as rather a joke. 'He never seemed to get in the right place', said Admiral Preston, 'and although the Minches do not cover much water, merchant ships seldom suffered from his attentions. We looked upon Amberger as a dud.'[5]

Controversy and mystery surrounded the tragedy of the *Hampshire* for many years and it was not until ten years later that, after constant questioning in Parliament, a stubborn and evasive British Admiralty eventually issued a White Paper on the sinking of the cruiser. It was really a white-washing paper, for it added little to what was already known and hid most of the facts. The most important of these hidden facts was that the Admiralty's right hand did not know what its left hand was doing: in the White Paper the Admiralty insisted that the mines were laid off Marwick Head by mistake, but they did not explain that the mistake was their responsibility.[6]

The Germans, who had learned of Kitchener's mission to Russia, had warned their Admiralty to take special measures. Lange's report was taken seriously and in an attempt to intercept and destroy the ship carrying Kitchener and at the same time to lure the British Fleet to destruction, ten mine-laying submarines were sent into action. Hall, on his side, played his own game with signals and his 'misinformation' tactics without telling his superiors. The signal which Lange had intercepted was one which had emanated from Hall's department and which was intended to mislead the Germans and to cause them to lay mines in this area, where in normal circumstances they would have harmed nobody and simply been wasted. Yet, instead of misleading the Germans, British Naval Intelligence had fallen into the very trap they themselves had set. No one had informed the Commander-in-Chief that mines might be laid in this area in consequence of the bait set for the Germans by the wireless message. The message had been sent in cipher in the very system which Hall had sold to the Germans through a double-agent. It was repeated four times so that the Germans should not miss receiving it.

This is the explanation of the mystery of the *Hampshire's* sinking; it also explains the Admiralty's reticence when pressed to reveal the secret report on the whole affair and the legend which persisted for many years that the British Secret Service had engineered Lord Kitchener's death. It was the NID trying to be too clever which caused the sinking of the *Hampshire*.

After the battle of Jutland the staff of Room 40 was increased and improved equipment for direction-finding provided. Carefully edited and amplified summaries of intercepted messages were passed through to Operations instead of the more or less literal translations previously given. Hugh Cleland Hoy was given the task of reading through the hundreds of intercepted messages and selecting those which should be passed on, this time taking particular care to note whether the information should go to the Cabinet, Operations, MI5, or Scotland Yard. In May 1916, Ewing had retired from his post as chief of Room 40, becoming principal of the University of Edinburgh.

Hall's greatest triumph and the one which brought him most political kudos was the 'Zimmermann telegram'. Partly as a result of the work of one of his agents, Alexander Szek, and two cryptographers in the NID, Nigel de Grey and the Reverend William Montgomery, Hall intercepted the following message, dated 16 January 1916:

BERLIN TO WASHINGTON.

Most secret for Your Excellency's personal information and to be handed on to the Imperial Minister in [?] Mexico with . . . by a safe route. We propose to begin on the 1 February unrestricted submarine warfare. In doing this however we shall endeavour to keep America neutral . . . [?] If we should not [succeed in doing so] we propose to [? Mexico] an alliance upon the following basis:

[Joint] conduct of war [joint] conclusion of peace . . . Your Excellency should for the present inform the President secretly [? that we expect] war with the USA [possibly] [Japan] and at the same time to negotiate between us and Japan . . . Please tell the President that . . . our submarines . . . will compel England to peace within a few months. Acknowledge receipt.

ZIMMERMANN.[7]

Arthur Zimmermann was the German Foreign Minister and the message he was sending was destined for his ambassador in Washington. Gaps in the deciphering still needed to be filled in, but clearly this was a threat of unrestricted submarine warfare. Zimmermann had sent his notorious cable by two channels to make sure it arrived safely: on what was known as the 'Swedish roundabout', which carried German telegrams first to South America, relaying them from there to Washington and Mexico City; secondly, by American diplomatic cables, a more direct route. But both lines passed through Britain where they were intercepted by Room 40.

Hall ordered that every effort should be made to fill in the gaps in the message, but, without waiting for the result of this, he took the partly de-coded message to Lord Balfour, who was by then the Foreign Secretary. Balfour decided to take no diplomatic action himself, but to give Hall a free hand to act as he thought best. It was a wise decision because only Hall could effectively explain the deciphering of the telegram to the Americans. The admiral took a copy of the message to his friend, Edward Bell, in the US Embassy in London. Hoy recorded that nothing could be 'more exasperating than those baffling blanks', but that 'at the third attempt the skill of the experts triumphed and Germany's secret—the greatest since she struck the first blow of the war—was clear'.[8]

The revised de-coding of the message now read:

We intend to begin on 1 February unrestricted submarine warfare. We shall endeavour, in spite of this, to keep the United States neutral. In the event of this not succeeding we shall make Mexico a proposal of alliance on the following basis: make war together, make peace together, generous financial support, and an understanding on our part that Mexico is to reconquer the lost territory in Texas, New Mexico and Arizona. The settlement in detail is left to you. You will inform the President, that is President Carranza of Mexico, of the above most secretly as soon as the outbreak of war with the United States is certain, and add the suggestion that he should on his own initiative invite Japan to immediate adherence and at the same time mediate between Japan and ourselves. Please call the President's attention to the fact that the ruthless employment of our submarines offers the prospect of compelling England in a few months to make peace.

Hall, however, was not exactly filled with joy when he read the revised decoding. While knowing that, if the message could be shown to be genuine beyond doubt, this was just the news to bring the USA into the war on the side of the Allies, he also realized that it would seem hardly credible that the Germans could think up anything as stupid as promising to give Texas, New Mexico and Arizona to Mexico. He felt sure the Americans would suspect that this was a faked message probably planted by the NID. Apart from this, there was also the risk that, in trying to convince the Americans of the genuineness of the message, the latter would learn all about Room 40. And as American security in such matters was practically non-existent then, this would be tantamount to telling every enemy and neutral nation that Room 40 was tapping cables.

Hoy's record of how the full text was obtained at the 'third attempt' was only partially accurate. Some outside help was needed if the Americans were to be convinced that the message was not planted, while at the same time guarding the secret of Room 40. Hall suspected that the 'Imperial Minister' referred to was the German diplomatic representative in Mexico City. So he sent a message to his agent in Mexico, succinctly explaining the situation and ordering him to burgle the offices of the Western Union Telegraph Company in Mexico City. So the files of the cable office were rifled and the copy of Zimmermann's cable secured. This supplied the missing links in the original message, making it abundantly clear that Mexico was involved. It also gave Hall the opportunity of claiming that he obtained the cable from Mexico and not through tapping in London. Thus he was able to cover up the activities of Room 40.

Even then the President of the United States, Woodrow Wilson, believed it was all a British plot and demanded further proof that the message was authentic. Hall suggested that, as Zimmermann had sent his message on American diplomatic cables, there should be a copy of the original telegram in the files of the US State Department. Psychologically, this was a touch of genius on Hall's part for the Americans had believed that the Germans would not abuse their neutrality if they were permitted to send cables on this route. Now they were to learn that the Germans had actually used this route to plot the dismemberment of the USA. The Americans found the cable, but were not able to decipher it without the help of the NID. This Hall gave them in a manner which entirely assuaged all doubts about the devious British. On 2 April 1917, the United States declared war against Germany. Hall's diplomatic-cum-espionage coup had succeeded where mere diplomacy had failed. It was a turning point in the war.

There were good reasons for the Americans being so mistrustful of Hall and the NID, even if the admiral had many friends among them. They were aware of his political intrigues and his concocted stories to fox the enemy and inside the State Department there was considerable disquiet about his role in the *Lusitania* affair. But it was his exploitation of the trial of Sir Roger Casement that created serious mistrust among some Americans close to President Wilson. This revealed Hall in a most unpleasant light.

The DNI had been determined to bring Casement to book since the early days of the war, employing large sums of money in obtaining intelligence on Casement's activities in Germany and elsewhere and even employing a yacht to spy around the west coast of Ireland, keeping watch for his return from Germany. Eventually Room 40 intercepted a message from Berlin saying that Casement would be landed from a German submarine off the coast of Ireland. As a result, in April 1916, Casement was arrested as he came ashore near Tralee. Subsequently he was tried in London and sentenced to death. There were various petitions for a reprieve, as Casement was highly respected both in Britain and overseas, not merely on account of his diplomatic services for which he had been knighted, but for his campaign against the ill-treatment of native workers in Latin America. To counteract the wave of sympathy for Casement, Hall privately circulated copies of a diary which, it was alleged, had been found in Casement's luggage: these were shown to MPs, journalists and staff at the US Embassy in London. The diary purported to show that Casement had indulged in homosexual practices with native boys in Latin America and the details were spelt out down to the minutiae of depravity. They were, of course, irrelevant to the charges against Casement or to naval intelligence and Hall was grossly overstepping his authority in carrying out this smear campaign. There was a strong suspicion in some quarters that the pornographic entries were interpolated into the diary text and that third person narratives were turned into first person descriptions of vicious practices. Dr W. J. Maloney, an American, disclosed in an article in the *Irish Times* in 1937, that Admiral Hall was responsible for circulating typewritten extracts from the diary. Further, he asserted that, by keeping the diary away from any expert who could possibly refute it and by instructing agents that they could show the material, or copies of it, to people, but must on no account let it out of their possession, 'the British Government that forged, planted, published, authenticated and used this atrocity diary to destroy their Irish enemy, Casement, sought to hide its falsity.'

The document was said by Sir Basil Thomson to have been found in a trunk left at Casement's former lodgings in London *after Casement's arrest in Ireland*. But this statement that the diary had been found for the first time hardly tallies with reports from the American ONI that the existence of the diary had been whispered for months by 'British naval circles in Washington' long before Casement had been arrested.

7
Intelligence and Submarine Warfare

Hall's hatred of the Foreign Office and diplomats in general undoubtedly proved his undoing in the long run. Admiral James admits that Hall

> ... had no right to handle the political messages [those which were intercepted] himself and that he should have sent them without comment to the Foreign Office. That is what a lesser man would have done when the first messages of a highly explosive character came into his hands, but Hall not only had complete confidence in his own judgement, but, as guardian of the secrets of Room 40, he would not take the risk involved in permitting any messages in their original deciphering form to leave the Admiralty.[1]

Balfour, when Foreign Secretary, was enormously impressed by Hall's ability to get along well with the Americans, but never again in history would a British DNI allot to himself so much power. Something of his influence in the latter half of the war may be gleaned from the fact that when the United States first entered the war on the side of the Allies, the US Navy depended almost entirely on the Royal Navy for any worthwhile intelligence on ships and submarine movements. Under Rear-admiral Roger Welles, as Chief of Naval Intelligence, the movement of submarines and plotted sinkings were recorded (the plotting system being handled by a telephone watch), but it seems to have been very ineffective. Admiral Sims was particularly scathing in his denunciations of the inadequacy of the whole system. He blamed the ONI and compared it un-favourably with the British system. He also argued that it was impossible effectively to direct the US naval forces from Washington owing to lack of intelligence. Tracey Kittredge in his *Naval Lessons of the Great War* wrote that the Navy Department

> ... resorted to many uncertain channels of information of varying degrees of reliability ... such as Allied attachés in Washington ... Armed Guard officers were given orders to collect, in a week or ten days of their stay in port in England or France, a vast amount of information concerning war operations and experience ... obviously beyond their capacity. ... The Department often based action on recommendations of Allied attachés or Armed Guard officers even when the recommendations differed from those submitted by Sims. Admiral Sims was in no case informed what information the Department was obtaining from these other sources, nor as to the action the Department took on recommendations.

Sims, in fact, had to rely almost entirely on London for the bulk of his intelligence for directing European operations. It was here that Hall played a vital role in keeping the American admiral informed. Increasingly, as the war lasted and the U-boat campaign was stepped up, submarine intelligence became all important. By the middle of 1917 the submarine battle posed two different problems for the combatants: for the Allies the task was to obtain detailed information on U-boat movements, while for the Germans it was to ascertain what measures the Allies were taking to counteract the U-boats. Radio interception provided a great deal of the intelligence on submarine dispositions, but not by any means all of it. A vast amount of information came from the captains of both Allied and neutral merchantmen and the skippers of trawlers. Some intelligence was also obtained from the discovery of new mine-fields off the Allied coasts: this not only indicated the presence of enemy mine-laying submarines, but, through analysis, enabled future patterns of mine-laying to be predicted.

Though German naval intelligence was rarely as spectacular, as ubiquitous or as well organized on a global basis as that of the British, there were a number of unostentatious successes which were chalked up. Perhaps their most useful spy inside Britain, from the viewpoint of naval intelligence, was Jules Crawford Silber, an agent who, if not brilliant, and indeed not even a professional, had the qualities which make for staying-power in espionage—patience, painstaking methods and sobriety. Silber's qualities as an agent shine through in his own account of his espionage in Britain: it is factual, low-key, discreet and even with a modicum of dislike for the work he was doing. In many respects it is by far the most honest of any spy's confessions. Silber, a German national, had spent a great deal of his life in South Africa and Canada. In the former country he had rendered service to Britain against the Boers in the South African War and his papers of identification had recorded this. When war broke out in 1914 Silber, who spoke perfect English and looked and behaved like an Englishman, offered his services to Britain in Canada. He was accepted and given a job in the postal censorship service—the perfect cover for a spy.

In every respect Silber was an amateur. He was not a long-term spy carefully dropped into another country with a pre-fabricated new identity, to await the right moment to produce results. Silber was torn between what he felt was his duty to his country and a certain liking for the British. He always had a guilt complex about his work against them. His conscientious-ness, his integrity and ability gained him promotion and he made friends very easily. Despite the fact that the British people developed a spy-mania in World War I, he seems never to have been suspected. Wisely he fulfilled a lonely role, refusing to operate with other German spies in Britain. As a censor, of course, he was in a position to pass through his own outgoing intelligence messages in whatever guise was necessary. He took the precaution (in order to get the right postmark) of sending himself letters from various points in London, using a 'commer-cial window envelope'. This allowed him to change the address by inserting a new letter after he had opened the envelope in his capacity as censor, then re-sealing it and stamping it with the censor's mark.

Silber had volunteered his services to the German Intelli-gence Service and it was because so much of what he obtained was of value to Naval Intelligence that he was unofficially taken over by them. With few worthwhile spies left in Britain, Silber became the favourite boy of German Naval Intelligence. He had never received any training in espionage, so that he was, in effect, a self-employed agent working for Germany. But he learned quickly and took few risks. Keeping his head, he varied his techniques, carefully reading through the British lists of suspects to whose correspondence he was to pay particular attention, and made full use of the information which the 'Suspect List' provided of addresses in neutral countries which were in touch with German Intelligence.

Proving himself to be rather more professional than many professional spies, Silber was testimony to the fact that the good amateur can beat them all. Having an extremely retentive memory, he only made notes when he left his work at nights. Here again he was ultra-cautious: he did not write out these notes at home, but went to another address where, apart from what he had remembered, he photographed documents he had 'borrowed' from the censorship department. The photographic material he bought at different shops all over London. He avoided every possible mistake which had been made by earlier and less fortunate German spies in Britain, thus continuing in his work undetected from 12 October 1914 until the end of the war, by which time he had been transferred to Liverpool. He remained in the censorship department until it was disbanded on 27 June 1919, when he was not only given a farewell party, but a certificate of service which described him as 'a very able man, a good linguist, thorough and competent and of exemplary conduct'.

Without possessing any special technical knowledge, Silber managed to use his office to slow down armaments production. Britain was purchasing considerable quantities of armaments from the USA and often these had to be made to particular specifications and drawings and details sent to British ordnance officers in America. Silber would study each drawing to decide which was the most vital part; then he would either manage to drop a blob of ink on a vital part of the drawing, or let some burning ash from his pipe fall on it, or temporarily delay the sending of the sketches. Sometimes, when he considered it to be serious enough, he would manage to 'lose' the documents altogether. His great scoop in naval intelligence came when he opened a letter in which a woman wrote about how glad she was to have her brother, a naval officer, temporarily stationed in a port near her home. He was, she said, working on some hush-hush project of the Navy about arming old merchant ships. Silber immediately detected the hint of some important development, probably in connection with anti-submarine warfare. Making an excuse to be away from his duties for a day or two, he took a train to the town where the girl was living and warned her that what she had written was in dangerous breach of security regulations. Not only was it dangerous for her, argued Silber, but it was equally dangerous for her brother who could be prosecuted and his whole career ruined. Silber stressed that he must know all that her brother had told her and promised that, if she was absolutely frank, he would see that her brother's career was not affected. Gradually, he got from the girl the whole story of the Royal Navy's new challenge to the U-boat, the Q-boat, or armed merchantman, which was used as a decoy ship and then, when a submarine surfaced, opened fire on it from guns which would normally be concealed behind hatches. Thus Silber was able to give German Naval Intelligence the first warning about the use of Q-boats.[2]

Nevertheless, the greater part of intelligence in the submarine battle was obtained from deciphering radio messages. The Germans made this task easier for their adversaries because they broadcast standard test messages in each cipher as it was introduced into service. Both sides consistently compromised new codes and ciphers by transmitting messages in the new form to ships and then repeating them in the old code or cipher because the addressee had not acknowledged or received the new one. This sometimes meant that, whereas the ship receiving such a message in a new cipher could not read it, the enemy was able to pick it up and translate it with ease. German thoroughness sometimes aided the British in making the fullest use of U-boat intelligence. For example, Hans Rose, commander of U-53, provided the kind of detailed factual report which the Germans required, but which, if intercepted, was of even greater value to the British. On one April day in 1918, Rose transmitted the signal '1—2—9—068a—U—53', which indicated that he had sunk one ship of 2,000 tons, had nine torpedoes left and was in quadrant 068 alpha at the western end of the English Channel. Armed with this information, all the NID had to do was to pinpoint the exact location of the U-boat, no difficult task as the details given referred to grid charts which were still being used until midsummer 1918.

The sinking, or capture, of a submarine, provided opportunity for much more intelligence. Some prisoners supplied a great deal of information not only about the construction of their submarine, but where she had been, what she had achieved and, sometimes, data on other submarines as well. Some intelligence came from neutral ports and, on one occasion, French Naval Intelligence scored a coup by masterminding the salvaging of a wreck of the German submarine UB-26 near Le Havre. The French discovered, among the U-boat's documents, charts of German minefields off the British coast in the Straits of Dover as well as along the Belgian coast. This information was immediately relayed to London and resulted in an offensive against U-boats the following month.

As the war progressed, so the means of obtaining U-boat intelligence was extended. Divers were employed to examine sunken submarines and craft were recovered from the bottom of the sea, French and Italian navies co-operating with the British in this work. Such opportunities were rare, as U-boats were usually sunk in waters where salvage and diving operations were impossible. The Germans blundered badly when they introduced a new naval signal-book in August 1916, and allowed the Zeppelins, which were under naval command, to carry the new code-books with them. In September 1916, a Zeppelin was shot down in Essex and a copy of the new signal-book obtained from it. A similar incident occurred the following year when the British again recovered naval cipher information from another Zeppelin that was shot down.

By 1917 the Allies were at last getting to grips with the U-boat menace and the increase in the amount of intelligence on submarine warfare resulted in a proportionately greater destruction of enemy craft. In 1916 some forty-four U-boats had been destroyed; by the end of 1917 this number had been trebled. Greater efficiency in deciphering enemy signals, the development of direction-finding and the recovery of documents from the wrecks of U-boats all played a part in this. When at last the convoy system was belatedly introduced, reports from ships in these convoys increased the number of sightings of submarines as well as providing checks on each other's reports. In the last two years of the war, directional wireless-plotting became a vital element in naval intelligence. The French Admiralty made rapid strides in developing its own intelligence network and deciphering teams. They managed to solve the German naval code and discovered that the Nauen wireless station regularly broadcast to U-boats the sailing times and destinations of French ships leaving Marseilles, basing this on information obtained by German naval spies in the French port. The French worked at top speed in deciphering these messages which were then taken by bicycle to the Ministry of Marine who alerted the harbour-master at Marseilles and enabled him to alter the routes and sailing times of those ships which had not yet left. Later the waterfront spies in Marseilles were caught.

The French opened up a chain of interception stations and were given some help by Room 40, though co-operation between the two Allied navies was not always as good or as close as it might have been. Hall not only maintained a tight control over Room 40's secrets, but often behaved arrogantly to the French. David Kahn writes that

... the French sent many of their naval solutions [of deciphering] to London, but Room 40 reciprocated as minimally as possible. Hall apparently never sent the *Magdeburg*, nor any other in-force codebooks to the French. His motives were understandable. England depended for her very existence on control of the seas. ... But Colonel François Cartier, head of the French cryptologic service, said Hall 'exceeded all decent bounds in his jealous hoarding of cryptanalytical secrets'.[3]

Co-operation between the Allies improved marginally after the United States entered the war, with both the British and French navies vying with one another in their desire to win favour with America. The Americans began to get a steady stream of naval intelligence from London and Paris. From January 1918, Admiral Sims was given a daily briefing by the British Admiralty, and Hall kept him supplied with warnings of U-boat movements. Yet it is clear from American records of the period that such information was masked in secrecy. Robert M. Grant states that the USA expected the U-boat campaign would be extended to American shores: 'Admiral Sims in London spent a good deal of time insisting to Washington that U-boats could not sail westward without advance information being supplied by the Admiralty [Britain's]. Since the Admiralty apparently did not tell him how the information was obtained, it is not surprising that his arguments were not entirely convincing.'[4]

Some indication of the paucity of the information which Hall allowed to be passed on to the French on the submarine war may be gleaned from a study of Rear-admiral Roger Welles' papers. As Chief Intelligence Officer, Welles decided it was essential to set up an additional naval intelligence network in France and he put Lieutenant C. A. Munn, a Reserve officer with a fluency in French, in charge of this. Welles recorded that, soon after the US entered the war,

> ... it became evident that the French Intelligence Service on the west coast of France was not preventing many sinkings off that coast and the Chief of Naval Operations ordered the DNI to establish an Intelligence service of our own in France for the proper protection of our transports. This was done with the full knowledge and in co-operation with the French service. Lieutenant Munn was stationed in Nantes and was provided by the ONI with sufficient funds to employ secret agents ... Not a single incoming transport was ever torpedoed off the coast of France ... Some spies were caught and executed.[5]

By the end of the War American co-operation with the French Navy was far better than the uneasy relationship which existed between the British and French navies.

Naval intelligence in this period was also directed towards gaining information on minefields. Two examples will perhaps suffice. In mid-1917 the British became aware that information about German swept channels in the Bight of Heligoland needed checking and correcting, as it appeared that no German submarines had been sunk on British mines for nearly three months. During the summer of 1918, when hints of mutinies aboard various German ships were coming in, both from intelligence sources and prisoners-of-war, a deserter from the German Navy stated that a large quantity of mines had been laid just outside Cuxhaven and that this was due to the fact that 'some members of the 5th Mine-sweeping Flotilla sold charts of the safe channels to the Allies, with the result that our submarines laid mines in them which caused several losses'.

A military staff officer of the United States, Colonel Richard H. Williams, provided a real scoop in naval intelligence in the latter stages of the war. He arrived at the site where a German Zeppelin surrendered in France, and, being a singularly thorough operator, insisted on probing further in the area of the swamp close to which the aircraft had touched down. Here he found a piece of a German map and, plodding on still further into the mud, eventually discovered other fragments of the same. Putting together all the pieces, Williams built up a picture of a cross-section code-map of the North Sea, the Irish Sea, the Skagerrak and the Kattegat, which he felt sure had some reference to the U-boat campaign. Eventually, through sheer persistence, he worked out that this provided all the clues that were desperately required by the Royal Navy. Williams's find was swiftly passed on to the NID and it resulted in a smart counterattack by RN submarines which ended in the destruction of a number of U-boats. It was one of the best examples of Allied co-operation in World War I and the initiative came entirely from the USA.

There is considerable evidence in German naval records that they tried to plant false information on the enemy. Some of the deserters who found their way to the British were highly suspect and, towards the end of the war, the NID wasted a lot of time checking their highly dubious statements. Much misinformation was provided, including details of U-boat construction and alleged increases in the number of U-boat flotillas, and E. K. Chatterton, in *Danger Zone*, records how one of these deserters told how eleven U-boats came out together from Wilhelmshaven 'all numbered in the hundreds . . . so there must be lots of new ones'.[6]

Admiral von Scheer was perturbed about the amount of intelligence which British submarines were obtaining, including details of channels swept by the Germans. He sent a memorandum to German Naval Intelligence in which he asserted

18 (*above*) On 2 March 1966 President Lyndon B. Johnson awards the National Security Medal to Frank Rowlett, special assistant to the Director of the National Security Agency, for his work in cryptology (*Associated Press*)

19 (*below*) The Japanese Purple Machine, used to great effect in the rapid production of encoded messages. Duplication of the Purple Machine was one of the triumphs of prewar US intelligence, although interpretation of the messages received was not always fully competent, resulting in the US failure to foresee the Pearl Harbor attack (*US National Archives and Records Service*)

CHERRY PICKER

7 OXIDIZER TRAILERS

2 FUEL TRAILERS

METALLURG ANOSOV

FUEL TRAILERS

MISSILE ERECTOR

DIVNOGORSK

BRATSK

20 A US Navy low-level photograph of the port of Mariel, Cuba, on 2 November 1962, showing a missile erector, 10 missile fuel trailers and seven missile oxidizer trailers; nine missile launch rings are waiting to be loaded onto the three ships at the dock (*US Navy*)

that the British had an excellent chart of the minefields in the Bight of Heligoland which seemed to be entirely up-to-date. 'This is vastly superior to any similar charts of Allied swept channels which we possess. We must produce equal results quickly. Presumably some of the intelligence gained by the British comes from documents recovered from wrecks of U-boats. This again needs looking into. I suggest that to make up lost ground we offer 500,000 marks for accurate charts.'

As far as can be ascertained, German Naval Intelligence merely circulated their agents in neutral countries and offered only 100,000 marks for such information. Admittedly Admiral Scheer was being wildly extravagant when he suggested so high a sum for what was at best an extremely vague briefing. Accurate charts of what? And of where? But German Naval Intelligence showed very little indication of knowing how best to set about this task. By getting in touch with their agents in neutral countries, they risked being given not what they wanted, but charts carefully planted by NID agents. Admiral Hall had already managed to sell a fake plan of a barrage in the Straits of Dover to a German agent for £2,000!

Mine-laying was an enormous problem in 1917 and this particular aspect of the war was won more in the field of intelligence than in Operations. Admiral Jellicoe recorded that 'during the month of April [1917] no fewer than 515 mines were swept up off the British coast, but at the loss of one mine-sweeper almost every day. April marked the peak of the mine-layers' activity and thereafter it steadily declined. The decline was due almost entirely to the effectiveness of the anti-submarine campaign and the consequent losses of the mine-laying U-boats.' He might have put in a word for the NID, but then Jellicoe was never a man of vision.

Yet it was Hall who again and again supplied the vital information warning of German plans for offensive action. Admiral Sir Roger Keyes recalled how he 'received information from Admiral Hall which pointed to a strong force of enemy destroyers being at sea', while on another occasion he spoke of a telephone call from Hall about 'a submarine, commanded by a very determined German officer . . . homeward-bound, and would probably pass through the patrol that night and might well try to do so on the surface'.[7]

One of the bravest and most useful feats which directly aided the NID was that of Shipwright E. C. Miller, a young diving instructor who possessed the invaluable combination of great courage and the ability to stand the pressure of water at greater depths than most men. To obtain intelligence of a material kind, Miller was sent to reconnoitre a U-boat sunk off the coast of Kent. He climbed into the sunken wreck through a hole in the hull and searched the vessel until he found an iron safe which he presumed, correctly, would contain the codes. Miller made a number of dives in search of further material, despite the unpleasantness of the task; referring to the dogfish which were very much in evidence, he said, 'They naturally resent any intruder, and on lots of occasions when they chased me I offered them my boot, and they never failed to snap at it'. But the result of Miller's work was that the NID obtained the latest German naval code.[8]

If the Allies in general and the British in particular acquired a vast superiority in naval intelligence in World War I, the Germans gained in the long term. The experience they acquired in this war was analysed and exploited in the years between the two wars while other naval intelligence services were declining, and so, by the advent of World War II, the Germans had gained an initial advantage. German Naval Intelligence concentrated on improving wireless communication and, had the war lasted longer, results might have shown they were gaining the upper hand in this field alone. U-boats were able to communicate over vast distances, in a greater degree than those over which Allied submarines could operate.

The German Navy, however, owed a great debt to the Austrian Military Intelligence, which, in many respects, was greatly superior to that of the Germans. It was the Austrians who gathered most of the intelligence on Allied shipping in the Adriatic and the Mediterranean, who sabotaged two Italian warships, and who also raided the Italian Consulate in Berne in the middle of the night and filched their documents.

Just how much the result of World War I owed to the NID it would be impossible to assess, but in the darkest days it was probably the NID alone which saved the Allied navies from total defeat. For there can be no denying that, throughout that war, the German Navy was much more on an offensive footing than the Royal Navy. The man who got the nearest to the truth in the immediate post-war years in assessing the work of the NID was an American, J. L. Leighton, who had worked on Admiral Sims' staff in London. In his book, *Simsadus*, published in 1920, he stressed that direction finding was the vital factor in the new style naval intelligence: 'It was the custom of submarines to communicate with their headquarters in Germany almost nightly by wireless. The messages were always in a highly secret code, and might, or might not, be eventually deciphered by the Admiralty. The chief interest in them was the opportunity they offered to locate the submarine which sent the message.'

To sum up, the work of interception and deciphering of messages, direction-finding of U-boats and the skilled professional assessment and analysis of the intelligence thus obtained was the quintessence of winning the anti-submarine war of 1914–18. It was unspectacular and exhausting, and often the skill that went into this unremitting task was hidden away in the records. Hitherto many active service naval officers had talked contemptuously about the NID and the ONI: now they saw that their lives sometimes depended on them and that without such organizations they could never hope to score so many successes in the battle against the submarine.

After the entry of the USA into World War I, Hall took pains to see that the Americans were given the fullest information by the NID set-up in Washington about German agents in America. As a result of this many of them were rounded up, yet credit should also be given to the ONI for their own efforts to detect enemy agents in the USA. Considering that internal security was something that had barely been tackled before by the ONI, the results were impressive. The ONI was at one stage, processing a thousand names a day in its security checks and the list of suspects eventually totalled 105,000 names. During the first six months of the US entry into the war the Navy rounded up 600 spies in the Great Lakes area alone.

Remarkable initiative was shown by Lieutenant Clifford N. Carver USN of the ONI, who helped to organize the offshore patrol for anti-submarine duties. He went far outside his brief to inform the ONI of the location of enemy property and

German smuggling methods. Rear-admiral Welles, who paid high tribute to him, stated that Carver's work was 'the direct cause of the establishing by the President of the Office of the Alien Property Custodian, with A. Mitchell Palmer at its head. The ONI furnished the Alien Property Custodian with information which resulted in the taking over of millions of dollars worth of alien property.[9]

Hall still needed all his skill as a diplomat to keep the Americans happy, to remove suspicions and at the same time to cover up his sources and methods. That suspicions were not easily dispelled is obvious from a message from Commodore Gaunt in Washington to Hall, in which the former said that when he was a guest of the Round Table in New York one member of the party 'openly said that the Zimmermann note was a forgery, and was practically unanimously supported by the whole bunch. I pointed out that both the President and his right-hand man had given their word that they knew it was not, and that it should be accepted as genuine . . . The above is an illustration of the way it was received over here, nineteen out of twenty men believed it was a forgery.'

1917 brought the Russian Revolution and, with the threat of Russia opting out of the war, a new strain for the Allies. The need for intelligence on Russian intentions was all-important and it was the navies of the USA and Britian which largely helped to supply this in the early stages. On the American side a great deal was organized by Colonel Breckenridge, the first Marine officer to become a naval attaché, who covered Scandinavia and the neutral ports there. He secured a great deal of important intelligence on Bolshevik plans. Curiously, Hall does not seem to have given much thought to the NID playing a role in Russia and for a long time the whole question of intelligence in that country was left to the naval attachés. However, the ultimate base for highly secret operations for obtaining Russian intelligence by the Royal Navy was at a tiny island named Osea, which lay in the estuary of the River Blackwater in Essex. Because of its isolated position, the Admiralty decided, in the early years of the war, to take over Osea as a base for coastal craft, which included a new style of naval ship, 'Skimmers', or, in technical language, Coastal Motor Boats. It was not until early in 1918 that the first special newly constructed motor-boats arrived. The aim was to give them a high speed, yet sufficient strength in construction to withstand the strain of vibration when running in a rough sea with a full load and to enable them to fire torpedoes in these conditions.

Service for the CMB's was open to volunteers only and it came under the command of Captain Wilfred Trench, obviously destined for bold action at the right moment. Captain Augustus Agar wrote of the CMB's that 'we were a wonderfully happy community on Osea Island. All minds were concentrated on the attack on the German fleet which was to be staged later that year. Our work was entirely in the open air, running torpedoes set to shallow water depth in the river, fitting out the boats, practising high speed manoeuvres in groups of boats or on the large stretch of water enclosed between Brightlingsea, Mersea and Osea Islands.'[10]

But it was not until February 1919, that Agar, then a lieutenant, was summoned back to Osea and told that he was to be used on a special mission concerning Russia—'the work will involve use of two CMBs. because great speed by sea will be essential. You alone will be in charge and you will have no one but yourself to rely on. It is of the utmost importance that not a soul, either here or in England, on the journey out, or even when you arrive in those waters, shall have any suspicion of your activities.'[11]

By this time Hall had departed from the NID and many of the tasks of naval intelligence had been taken over by the Secret Service. Agar, for example, was told to report to Captain Sir Mansfield Cumming RN who was head of that service. For, by early 1919, most of the British missions and consulates in Russia had left. Agar was later awarded the VC for his part in running the new-type coastal motor-boats to make contact with British agents in Finland and Russia. Twice he ran the gauntlet of the Kronstadt forts to bring his courier into shore to link up with Paul Dukes, then head of the British Secret Service section inside Russia. On one occasion Agar took on the might of the Red Navy in his tiny motor-boat and he actually sank the cruiser *Oleg* by torpedo.

However, this was at no time a Navy-controlled operation, as Agar makes clear in his own narrative of the Baltic adventures: 'On arrival at Biorlo the Admiral received a cipher message from

"C" [Mansfield Cumming] instructing us to cease all Secret Service activity with Petrograd and to use Terrioki only for official liaison work which confirmed the arrangements I had already made.'[12]

Another gallant naval officer who worked for the British Secret Service was Captain Francis Cromie who earlier, as commander of the E-19, won fame by penetrating the Baltic from England. He was shot dead by Cheka agents while trying to resist arrest in Petrograd, but not before he had himself killed a number of Chekists.

During World War I the British lost a submarine, L-55, in about a hundred feet of water in the Gulf of Finland. Despite the fact that the NID were warned that the Soviet Government had taken an interest in this subject, no steps were taken to retrieve it, or even to win the co-operation of other powers to have salvage operations carried out. It is true that at that time—in the early 1920s—the Russians did not know exactly where the submarine was lying. But, shortly after the disappearance of Sidney Reilly, a British secret agent in Russia, in December 1925, it became known in London that the USSR had discovered where the craft was in the Gulf of Finland and that Soviet technicians had taken soundings in the area. Two years later the Russians actually raised the L-55 and so discovered all her secrets. Three years were spent studying and repairing the submarine which was finally put into service with the Soviet Navy.

8

Germany Solves British Ciphers

Clausewitz once said that 'a great part of the information obtained in war is contradictory, a still greater part is false, and by far the greatest part is of a doubtful character'. While this maxim could be aptly applied to World War I in many matters it became increasingly true in those years of uncertain peace between 1919 and 1939.

Among some of the western powers political prejudice prevented an objective approach to naval intelligence. This was particularly true of the British NID which suffered in this period from having totally unsuitable men in charge of it, usually looking for the wrong enemy in the wrong place. But at least the American Naval Intelligence took a cold, hard look at its own defects and decided that one lesson of World War I was that the ONI needed to develop its own deciphering department which could cope with messages on a global basis. The man selected for organizing this was Herbert Yardley who claimed that, between 1917 and 1929, he 'broke' nearly 50,000 diplomatic telegrams involving codes of several countries.

It was not until the latter part of 1918 that Yardley went to Europe to learn what he could from America's allies. He got little help from Hall, but much more from the French. When he returned to the USA and organized what became known as the 'Black Chamber', a medieval title for what was a modern set-up, Yardley's know-how was technically under military control. But, as he swiftly discerned that America's really vital intelligence interests lay in the Far East, his work became of increasing value to the US Navy. It had been in counter-intelligence at home that the US Naval Intelligence Office had excelled during the war when it worked closely with the Department of Justice. The ONI had suffered from demobilization and, by October 1920, its personnel numbers were down to some eighteen officers and a few civilians. There was a swift succession of directors, Captain C. C. March relieving Captain Kimball in 1919, to be followed by Captains W. D. MacDougall and Dudley V. Knox within two years. In the early 1920s the post was filled by Rear-admiral Niblack, a stickler for old-fashioned protocol and one who disapproved of 'all this damned spying and prying'. He was eventually sent to London as naval attaché.

The cryptographic section was reconstituted and, realizing how unfavourably this work had been compared with that of the British in World War I, assistance from the universities was sought. The cryptanalyst section of the US Navy became known as OP-20-G, an abbreviation for the G Section of the 20th division of OPNAV, the Office of the Chief of Naval Operations. This section was directed by Commander Laurence P. Safford, who was easily the outstanding cryptographical expert in the US Navy, and who, in 1924, set up the communications-intelligence organization. Though Safford had spells of service at sea between 1924 and 1929, he returned to this section and played an enormous part in its development. He kept close links between Intelligence and Operations, developed a research system into foreign codes, explored the possibilities of cipher machines to boost efficiency, analysed reports received and aimed at making available to the Fleet a regular summary based on intelligence reports compiled from radio research.

It was Yardley, however, who increasingly stressed to the authorities the growing threat of Japanese naval power. His biggest coup was brought off during the Washington Naval Conference of 1922, called by the USA in an effort to limit Japanese naval power in the Pacific. The Japanese delegates to this conference had been given the most careful and detailed briefing which laid down the maximum ration of power for which they should aim and the minimum for which they might settle. It was of vital importance for US Naval Intelligence that they should have the answers to these questions before the conference got under way. Luckily, Yardley had devoted most of his time to the problem of solving Japanese codes and ciphers.

He set up a sub-section of his department to concentrate on this alone and for some weeks wrestled with the intricacies of the Japanese language and the imponderables of how this could be used in codes. In World War I many people had nervous breakdowns as a result of the strain of their work, but Yardley, while equally under strain, was obviously a much tougher individual than the average decipherer: 'I had worked so long with these code telegrams', he wrote, 'that every telegram, every line, even every code word was indelibly printed in my brain. I could lie awake in bed and in the darkness make my investigations—trial and error, over and over again.'[1]

Yardley's task was not made easier by the fact that from 1919–20 the Japanese had employed a Polish expert to revise their cryptographic systems and had introduced eleven different codes. But Yardley made a successful intercept of a telegram of 5 July 1921, from the Japanese Ambassador in London to Tokyo, which provided the first indication of a conference on naval disarmament. From then on Yardley kept the State Department and the US Navy Department fully informed. Everything was analysed concerning the preliminary messages which involved the question of what should be permissible tonnages of naval ships for the USA, Britain, France, Italy and Japan. As Yardley himself, somewhat melodramatically, but none the less truthfully, wrote at the time: 'Though the blinds are drawn and the windows heavily curtained, its far-seeing eyes penetrate to the secret conference chambers at Washington, Tokyo, London, Paris, Geneva, Rome. Its sensitive ears catch the faintest whisperings in the foreign capitals of the world.'

The result of Yardley's probings was that he was able to advise the Americans that, if pressed, the Japanese would yield. The result was that the Japanese capitulated and accepted the ration proposed by the USA, which was that of 10—10—6—3·3—3·3 for the USA, Britain, Japan, France and Italy respectively. Yet whether Yardley's efforts, or rather the way they were interpreted by the US Navy, were worthwhile is problematical. The emphasis at this time was supposed to be on disarmament: as far as the Japanese were concerned, it was a one-way disarmament and against their own interests. As Fletcher Pratt aptly remarked: 'The tale had not a little to do with the Japanese denouncement of the naval treaties.'[2]

This could be described as a very short-lived triumph and in any event was probably an indication of short-sighted interpretation of naval intelligence. Japan had been an ally of the Western powers in World War I: all that Yardley's intelligence had resulted in was a deliberate deception of an ally by underhand methods, and a rift between the two nations. In the long-term Yardley's work was probably of enormous importance, but in the short-term it was disastrous. The Japanese were not slow to realize they had been duped and their consequent distrust of the United States gradually developed into hostility and finally into a renouncing of the Naval Treaty and preparation for war.

Not surprisingly there were some American politicians who began to view the Yardley 'Black Chamber' with distaste and positive hostility. They raised the question, which Hall's adversaries had also made, that there was something immoral about the interception of other people's ciphers. Yardley's powers were drastically cut in 1925 and, when Herbert Hoover became President, he was gradually edged out of office. Henry Stimson, then US Secretary of State, was adamant that Yardley's tactics were indefensible and in 1929 the 'Black Chamber' was closed down. Yardley got his own back by writing a book in which he revealed how he decoded Japanese messages during the Naval Conference. It was a foolish, even an unpatriotic, gesture and Yardley probably did as much as any man in giving the Japanese an excuse for their subsequent hostility to the USA.

The Japanese stepped up their own naval intelligence organization, creating networks of espionage all around the globe and at the same time revising their cryptographical methods. British Admiralty records of the period suggest that the NID had little comprehension of the extent of Japanese espionage in the years between the wars, or how far Japanese naval intelligence had developed. In every British colony in the Far East there was a resident director of Japanese naval intelligence of high rank who was able to pinpoint weaknesses, thoroughly assess the whole strategic position and at the same time ensure that there was a permanent team of agents to keep such information up to date. It was Japanese Naval Intelligence which was able to inform Tokyo that Singapore was indefensible, that Hong Kong could easily be taken and that the whole of Malaya could be occupied within a short span of time.

Japanese progress in cryptography was slower and, despite its improvements, the Americans were still able to pick up Tokyo diplomatic traffic for a long time. In the late 1920s the Americans, Dutch, Germans and Swedes all produced cipher machines, incorporating cipher wheels, which could be operated by typewriter keyboards. The Japanese bought these machines, adapted and improved upon them, introducing what came to be known as the 'Purple Machine'. The Purple was swiftly adopted for Japanese Naval Intelligence and for their Foreign Office, but its use was confined to thirteen embassies overseas. For some years it defied American attempts to crack it and, in the end, the task of solving this enigma was assigned to one William Friedman, son of a Moldavian Jewish family who had emigrated to the USA in the 1890s to escape the pogroms. Meanwhile the ONI had set up their own answer to Room 40 with Rooms 1649 and 2646, bringing in all their Japanese language specialists to lend assistance. One of the chief of these was Lieutenant Ellis M. Zacharias who, after some months' training in Washington in 1926, was sent to Shanghai where he took charge of the intercepting of Japanese naval traffic. Years later Zacharias stated that

> ... my days were spent in study and work among people with whom security had become second nature. Hours went by without any of us saying a word, just sitting in front of piles of indexed sheets on which a mumbo-jumbo of figures or letters was displayed in chaotic disorder, trying to solve the puzzle bit by bit like fitting together the pieces of a jigsaw puzzle. We were just a few then in Room 2646, young people who gave ourselves to cryptography with the same ascetic devotion with which young men enter a monastery.[3]

In the immediate post-war years the enigmatic Wilhelm Canaris moved in the same kind of obscurity that typified his service in the last years of World War I. Nobody, not even in Germany, was ever quite sure what Canaris was up to and hence many legends sprang up around his name. He had a tremendous admiration for the British in this period and is even said to have given some indirect assistance to the British NID, while he never took much trouble to hide his contempt for the Nazi leaders from his intimate friends. During the 1920s he made a study of British naval intelligence methods and it was partly through his influence that the *Oberkommando der Kriegsmarine* started to build up a deciphering organization which would match that of Room 40. The OKM, as it became known, soon established a reputation for breaking down ciphers and, long before World War II, had solved some of the most secret of British naval codes.

But where Germany continued to suffer in the field of naval intelligence was in its failure to set up a really powerful NI organization as effective in its own right as other branches of national intelligence. For example, the Cipher and Monitoring Office, *Chiffrier und Horchleitstelle*, came under the Ministry of Defence as part of the *Abwehr*, which meant that it concentrated mainly on military intelligence. It lacked the specialization and expert knowledge essential to an organization serving the Navy. Nevertheless, paradoxically, it had become a tradition in Germany that a senior naval officer should be head of the *Abwehr*, the German Secret Service and, perhaps to compensate for the fact that the German Admiralty had no comprehensive, highly organized Naval Intelligence Service of its own, the Navy continued to press for one of their own men to hold this post. It was not until 1934 that Canaris, then an Admiral in command of the shore establishment, *Swinemunde*, was appointed head of the *Abwehr*. The previous holder of the office, another naval officer, was regarded as unsympathetic to the Nazis. It was ironic that his successor should be even more hostile to them, though cleverer at disguising the fact. And, if he made snide jokes about the Nazis to his closest friends, he knew how to handle Hitler even when the latter was in one of his most belligerent moods. However, the German Navy benefited least from Canaris' move to become head of the *Abwehr*. There is no record that he made any real attempt to improve the sources of intelligence which were essential to the Navy, despite his vast experience in this field. His political and diplomatic contacts abroad enabled him to pass on to the German Admiralty warnings which they often neglected. For Canaris the menace of communism was of far greater importance than extending the frontiers of Germany and, throughout the 1930s, he expressed the belief that, whatever war Germany entered into, it was essential to keep Britain out. There were links between the British NID and Canaris right up to 1939, though these were mainly through Spanish channels, the chief contact being Juan March, the millionaire and former head of a smuggling ring that had been won over to the side of British naval intelligence in World War I. March was a friend of Canaris and the two men's views were almost identical. When Juan March escaped from Spain to Gibraltar when Republican forces in the Civil War demanded his punishment as 'an enemy of democracy', it was the NID who tipped him off and arranged for his escape from the Alcara de Henares prison where he had been held on charges of alleged tobacco smuggling.

One of the shrewdest minds in the Gibraltar section on British naval intelligence was Don Gomez-Beare who later became British naval attaché in Madrid during World War II. He was always in close contact with Juan March and through this was able to pass on a great deal of what Canaris was thinking. At times it seemed as though Canaris was inviting the NID to open secret communications with him, but with Canaris one could never be sure what his motives were. Thus the British held back, largely because they then had no DNI of the calibre of Hall who would undoubtedly have probed further into the possibility of a secret understanding with Canaris. In the years between Hall's departure and 1939, there had been eight directors of Naval Intelligence in Britain, none of them in any way distinguished.

These years between the wars had resulted in a neglect of the true functions of the NID through extremely bad staffing in the senior posts and a general carelessness in signal security which existed throughout the Navy. As early as 1936 German cryptanalysts penetrated the wireless security of British ships in the Red Sea and this failure was not completely overcome until the middle of 1943. Its worst effects, as will be seen, resulted in the disastrous Norwegian campaign of 1940. The laxity in signal security also extended to an appalling slackness in almost everything else concerning intelligence. Sir Barry Domville, DNI from 1927–30, was a member of the pro-German organization, The Link, who, in 1940, was arrested under Regulation 18 B, largely on account of having been chairman and founder of this society. It is true that he did not come under the Nazi influence until 1936, six years after he had left his post as DNI, when he attended the Nuremberg *Reichsparteitag*, but the fact that such an unstable character was even selected as DNI reveals the inadequacy of Admiralty methods of choosing intelligence chiefs.

In the latter part of 1938 Juan March reported to a member of the NID that Canaris had told him that he had 'already penetrated the NID and I find it is not so circumspect as in Admiral Hall's day. . . . I should prefer to deal with the Royal Navy, to come to an understanding with its Intelligence Department, but how can you deal with an organization which changes its Directors so frequently?' There are obscurities in these alleged statements of Canaris: it is even possible that, in translating Canaris's Spanish into English, his original German thoughts were somewhat mutilated. But it is clear that he wanted some kind of an accord with the NID, though for what purpose is far from clear. Later, in March 1939, the British Foreign Office had reports from Berlin that the German Air Force might make a surprise attack on the British Home Fleet. On the strength of this the Admiralty ordered that the Fleet's anti-aircraft guns should be manned. The Cabinet also agreed that the First Lord of the Admiralty, Lord Stanhope, should refer to this in a speech he was about to make. Stanhope, a peer with little political sensitivity and at best a careless orator, exacerbated the whole situation by a late night speech on 4 April 1939, when an astonished gathering heard remarks which suggested panic decisions in Whitehall: '. . . shortly before I left the Admiralty it became necessary to give orders to man the anti-aircraft guns of the Fleet so as to be ready for anything that might happen. Long before guests came aboard this ship sixteen anti-aircraft guns could have given a warm welcome to anyone who happened to come this way.'

Sixteen anti-aircraft guns! The Germans must have chuckled gleefully at the idea of a mere sixteen anti-aircraft guns being brought into action against them. Chamberlain, the Prime Minister, tried to prevent the publication of this part of Stanhope's speech by citing the 'D' notice procedure, but while some acquiesced, other newspapers ignored the request, mainly on the grounds that the report had already been broadcast on the BBC Empire programme. The truth was that the First

Lord had never consulted the DNI on his speech, despite the fact that it was suspected by some in the NID that Canaris himself had been responsible for planting the rumour about a possible surprise attack on the British Home Fleet. What Canaris's purpose could have been on this occasion is again obscure, but it is probable that he hoped the Royal Navy would react in a less hysterical manner than the First Lord indicated and that they would treat his information as confidential and act accordingly. What is certain is that Canaris did all he could to warn the Royal Navy of the risks of war and the importance of their being seen to be sufficiently strong to deter aggression. This he did sometimes by leakages from Spain to the NID, more rarely by intermediaries in Holland and mysterious envoys to London. The NID were singularly inept in handling these reports, the trouble being that, while it was well informed from Spain, it was getting contradictory reports from inside Germany where its network was inefficient.

Meanwhile German Naval Intelligence, in its cumbersome and pedestrian way, was preparing for war. Deciphering methods were steadily improved, though interpretation of the intelligence received was not always correct. It is clear from German naval records that the French diplomatic code had been broken in 1937, and the breaking of the British naval signals traffic in the Mediterranean was of great importance. But a vast amount of intelligence was obtained simply enough through listening in to telephone conversations inside Germany, including British, French, Italian, Japanese, Belgian and Yugoslavian embassies, which also provided a good deal of purely naval information. At the same time the German Naval Intelligence was also involved in preparing plans for sabotage operations in the United States. However, after about the middle of 1939 the High Command in Germany became less interested in naval intelligence. This state of affairs continued until quite late in the war and, when British Intelligence officers obtained details of questionnaires given to captured enemy agents, it was noticeable that 'naval questions were on the whole less numerous than might have been expected. They concerned mainly His Majesty's ships, particularly aircraft carriers, movements of ships, and, later on, convoys and ports, docks and shipbuilding.'[4]

The centre of intelligence of all the powers spying on Germany in this immediate pre-war period was the Luetzow Platz in Berlin where both the British and Americans had 'cover' offices, American ONI maintaining their top agent in Germany here, under the guise of a businessman in premises occupied by a Frigidaire showroom. However, at this time, it was German Naval Intelligence, acting mainly on their ability to solve some of the most secret of British Admiralty codes and ciphers, which continued to score most successes. The lead they had gained in deciphering enabled the speedy German surface raiders to keep away from the British Home Fleet in the early stages of World War II.

While Neville Chamberlain has so often been blamed for the policy of appeasement which led to the war, and Churchill hailed as the supreme war winner, it is perhaps fair to point out that in one respect Chamberlain's sagacity actually helped to stave off a German invasion, while, if Churchill's advice on the subject had been taken, a much more dangerous situation could have been precipitated. Chamberlain had wisely decided, before war occurred, that it was time to establish a greater measure of goodwill between the United Kingdom and the independent state of Eire. Part of the agreement which he made was to cede the British naval bases in Southern Ireland to the Irish Government. This plan was foolishly attacked by Churchill (not then in the Government) and indeed there were times early in the war, after he became Prime Minister, when he seriously considered forcibly taking back those bases. Fortunately sanity prevailed and the Prime Minister was overruled. Opinion inside the NID was divided on this subject for a long time, not least because of a lack of worthwhile naval intelligence from Ireland and a misunderstanding of the whole position. As late as 24 November 1940, the war diary of the German Naval Staff noted that 'political information reinforces the impression gained from radio interception of an imminent operation by Britain against Ireland. The British are using allegations of a planned German occupation of Ireland to justify this', while on the following day it was stated that de Valera was doing all possible to prevent war spreading to Ireland. In fact Hitler had already made up his mind against any such plan unless forced into it by the British.

21 (*above*) An artist's impression of the deep-submergence research vehicle *Alvin*, lent by the US Navy to the Woods Hole Oceanographic Institution for use in Navy-sponsored oceanographic studies. *Alvin* can take a pilot and an observer to depths of about 1000 fathoms for periods up to twenty-four hours (*US Navy*)

22 (*below*) A photograph taken from *Alvin* at a depth of about 400 fathoms showing the parachute-shrouded nose of the thermonuclear weapon that fell into the sea off the coast of Spain following the midair collision of two US Air Force craft in early 1966 (*US Navy*)

23 (*above*) A photograph of the deep ocean floor taken in 1966 from the US submersible *Trieste I* (*US Navy*)

24 (*below*) The *Hughes Glomar Explorer*, used in the partial recovery of a sunken Soviet submarine in 1974 in the Pacific to the northwest of Hawaii (*Associated Press*)

Belatedly, from an external intelligence source, the NID was given two extremely significant reports which helped to elucidate this dangerous issue. The first was that, as long as Eire did not allow British naval ships to use her bases and remained neutral, and as long as the USA stayed out of the war, Germany would make no move to Irish territory. The Germans felt that the considerable Irish influence in the United States would be brought to bear against them if they invaded Eire. The second report was that the Irish were bamboozling German agents in their own game of misinformation almost as effectively as the British.

Dr John de Courcy Ireland, one of Ireland's most distinguished naval historians, has this comment to make on what might have happened if Churchill had had his way and tried to take back the former British bases in Ireland:

> If Eire had come in with Britain in 1939, there would almost certainly have been civil war here, convinced Republicans being driven to take a pro-German line. If the British had either taken the bases by agreement, or seized them, they would have been fighting both the Irish and the Germans. They would never have had time or material to equip these bases and, in doing so, they would have been neglecting the vital defences of the United Kingdom itself.[5]

One can go much further than this. Germany had a plan to make landings in Eire in certain circumstances. If the British had tried to seize the Irish bases, those landings by parachute would almost certainly have been successful. What might have been equally serious was that the Irish counterespionage organization would not have been able (or even willing) to snuff out German espionage in Ireland as effectively as in fact it did after the Irish declaration of neutrality. Only after the reorganization of the NID, in the late summer and autumn of 1939, were the voices of their Irish agents sufficiently heeded to realize how Irish agents of the NID had already infiltrated the German network in Dublin and were working effectively with Republican colleagues.

It was not until early in 1939 that it slowly dawned on the British Admiralty that the NID was at a disadvantage compared with the German Naval Intelligence's working relationship with other sections of German Intelligence, all operating on a war footing in peacetime. It was then seen that the recruitment of non-naval personnel was as essential as it had been in 1914. It was Admiral Sir Roger Backhouse, then First Sea Lord, who recommended Captain John Godfrey for the post of DNI in January 1939. Godfrey received a terse and unhelpful signal from the Naval Secretary to the First Sea Lord, saying: 'I expect you will be requested to come to the Admiralty to relieve Troup as DNI. I hope this will suit you.'

And that last sentence perhaps sums up the mental lassitude inside the Admiralty itself at this time. Godfrey was never to achieve the calibre of an intelligence chief such as Hall. He was subservient to a marked degree within his own Service, but stubborn and unimaginative in dealing with the Army and the RAF. By all accounts he was more frightened of Hall's achievements than inspired by them and, though a competent administrator, he never really grasped the significance of changes in the cryptographical war. He started his stint as DNI with an inferiority complex, admitting that 'experience soon convinced me that I had an awkward commodity to sell, that in 1939 the cupboard was bare and the DNI extremely vulnerable'.

9
The Misinformation Game

That the German Navy was quickly off the mark in intercepting important signals at the beginning of World War II is obvious from excerpts from the records of the German Naval Staff. On 5 September 1939, it was recorded that the German Naval Intelligence monitoring service had reported the rendezvous positions and routes signalled by the British Admiralty to incoming ships in the Atlantic and that this information had been transmitted to U-boats in the Atlantic.

Five days later German Naval Intelligence recorded that a 'British aircraft shot down on 4 September has been raised. British *Faut*[?] salvaged, and with its help the positions of *Ark Royal*, *Nelson* and *Sheffield* [Home Fleet] near Dundee have been fixed'.[1]

Yet the story of the allegedly most splendid feat in German naval intelligence in these early days of the war is still a subject of considerable controversy, of misleading statements and some quite extraordinary misinformation. It is, when summed up, the story of the spy who never was. It concerns the sinking by the Germans of the British battleship, *Royal Oak*.

Deception plans and false information played a not inconsiderable part in World War I and indeed von Rintelen alleges that it was a deception plan by the British which led to the battle of the Falkland Islands in 1914, though there is little confirmation of this. But in World War II such tactics became almost a way of life for the intelligence organizations and for those of the navies in particular. On 14 October 1939, round about midnight, the U-47, commanded by Lieutenant Gunther

Prien, surfaced in Kirk Sound at the north-east entrance to Scapa Flow and, gliding between the block ships under the noses of the battery of guns guarding the entrance, fired three torpedoes at the *Royal Oak*, then swung round and attacked a second time. The second attack caused the ship to capsize and sink with the loss of twenty-four officers and 809 men. Prien escaped from Scapa Flow without any difficulty and returned to Germany to be greeted as a hero and awarded the Iron Cross.

This was not only a devastating blow to the Royal Navy, but to the War Cabinet as well, for it raised the whole question of lack of security and inadequate defences at Scapa Flow. Churchill, who had only just been appointed First Lord on the outbreak of war, immediately detracted attention away from the Admiralty to MI5, the counterespionage organization. It was undoubtedly a brilliant and daring coup by the German Navy, but it clearly indicated that Prien could not have carried it out so successfully without having had detailed intelligence, both of what ships were in the Flow and of the approach channels, block ships and other defences. The deduction was that there must have been a German spy in the vicinity of Scapa Flow and demands were made that he should swiftly be found. When it was reported back that there was no trace of such a spy, it was not the NID which was blamed, but Major-general Sir Vernon Kell, head of MI5, who, shortly afterwards, was retired from the service. Yet subsequent inquiries showed that Kell was almost certainly not to blame.

Most British naval historians are curiously silent on the *Royal Oak* episode, or dismiss it briefly. Donald McLachlan, who served in the NID, made no reference whatsoever to the subject in his book, *Room 39*. In the *Saturday Evening Post*, in the spring of 1942, an article by Curt Riess was published in the USA, declaring that the mysterious spy who was able to supply the information for Prien's coup was Kapitan Alfred Wehring, a former German naval officer. The article told how Wehring, changing his name to Albert Oertel and his identity to that of a Swiss watchmaker and repairer, was sent to Kirkwall in the Orkney Islands in 1927 specifically to gather intelligence on Scapa Flow and its defences. Having won the respect of the community in which he lived and being certain he was in no way suspected, Wehring sent in a steady stream of reports to

Germany and, early in October 1939, reported on the deficiencies of Scapa Flow's defences with the result that Admiral Karl Doenitz, in charge of U-boats, ordered the U-47 to penetrate the Flow and sink the *Royal Oak*. The article even stated that Wehring had become a naturalized British subject under the name of Oertel. This same story of the mysterious super-spy was repeated by Walter Schellenberg, head of the *Sicherheitsdienst* and later successor to Canaris, in his post-war memoirs. Referring to Oertel, Schellenberg wrote:

It was in the beginning of October, 1939, that he sent us important information that the eastern approach to Scapa Flow through Kirk Sound was not closed off by anti-submarine nets, but only by block ships lying relatively far apart. On receipt of this information Admiral Doenitz ordered Prien to attack any British warships in Scapa Flow.[2]

The story was also enlivened by an account of how Oertel drove by car to the vicinity of the north-east entrance to the anchorage and signalled to Prien by flashing the headlights of his car. If this story was true, of course, it was highly damaging to the NID, MI5 and the Special Branch. There was a good deal of superficial evidence long after the war that it was indeed true, not merely because Schellenberg confirmed it, but because it was accepted by a number of American historians as having been corroborated, and also because the British made no efforts to deny the story and, unofficially, hinted that it could well be accurate. Yet there is no vestige of truth in it. No trace of 'Alfred Wehring' can be found in any of the registers of the German Navy, or even of the *Abwehr*, nor is there any reference to an 'Albert Oertel' either in German Naval Intelligence documents or *Abwehr* records. My own inquiries in Orkney, when carrying out researches into the mystery of the sinking of HMS *Hampshire*, first led me on to the trail of the mysterious Oertel. Various inhabitants of the islands had heard the story of the Swiss watchmaker and they all refuted it. It is now fairly certain that the Oertel story was planted by German Naval Intelligence in the United States, in order to discredit Britain, shortly after America entered the war. British security authorities, including the NID, checked up on it in America as soon as the article was published, naturally being perturbed that it might be true. Eventually they traced its origin to an emigrant from Central Europe, but, because the narrative to some extent tallied with the facts, some members of the NID tended to believe it was true rather than a hoax. But what most tended to make the naval authorities believe in Oertel was that Prien's daring escapade suggested that detailed knowledge had been obtained and that this was of such a kind that it could not have been gleaned from aerial reconnaissance, but only from espionage inside Orkney.

Others who have delved into this mystery, besides myself, will testify that Alfred Oertel was the spy who never was. Ladislas Farago writes that '. . . the watchmaker who was supposed to have helped Lieutenant Prien to his victory in the Flow came from somebody's imagination. It was not especially difficult to establish that even Schellenberg's tale, cited as one of the great feats of the German Secret Service, was nothing but a hoax, perpetrated on the British to add insult to their injury and to compound confusion.'[3] R. Wright Campbell, who has made an ingenious novel out of the whole story and who spent some time researching it in Orkney, wrote to me saying that the affair of Oertel 'was not a tricky German plot, but that of a hungry German writer. . . . The only watchmaker in Kirkwall had been born into a family who had been in Orkney for seven generations.'[4]

The truth was that the sinking of the *Royal Oak* was a perfect example of extremely sound naval intelligence planning, the credit for which certainly does not go to Walter Schellenberg, or to any super-spy in Kirkwall, but almost entirely to the SKL-3 section of German Naval Intelligence. Admiral Doenitz had always taken the view that one of the great failures of the German Navy in World War I had been not to take swift action against Scapa Flow immediately after war broke out. Long before World War II started—at least several months previously —he had given orders for the drawing up of detailed intelligence reports on Scapa Flow and its defences and for these to be kept up to date monthly. Thus, long before the mythical Oertel was supposed to have reported the fact, Doenitz knew that anti-submarine nets had not been laid at the north-east approaches to Scapa Flow. As a result of this Doenitz began to plan for a U-boat raid on the British base immediately after the outbreak of war, hoping, ideally, to destroy at least two or three capital ships. 'I had always had in mind the idea of an operation against Scapa Flow,' he stated in his memoirs.[5] Nevertheless, much of the intelligence that came in lacked corroboration and, though the reports on Scapa Flow were kept up to date as far as possible, it was not until the end of the first week in September, after war had broken out, that Doenitz was in possession of sufficient evidence to make positive plans. Had he obtained these details a few weeks earlier, a much bigger disaster might have hit the British Home Fleet. Until then SKL-3 had made their usual fatal error in assessing intelligence on the British Navy when reports showed that certain defensive measures had not yet been taken by the British—for example, the placing of anti-submarine nets, extending the scope of block ship defences—they gave the Royal Navy credit for greater efficiency and speed in carrying out such essential tasks than was actually due to it, stressing that, by the time their reports were submitted to Doenitz, it was almost certain the deficiencies in the British defences at Scapa Flow would have been remedied.

Doenitz, however, was not deterred by the ultra-cautious tone of these reports from his intelligence officers. A lesser man might have abandoned his plans, but Doenitz consulted his U-boat commanders, especially the captain of the U-16 ,which had just returned from a cruise in the vicinity of Orkney. The latter stated that there was a narrow channel, about 50 ft wide, leading into Kirk Sound, which appeared to be navigable for a U-boat, and also supplied the latest data on patrol vessels, prevailing currents and block ships. It was at this stage that Canaris himself—most unusually and untypically during his command of the *Abwehr*—supplied to the German Navy even more important intelligence. Prior to war breaking out, Canaris had taken the view that a clash between the British and German navies would be an appalling blunder. Now he was of the opinion that the German Navy desperately needed to prove it could strike a telling blow against the British. Canaris had a long memory and he recalled how, in the months before World War I, Steinhauer had gone to Scapa Flow himself, posing as a fisherman, to take soundings and make reports on the defences. So the admiral ordered that a similar attempt should be made in 1939, Commander Menzel of the naval section of the *Abwehr* being told to make arrangements for such reconnaissance.

'Don't send a fisherman to Orkney,' warned Canaris. 'The British won't fall for that a second time. But make sure that a fishing or freighter skipper gets the information we require.' The results were better than anyone in Berlin expected. One of the *Abwehr* spies in the merchant navy visited Kirkwall late in August 1939 and reported back to Germany that there was a lack of anti-aircraft batteries along part of Orkney and that it was common talk in Kirkwall that the defences of the anchorage were very poor, some of the boom and anti-torpedo defences being in need of repair, while on the eastern approaches they were non-existent. All this was enough to enable Doenitz to order Prien to carry out his attack on the *Royal Oak*.

There is only one other question which remains unanswered. In the story of the mysterious and non-existent Oertel, it was stated that he had driven his car up to the anchorage to flash his headlights and signal to Prien. It was this incident which caused the British investigating the *Saturday Evening Post* article to be inclined to accept the story as being at least partially true, because it transpired that an unidentified driver of a car with headlights switched on had been seen in Orkney in the vicinity of Kirk Sound at the time the U-boat was approaching it. There was further confirmation of this in Prien's log in which he noted that, at 1.20 a.m. on 14 October 1939, 'I must assume that I was observed by the driver of a car which stopped opposite us and drove off towards Scapa at top speed'. Ladislas Farago, who delved deeply into the *Abwehr* and other German files, comments that 'obviously the driver was not a spy'.[6]

Yet this deduction does not seem to be 'obvious'. Prien would not have been told if German Naval Intelligence had sent an observer to check up on his exploits. He would only have been told if he was to expect a signal from an agent ashore. What is interesting is that the mysterious driver proved as elusive as the fictitious Oertel: he was never located. Is one possible explanation that the car driver was one of Canaris's undercover agents whose job it was to frustrate Prien's mission? Bizarre as such a theory may seem, it is not improbable. No intelligence chief could play a double-game better than Canaris. He was devious, cunning, clever and complex in his thought processes. Canaris would go along with Doenitz to a certain extent, but from what we know about him it is more than likely that he would not wish to see the Royal Navy suffer too heavy a blow. One ship lost, perhaps, but more than that would be unthinkable. Did he send an agent in a car to flash his headlights and then drive off with the aim of frightening Prien into believing he had been discovered, thus making him stop at one act of sabotage, instead of sinking other capital ships?

The lead which the Germans had established in naval intelligence, prior to the Norwegian campaign, enabled them to plan for this with confidence and skill. It also helped the German Navy to keep away from the British Home Fleet and to make surprise attacks on enemy shipping, including the sinking of six submarines in the Skaggerak area. Hitler's plan to invade Norway in the spring of 1940 had been worked out months before it actually happened, but no date had been set for it. What precipitated the invasion was Doenitz's *Beobachtung-Dienst* (Observation Service).[7] This organization within German Naval Intelligence intercepted British messages which showed that there was a scheme, approved by Churchill as First Lord of the Admiralty, to mine the approaches to Narvik and to occupy that port and stop German ore shipments. Details given in the intercepted signal enabled the Germans to alter their own plans and speed up their implementation.

On 20 January 1940, Churchill had indulged in some wishful thinking propaganda that belied the facts of life. He made a broadcast in which he alleged that 'half the U-boats with which Germany began the war have been sunk, and their new building has fallen far behind what we expected'. This was a half-truth translated into a dangerous optimism. The British Admiralty, it is true, had been misled before the war into believing that the Germans had more U-boats than in fact existed and it took some time for the NID to change this viewpoint. Even so the NID never shared Churchill's publicly declared opinion in this period. There was a marked controversy between the NID and Churchill on this subject early in 1940, and in the reports of the DNI to the Chief of Naval Staff this was fully reflected, most notably in the statement that it would be 'most unwise optimistically to assume that the Germans will lose 52 U-boats in the next six months'.

Having intercepted British messages, the Germans decided that the NID could not have realized the vital problem of the German Navy—that their transports to Norway were weakly guarded. Their answer was to send out a decoy force to lure the British into believing that they intended to defend Narvik at all costs. News of the decoy move was leaked to Britain. It was one of the most effective misinformation ploys of the early years of the war. The British fell into the trap and concentrated their naval forces to the north of Norway That the German Naval Intelligence Service knew most of the moves the Royal Navy were planning at this time is clear from the following signals which they intercepted:

16 February 1940: In view of the enemy activities inter-cepted by our monitoring service and the report from the supply ship *Altmark* Group West and the Naval Staff agree that the enemy will use every means and has already taken measures with his naval forces to catch the *Altmark*. The previous assumption of the total safety of the Norwegian ter-ritorial waters can no longer be accepted in any circumstances.

13 March 1940: On this day the Naval Intelligence Service de-coded a British Admiralty signal which put British destroyer units under the C-in-C Home Fleet, and it was noted in Berlin that this strengthening of destroyer units allied to a concentration of Royal Navy ships at Scapa Flow was significant of hostile moves in this sphere of war: . . . our radio reconnaissance [units] have again succeeded in intercepting details of the new deployment of the British submarines, by decoding signals, and they conclude that, contrary to the previously observed [pattern of] distribution of submarines in the German Ocean [North Sea] there are today fifteen British submarines (twice to three times as many as at any time before) lying in wait off the Skaggerak . . . either this is a flank protection for a major landing operation planned by the enemy in Norway, or the enemy has learned of some of the preparations on the German side and fears a German operation against Norwegian territory.

Similar messages went out over the whole of this period, warning the German Fleet of exactly what the British were planning. Only on 23 March 1940, was it recorded in Berlin that 'the main British radio cipher system has changed its code' and the Intelligence Service indicated that it would probably be a fortnight before British messages could once again be intercepted and read. While the Royal Navy sailed north to Narvik, German ships, totally unhampered, crossed the Skaggerak without meeting any opposition. The decoy force was spotted by the Royal Navy on 7 April, and Churchill ordered the Home Fleet to sail to Narvik. The Germans immediately sent in their transports to Southern Norway and, without opposition, made landings.

Failure by the British to realize the extent to which the Germans were intercepting and decoding so much of their naval signals traffic was also a major factor in the calamitous Norwegian campaign. There was also a lack of professionalism in the drafting of intelligence messages for the Home Fleet, these sometimes revealing a failure to interpret information received in such a form that it would be a reliable guide to operational forces. One such signal emanating from the Admiralty on 7 April 1940, mentioned reports of a German expedition being prepared, notably from Copenhagen, which suggested it would arrive at Narvik the following day. Yet the Admiralty proceeded to depreciate the reports by adding that they were 'of doubtful value and may be only a further move in the war of nerves'. This would seem to have been a fault directly attributable to the NID, who should have reacted more positively to the fact that, apart from other reports, the really vital intelligence message came from the British Consul-general in Copenhagen.

Godfrey made some wise appointments in the NID, but in one respect he was especially pig-headed and slow in coming to terms with technical developments. There was the question of the Navy's role in relation to 'Ultra', the enemy-cipher-breaking project by which the boffins at Bletchley Park, aided by the invention of a Polish defector, intercepted top-grade German signals. This whole operation was, of course, initially linked with the Government Code and Cipher School of which Commander Denniston was chief. While the Army and the RAF had shown immediate and enthusiastic interest in the scheme, the reaction of Godfrey, the DNI, had been tepid, to say the least. The NID still regarded itself as the senior Intelligence Service and a law unto itself and Godfrey unfortunately upheld this outdated traditionalism. He was the last to give a reluctant 'yes' to the project for a Combined Services unit. Group-captain Winterbotham wrote:

> It was only a little while after I had got the Army and RAF components operational that the German naval Enigma was broken. I knew it would not have been any good trying to get John Godfrey, the DNI, to come in earlier. He wasn't at all keen even now. . . . I managed to persuade him to send one naval officer to join the party at Bletchley. Despite the fact that Lieutenant-Commander Saunders was a brilliant German scholar, the DNI insisted that naval signals should still go to the Admiralty in the original German, notwithstanding the fact that those that concerned the U-boat traffic or German ship movements were already being translated by Humphreys and being sent to Coastal Command of the RAF.[8]

This attitude robbed 'Ultra' of much of its efficacy as regards the Navy in the early stages, but eventually it proved a war-winner. Marshal of the RAF, Sir John Slessor, referred to the fact that 'characteristically and not always with happy results, the Admiralty were allowed to keep these Signal Intelligence matters in their own hands'.[9]

While German naval intelligence largely depended on its professionals under Doenitz and haphazard and sometimes erratic help from the *Abwehr*, British naval intelligence increasingly relied on other branches of intelligence such as Ultra and, later, the operations of the 20 Committee.[10] The NID role was more subdued than in World War I, though still vitally important. The reorganization of British intelligence in other fields took away from the NID many of the powers of deception and espionage which Hall had totally controlled in 1914–18.

It was B Division of MI5 which enabled the Admiralty to carry out its deception work in the war. Though this was all very different from Hall's incursions into diplomacy, and much less linked with political espionage, it was also more closely concerned with basic essentials of naval intelligence and counter-intelligence. It was recognized by B Division that 'misinformation tactics' were more easily adapted for the Navy than for the Army, where detailed co-ordination with other services was essential. Deception for submarine warfare, or for protection of convoys, was relatively easy. One of the most important aspects of such deception work was that of falsifying figures concerning ship-building. One example of this was that, late in 1942, the Admiralty agreed to the admission of two aircraft carriers to C-in-C, East Indies, when in fact this command had none. In the years 1939–42, when Britain was alone in standing up to Nazi aggression, it became vital to practise deception on a wide scale in order to survive. The stark truth was that almost nothing could have stopped the Germans from successfully invading Britain in the mid-summer of 1940, had they made up their minds to do so. More important than any military or naval action was the need for a massive and convincing deception operation to bewilder the Germans and make them believe that Britain was far stronger than she was.

Whereas the NID was quick to realize that the respect in which the Royal Navy was held by the Germans could prove to be a deterrent to the invasion proposals of some of the Nazi leaders, the latter failed to appreciate that the Royal Navy was much more vulnerable than even their most optimistic intelligence reports suggested. It was this psychological factor which caused German naval intelligence to decline, while that of the British gained in strength. Much of the early 'misinformation' concerned defences, such as the putting out of reports on non-existent minefields and the use of anti-torpedo nets by merchant ships. It was aimed at disguising the basic principle that the torpedo was caught by the tail and not stopped by the head, and that, by considerably disguising the efficiency of the nets, they were able to delay the introduction of effective counter-measures. Using agents of other branches of intelligence, the NID was able to pass on misleading information on this subject to the Germans, despite the fact that many British merchantmen, fitted with the latest anti-torpedo nets, visited ports where German agents were operating.

The highly successful operation of the double-cross system of espionage was, of course, a triumph for many people, most notably Sir John Masterman. While it had many purposes and was of great assistance to the Royal Navy, its main function was to gain control of enemy agents both inside and outside of Britain and to turn them into double-agents, feeding false information back to the enemy, while passing back details of enemy activity to Whitehall. Most German agents who were trapped in this way were successfully turned over to the Allied side and some of them brilliantly maintained the role of double-agents to the end of the war, giving enormous help to the Allies. One such agent, code-named 'Tate', or Agent 3725, was an experienced wireless operator named Wulf Schmidt who fulfilled his double role for more than four and a half years. He had landed in Britain by parachute in September 1940, was interrogated by the intelligence authorities and turned into a double-agent of great value to the NID. Sir John Masterman described 'Tate' as 'one of our most trusted wireless agents . . . for he transmitted and received messages to and from Hamburg from October 1940, until May 1945'.[11]

According to the German writer, Gunter Peis, Tate was allowed to leak accurate information on the Dieppe Raid plans in advance to the Germans, presumably in the hope that they would then be more likely to accept inaccurate information on the dates and whereabouts of landings in North Africa and Normandy later on. However, there is no absolute confirmation of these allegations, though they are by no means improbable and they should be borne in mind in relation to the narrative of bad security on this raid mentioned in Chapter 11. What is certain is that, even as late as the spring of 1945, Tate was sending messages regarding minefields at sea which were instrumental in closing an area of 3,600 square miles to U-boats. In the last months of the war a vast amount of deception work was carried out by these double-agents for the Admiralty, especially in connection with the final German U-boat campaign. By then it was realized that German submarines no longer had to come to the surface to recharge batteries as the snorkel apparatus enabled them to do this underwater. This made the hunting of U-boats difficult and the only solution to the problem was the laying of deep minefields which would trap the U-boat, but over the surface of which ships could pass in safety.

The NID needed to convince the Germans that there were far more of these deep minefields than in fact existed. Tate was the instrument for carrying out this deception which consisted of his reporting to the Germans the details of totally fictitious mine-laying in certain areas. It would seem that the Germans were sufficiently impressed by Tate's reports to act upon them for, even as late as 2 May 1945, he was receiving a message from Hamburg in which German Naval Intelligence Service urged him to maintain contact and keep them informed on mine-laying. Tate was outstanding, being awarded an Iron Cross by the Germans and managing to persuade the British to trust him to the extent of allowing him to live with a family rather than keeping him under supervision in prison or a 'safe house'. While some double-agents succeeded for a year or two, or perhaps a few months, most came under suspicion by the Germans sooner rather than later. Yet Tate managed to persuade them to trust him, even though, when they thought he was operating in London, for most of the war he was stationed at Wye in Kent. He still lives in Britain, his identity well concealed, and within 3 miles of the Tower of London where at least eight of his former German colleagues were hanged.

The most spectacular deception operation of the war was probably operation 'Mincemeat', the ghoulish code-word for the 'man who never was', the fictitious major of the Royal Marines whose corpse was jettisoned from a British submarine off the coast of Spain and allowed to float ashore. The Spaniards recovered the body and, as British Intelligence guessed, passed on the information of what was found in his briefcase (chained to his person) to the Germans. That 'information' was to mislead the Germans into believing that the Allied landings would come in the eastern Mediterranean and Sardinia rather than Sicily. This story has been told over and over again by countless authorities, but it is worth making the point here that the NID played a major role in successfully launching this deception, as well as masterminding the crucial task of handling the affair in Spain.

The surprising thing about the 'man who never was' operation was that while the most thorough precautions had been taken to ensure success, there was a curiously amateurish approach and lack of security in the quest for a suitable corpse for 'Major Martin RM'. Lieutenant-commander Ewen Montagu RNVR, who was one of the principal planners on the naval side, admitted:

> At one time we feared we might have to do a body-snatch . . . but we did not like the idea, if we could possibly avoid it. We managed to make some very guarded inquiries from a few Service Medical Officers whom we could trust, but when we heard of a possibility, either the relatives were unlikely to agree, or we could not trust those whose permission we would need not to mention to other close relatives what had happened.

Many people must have heard of the quest for a body. Luckily all went well and eventually the right corpse of the correct age, height and weight was found, thanks to Sir William Bentley Purchase, the Coroner for St Pancras. Yet even Bentley Purchase was worried about the security aspects of the affair, though that was not his responsibility. His biographer states: 'Purchase's action in providing the body had the sanction not only of the Government, but the man's own relatives, but he was still worried about the effect on public opinion of the unorthodox disposal of a body which had been in his keeping.'[12]

Yet the whole operation, which built up a most detailed picture of the mythical major, down to giving him a girlfriend whose photographs and letters were found on his person, and a bank overdraft, might well have foundered, but for the high efficiency of the NID organization in Spain. In no country in Western Europe was the NID so effectively served as in Spain during World War II. There were two men of remarkable energy, initiative and cunning—Commander Alan Hillgarth, the naval attaché in Madrid, who had a keen appreciation of diplomatic and political problems in the area, and the attractive, lively Don Gomez-Beare, a gregarious, party-loving character whose principal bailiwick was Gibraltar, but who travelled far and wide inside Spain, indulging in a number of hair-raising espionage activities. It was Gomez-Beare who was sent post-haste to Huelva, near where the body of 'Major Martin' was floated ashore from a British submarine (tide tables and details of currents having been carefully studied beforehand), to beg of the Spaniards that no unauthorized person, especially German agents, should be allowed access to the body and the papers in the briefcase. He was able to convey to the Spaniards in nods and winks and a few discreet phrases that the major had been carrying vital papers which must not fall into the hands of the enemy. He made it clear that he was not asking for the papers immediately, but only for them to be kept away from the enemy. These tactics worked, as Gomez-Beare knew they would, and the Germans were allowed by the Spaniards not only to see the papers, but to photograph them before they were handed over to the British.

An examination of German naval signals in the first year of the war reveals a confidence and efficiency which were lacking later on. Yet even on 21 August 1940, there was a hint that the era of easy reading of Allied messages was over: the war diary of the German Naval Staff records that, as a result of the simultaneous change-over by all codes and ciphers of the Royal Navy, 'it is no longer possible to reckon with results from decoding for the time being'.

The German Naval Intelligence commentary on this was that it was . . .

the heaviest blow to our radio monitoring since the beginning of the war, and had hitherto just caused our decoding service temporary difficulties by cipher changes introduced from time to time. The activities of our radio monitoring and decoding services were considerably facilitated by the capture of quantities of enemy documents, so that we had nearly complete knowledge of the enemy's radio traffic. It was to be expected that the enemy would sooner or later change his coding system, to re-establish wireless security: now it is clear that this step has now been taken, a year after the outbreak of war. We cannot count on the monitoring service being able to deliver new information for at least six months.[13]

The man appointed to NID 10, the section concerned with intercepting and studying enemy signal traffic, was a versatile character, Commander Wilson. He had been a biologist, pharmaceutical chemist, solicitor, accountant and the Keeper at the Victoria and Albert Museum. But by far the most *avant garde* figure in the NID was Ian Fleming, the creator of James Bond, who was appointed chief assistant to the DNI on the recommendation of Sir Montagu Norman, Governor of the Bank of England. Fleming, who had been a stockbroker and a Reuter correspondent in Moscow for brief spells, soon became one of the most effective executives of the NID, nursing (or, to use his own phrase, 'jollying') Godfrey along and coaxing him through the pitfalls of the outer world of intelligence. When Godfrey was succeeded by Admiral Rushbrooke in 1943, Fleming remained as personal assistant. He had a wide range of cosmopolitan contacts, was full of bright ideas (many of which bordered on the bizarre) and he supplied an imaginative and lively approach to the whole sphere of naval intelligence. Years later Godfrey described his Personal Assistant as 'a war-winner': this was no carelessly phrased piece of flattery, for Fleming could easily have justified this remark by his ideas alone. Indeed, many war-winning ideas which others claimed to be their own were almost certainly products of Fleming's inventive mind. He was always much more concerned for other people to get the credit than for himself. Possibly this was why he shone in smoothing over personality clashes, pacifying senior officers and in general liaison work, especially with the Americans with whom he got on immensely well.

Fleming was an Establishment figure who did not hesitate occasionally to cock a snook at the Establishment (taking a German prisoner-of-war to a West End restaurant, wining and dining him while seeking information was one example). In some ways he was more like Hall than either Godfrey or Rushbrooke and, like Hall, he sometimes took the risk of dabbling in espionage affairs outside his own department, even daringly playing secret service games of his own. Nobody knew better than Ian how to go above the heads of his immediate superiors to get what he wanted and he had a positive genius for cajoling people to undertake assignments without their ever having the slightest idea of the purpose of the operation. This applied to people outside the NID as well as those in it. When serving in the Mediterranean in the Royal Navy early in 1943,

I received a roundabout request from Fleming to visit the kasbah of Algiers (then strictly out of bounds to Allied Forces) to make a street map of the area. It seemed to be an odd requirement, as maps of the kasbah could be obtained in Algiers. Only after some hair-raising nocturnal adventures did I grasp the fact that there were German agents hiding out in the kasbah and that Fleming wanted a rather special map which would show their locations.

In the early winter of 1939–40 there was a plan to block the Danube to German ships. A small team of officers, attached temporarily to the NID, was sent to Bucharest, charged with closing the German's principal oil lifeline from the Black Sea by blocking the Iron Gates, 25 miles of dangerous narrows on the Danube between Rumania and Yugoslavia. The plan was to block the Danube with sunken barges. What is not quite clear about this scheme is to what extent, if any, it had Cabinet clearance, though Sir Robert Bellairs, co-ordinator of intelligence to the War Cabinet, was aware of it. The whole affair was somewhat of a dismal failure, undertaken with hasty improvization and insufficient planning, which may be one reason why officially it has never been admitted, though in 1975 Merlin Minshall lifted a corner of the curtain of secrecy which still masks the operation.[14]

The two main operators in the Danube Plan were Lieutenant-commanders Merlin Minshall and Michael Mason, both RNVR. Minshall, described by his enemies in the Service as 'a bloody pirate' because of his daring and sometimes ruthless escapades against the Germans, was essentially the type of character who fits the Secret Service agent of fiction. A racing motorist before the war, a first-class shot and karate expert, he was a natural choice for the Bucharest mission. Michael Mason, the senior member of the team, was an equally good shot, an amateur boxer of some distinction who, after being educated at Eton and Sandhurst, found himself in Word War II in the Navy, not the Army, but was sufficiently adaptable to fill a variety of roles from intelligence operative to commander of a landing-craft flotilla. According to *Who's Who*, he had spent a great deal of his life travelling 'extensively, mostly in wild places' and he had also been commodore of the Royal Ocean Racing Club. Like Minshall, Mason was a courageous officer who,

163

from my own personal knowledge of him in action, was totally without fear. Nevertheless, the respective accounts of these two operators differ considerably.

That there was erratic planning of this project seems indisputable and it also led to dissension between at least one of the operators—Minshall—and the NID. Minshall was presumably chosen because he knew the territory well, having actually travelled along the Danube in a Dutch barge prior to the war—narrowly escaping death by poisoning at the hands of a beautiful Nazi agent, according to his own account of this. When he arrived in Bucharest he had false-bottomed suitcases packed with detonators and high explosives disguised with the familiar red and gold foil of Mackintosh's toffee de luxe, while further gelignite was to be shipped out in a diplomatic bag. He tells how, having failed to bribe Iron Gates pilots with gold sovereigns, he commandeered half a dozen British ships lying in Braila harbour and then had a crew of British ratings brought out from Britain to man them.

Minshall claimed that he got his convoy out of the harbour only after surviving two attempts to kill him by German agents, one of whom he disposed of by dropping poison into his wine. But, as a result of the Germans siphoning fuel out of his boats under cover of night, the boats ran dry before they reached the Iron Gates and were arrested. Minshall says he himself escaped arrest by evading the convoy in a naval launch in which he was following. He salvaged something from the operation by filling the launch with explosive and ramming it at high speed into the railway embankment. This account of the operation is disputed both by Lieutenant-commander Mason and Sir Alexander Glen, another RNVR officer who, at that time, was operating in naval intelligence in Belgrade. Mason claims that the initial project was to blow up the Rumanian banks of the river at the Iron Gates so that they would be impassable to German barges. This plan was ruined through another agent talking too much and, in desperation, some thirteen tons of gelignite were shipped out of Bucharest in 1940 on the Orient Express through Italy, in cases labelled as the Ambassador's luggage. Mason also claims that, in company with another agent, a Rumanian, he had to deal with two men who had been watching him in the dining-car of the Orient Express: 'I knew they'd be waiting to jump me in the corridor and there they were. I hit one under the heart and one in the jaw and out they went. I beat them insensible and threw them off through the lavatory window.'[15]

Sir Alexander Glen states that

> ... certainly the Admiralty recognized the importance of the Danube very early indeed, not only in itself, but in conjunction with the Rumanian oil wells, both so vital to the German economy ... Captain Max Despard, whose assistant I was [as assistant naval attaché in Belgrade at the time] played a vital part in planning both operations. But it is Ian Fleming who is and must be the central figure. .... Michael Mason had physical and mental attributes that would have stretched Bond at his very best ... Dunstan Curtis had a part—elegance and courage in a nicely under-statement way ... But much of Bond lay in Fleming himself, in his own sharp mind, his imagination and his frustrations, too, at being tied so often to a desk job as DNI's personal assistant.[16]

This operation was not one of Fleming's successes, but he learned a great deal from it. In any event the blocking of the Danube in 1940 could only have had a temporary effect and might have had unfortunate political repercussions in Yugoslavia later on. It was not until the RAF laid mines in the Danube in 1944 that German traffic on the river was drastically cut down.

In January 1941, a Special Activities Branch of the American ONI was set up under Commander J. L. Riheldaffer as a precautionary attempt at securing naval intelligence on Germany while the USA was still neutral. Counterespionage activities had also been stepped up in the ONI and, between 1936 and 1940, twelve convictions for espionage inside the USA were obtained. Four of these were the direct result of investigations by the ONI. Inside the ONI, however, general intelligence-gathering had been adversely affected by the poor quality evaluation of the information, due partly to the fact that, between the outbreak of World War II and the Japanese attack on Pearl Harbor, there had been no fewer than five directors of the ONI. The British had changed their directors frequently enough in peacetime, but at least in wartime they kept a DNI in office long enough to be able to come to grips with the situation. But in Washington, Admiral W. S. Anderson left the directorship in January 1941, to be replaced temporarily by Captain James, who stayed until March of that year, when he was succeeded by Alan Kirk who stayed until October.

Kirk, then a captain, had been naval attaché in London at the beginning of the war, and Godfrey, as British DNI, had, on Fleming's prompting, gone out of his way to cultivate his acquaintance. No doubt he hoped to alert the Americans to what would, in the long run, be common problems for the USA as well as Britain. Kirk began his period of service as naval attaché in London with grave doubts as to whether Britain would continue the war. In June 1940, he was convinced that Germany would triumph, probably being influenced by the defeatist opinions of Ambassador Joseph Kennedy. But he struck up a close friendship with Godfrey who possessed enormous tact and patience, and gradually began to co-operate with the British to a remarkable degree. The British knew that the Americans had had great success in deciphering Japanese signals and more than anything else the NID wanted close, unofficial co-operation with the US Navy in intelligence matters, or an exchange of information. Donald Maclachlan revealed that 'as early as 1940, during the disasters of the Dunkirk summer, Room 39 [the World War II version of Room 40] originated a proposal that the Admiralty should offer to Washington an extensive revelation of naval secrets'.[17]

Some progress was made and eventually the US Naval Mission in London grew from six to forty and a limited degree of co-operation on intelligence matters was achieved. There had to be a great deal of tact, forethought and even downright hypocrisy in much of this co-operation as there was always the danger that some talkative, isolationist-minded, American naval officer would compromise the whole operation if there was any suggestion of trading secrets. To safeguard this it was agreed that whoever on the British side passed intelligence on to the Americans must not ask for anything in return, nor must he ever be the recipient of any intelligence proffered from the American side. One set of British officers would pass on the information, an entirely different set would receive it. This arrangement was dubbed 'the Anglo-American musical chairs' by Fleming who urged on Godfrey a plan for attaching US naval officers to the NID. With this revolutionary policy in mind, Godfrey went to Washington for talks with Kirk who was then head of the ONI. He found an improvement in the US naval intelligence system since Kirk had taken over, but realized there were grave deficiencies which could take several months to overcome. A report from an independent observer for the NID, dated 10 May 1941, stated that 'Kirk has undoubtedly made some improvements, but the whole set-up of naval intelligence in Washington is lacking in urgency, riddled with red tape, with consequent delays in assessing intelligence, and the whole method of handling reports (many of which are badly written in bureaucratese, diffuse and incomplete) is deplorable. Far too many people are involved in handling the traffic and the result is very often incomprehensible appraisals of intelligence. If the United States were to be attacked by a foreign power, it would take US Naval Intelligence at least forty-eight hours to react to the situation.'

This may have been a harsh and somewhat prejudiced judgement, but it was not far from the truth. Despite this, co-operation between the American and British naval intelligence services continued. One of the errors which led to the Pearl Harbor crisis was that the Americans, unlike the British, had then not evolved a system for grading and assessing naval intelligence, thus really vital information of inestimable value was mixed up with inaccurate, or even totally untrue reports, sometimes mere opinions without facts. One of the worst features was that opinions were sometimes preferred to facts.

Admiral Kirk, as eventually he became, had a highly successful war and he remained in close touch with the NID. Luckily for Godfrey, Kirk was appointed as Chief of Staff to the US Naval Headquarters in London in 1942. Later he rounded off his war career by commanding the US naval assault group in the Normandy landings and it is a tribute to his political acumen that, after the war, he was appointed as US Ambassador first to Brussels, then to Moscow.

10

Lessons of Pearl Harbor

The surprise Japanese attack on Pearl Harbor, the US naval base in the Hawaiian Islands on 7 December 1941, is still an object lesson in how costly naval intelligence failures can be. This is just as applicable today as it was then and, indeed, ever since the days of World War I when Admiral Jellicoe said that the Grand Fleet could win or lose the war in a single afternoon.

Japan's aim was to destroy the United States Pacific Fleet while it was still at anchor and thus be able to complete the conquest of Asia and the Pacific Islands unhindered. The attack might well have resulted in even greater disaster: the tragedy was that it should and could have been avoided. American naval intelligence still lagged behind that of Britain, Germany and Japan right up to the time of the Pearl Harbor attack, which finally produced some drastic reorganization. It was not so much that it was downright bad as that it had not improved fast enough. On a purely peacetime basis probably the ONI had done a reasonable job, but it simply was not good enough for a nation which needed to be on a war footing. Where it failed most was that there was no proper system of grading intelligence reports. In other words, the really first-class report was given no better rating than the dubious item of intelligence. This had inevitably bred a mistrust of intelligence —a feeling on the operational side that the system was one of 'hit and miss'. There had been a setback to American naval cryptanalysis when Yardley's Black Chamber was de-commissioned in the 'isolation' era of 1929. Yet, despite this, the USA had succeeded in building several duplicates of Japan's famous

Purple Coding Machine, a most complicated apparatus which had long fascinated the Americans. The Japanese used this machine for diplomatic cable traffic which had the great advantage of speed. Basically, the Purple Machine consisted of what resembled two electric typewriters, separated by cipher wheels and a plug board, the plain text being typed on one typewriter and the cipher text automatically reproduced on the other. It had taken the Americans some few years to copy the machine and the story that it was miraculously developed within eighteen months, entirely from brilliant theoretical work, is erroneous. Highly intelligent deductions were made, but they were all based on a hazardous and highly skilled espionage operation. A naval spy smuggled a miniature camera into one of the twelve Japanese embassies and consulates which possessed a Purple Machine. This operation was then repeated in two other embassies until Naval Intelligence had three different photographs to work on. These were 'blown up' to a scale ten times higher than the actual size of the machine. It was from these photographs that the final deductions were made. But they already had much data to work on as the 'Red' or 'Orange' Machine, which had preceded the Purple Machine, had been solved earlier when Lieutenant Jack S. Holtwick Jr, a US naval decipherer and analyst, had built a machine to solve the diplomatic code of the Japanese which was cancelled by Tokyo in 1938.

The task of breaking the Japanese cipher system was then relatively easy because of the simple fact that, as the Japanese alphabet consists of more than 50 letters and 2,000 hieroglyphics, the Japanese sent their codes in Roman letters. Thus there was no reason why the Americans, and especially the ONI, could not decipher all Japanese messages on the diplomatic circuit long before Pearl Harbor. The fault lay in incompetent interpretation of some messages, a lack of political acumen and, in some cases, gross negligence. The ONI had been extremely dilatory early on in setting up agents inside Japan. Even the naval attachés sent to Japan were not always of a high calibre. On the eve of Pearl Harbor, the American naval attaché in Tokyo reported that any surprise attack was highly improbable because there were thousands of Japanese sailors in the city and they could not possibly be recalled speedily. Ladislas Farago in *War of Wits* reveals that these sailors were

169

actually soldiers dressed in naval uniform purposely to deceive.

In the months before Pearl Harbor the Japanese had been consistently disguising their intentions to launch an attack on the United States by making peace overtures and even sending envoys to Washington to discuss plans for better relations between the two countries. Yet, in spite of all the hints of sweet reasonableness, it should have been apparent that the Japanese were playing a double-game as they were still being obdurate in getting down to the details of an agreement. In fact the talks were largely a plot of Japanese Naval Intelligence, as Admiral Isoroku Yamamoto, C-in-C Combined Fleet of the Imperial Navy, had finalized his plans for the Pearl Harbor attack as early as September 1941. The diplomatic talks were mainly delaying tactics while the Japanese completed their preparations. Yamamoto was a brilliant tactician and a realist. His view was that, if Japan went to war with the USA, there was no chance of winning it unless the US Pacific Fleet could be destroyed at the outset.

In the mid-summer of 1941 the US Navy had sent Captain Joseph Rochefort, an expert in cryptanalysis and wireless techniques, as well as being adept in the Japanese language, to reorganize naval intelligence at Pearl Harbor. His qualifications for such work had long been neglected, for as far back as 1925 he had been a key figure in the US Navy's cryptanalysis section. The organization he took over in Pearl Harbor was then known as the Radio Unit of the 14th Naval District in Hawaii. His instincts told him that this was far too blatant a title for what should be a very hush-hush set-up, and he changed it to that of the Combat Intelligence Unit. To the uninitiated this might seem just as obvious, but not, at least so Rochefort opined, to the somewhat literally minded Japanese. He at once made it his aim to find out the dispositions and operations of the Japanese Navy.

Rochefort developed this unit into a much broader conception of what intelligence was all about, not merely concentrating on radio traffic and deciphering, but seeking details of the Japanese Navy's top secret codes, direction-finding and skilled analysis and assessment of intelligence. But, by the end of the summer of 1941, the Japanese, knowing how much depended upon disguising their war plans, set up their own deception tactics. In the first instance it was a massive exercise in confusing the Americans as well as the British. The Japanese Navy pushed out an increased number of radio messages, deliberately intended not only to confuse, but to waste the time of the decipherers, to realign their own forces under new call-signs and Fleet unit numbers. It was all highly skilful confusion, with messages being repeated to false destinations, and with, of course, no replies or acknowledgements coming in. Aircraft carriers were ordered to keep radio silence so that the Americans were led to suppose that the carriers were being retained in Japanese ports.

The Americans intercepted the traffic all right; the trouble was they got their deductions all wrong. They had listening posts not only at Pearl Harbor, but at Guam, in California, Long Island, Corregidor, Maine, Maryland and elsewhere. They also gained ample information about Japanese espionage in the Hawaiian Islands which should in itself have alerted them to the probabilities of a surprise and treacherous attack. As early as the spring of 1941, a junior naval officer of the Imperial Japanese Navy, Takeo Yoshikawa, had been sent to Honolulu as a spy under the cover-name of Tadasi Morismura (sometimes known as Ito Morimura). He had been invalided from active service on medical grounds and was assigned to the American desk of the Third Division of the Japanese Naval Intelligence, a corps comprising some thirty officers. Yoshikawa was not perhaps so professional a spy as Sorge had been inside Japan, but he was adaptable, versatile and obtained results, though the latter sometimes attracted the attentions of the US Naval Intelligence as his heavy drinking and his promiscuity were not far short of exhibitionist, and the messages he sent back to Tokyo were not even in naval code, but in that used by the diplomats to which the Americans had access. In fact Yoshikawa was being quite correct in using the diplomatic code because his cover was that of a vice-consul in Honolulu. But he should have been detected long before he was able to do any real damage. The extraordinary thing was that US Naval Intelligence missed the fact that Yoshikawa was keeping Tokyo informed as to which US warships were in Hawaiian waters and where they were situated. But they did learn all about his love life by tapping his telephones.

Yoshikawa, a likeable and amusing character, is said to have made the crack that 'a spy without a love life is a spy doomed'. He also claimed that US Naval Intelligence officers were voyeurs first and spies a very bad second. Obviously he believed that an ardent and persistent love life was an admirable cover. He also avidly studied US naval and technical reports which were freely available as well as a mass of technical journals; he had an eye for detail as well as a mass observation technique for gathering the names, numbers and technical idiosyncracies of ships, and he worked closely with a German agent, Dr Friedel Kuehn and his daughter, Ruth, members of a family who posed as refugees from Hitler. Ruth even signalled messages to him, having set out to make dates with American naval officers. While Yoshikawa was not by training a professional spy, he had surprisingly versatile talents in that field: he disguised himself sometimes as a barefooted Filipino labourer, while at others he played the role of a Japanese nightclub 'Champagne Charlie'. He was a skilled photographer, taking pictures of US ships from the hills and even hiring a small plane to take aerial photographs of the hangars at Wheeler and Hickam airfields.

Nobody in the US Naval Department seemed to have realized that Japan was the least likely of any of the great powers to observe the Hague Convention that hostilities between two countries must not begin without a positively worded warning. Curiously enough, the Japanese did try to comply with the Hague Convention in the most cynical manner possible. They had sent an ultimatum to Washington at 1300 hours Washington time, while launching their attack on Pearl Harbor at 0730 hours Hawaiian time (1330 hours Washington time), thus giving the United States a mere half hour's warning of a possible attack, far too short notice for any effective countermeasures, even if the Americans had known where the attack was to be made. The vital ultimatum was sent in Purple and the Japanese code clerks in their embassy in Washington were deciphering it at the same time as the US Navy was breaking it down in a nearby building in the American capital. The actual text of the message was that 'the Japanese Government regrets, in view of the attitude of the American Government, it considers it impossible to reach an agreement through further negotiations'. It was a subtle way of declaring war. Yet the US

Navy failed to realize the implications of the message. As one of the Naval Operations Staff commented: 'we wondered why the Japanese had insisted on the message being delivered at 1330 hours'. US Naval Intelligence made the correct deductions rather more quickly: they realized they had picked up the message seven hours before the deadline, that this almost certainly meant war and that, if an attack was to come, Pearl Harbor was the obvious target.

All this should have been obvious to Naval Intelligence days, if not weeks, beforehand. That it was not appreciated was due to abysmally bad interpretation of naval intelligence. In January 1941, Ambassador Grew had indicated from Tokyo that if there was a break in Japanese-American relations, Japan would almost certainly make a surprise attack on Pearl Harbor. Yet the ONI disregarded it as 'just another rumour'.[1] The signing of the Russo-Japanese Pact should have added further point to the warning. Even the work of the US cryptographers in breaking Japanese diplomatic traffic was largely discounted. For example, in September 1941, the ONI was given a deciphered message to the Japanese Consulate in Honolulu asking for full details of the location of ships in Pearl Harbor. Astonishingly, this message was not even sent to Pearl Harbor for information, despite the fact that the request was repeated the following month, when there was a demand for twice-weekly reports on ship locations. So the US Government waited on developments, while the US Navy totally failed to warn Pearl Harbor.

The Pearl Harbor attack was a brilliant success for Japanese Naval Intelligence and not dependent on Yoshikawa alone. They had built up a network of naval spies recruited from the Black Ocean, Black Dragon, East Asia, One Culture and White Wolf secret societies. They had hundreds of agents in the whole Pacific area, though not thousands as has sometimes been suggested. Japanese Naval Intelligence had also bought its way into controlling several brothels patronized by US naval personnel. Allen Dulles has recorded that they became 'a highly efficient and dangerous presence in the intelligence world'. Thus the Japanese knew that on a Sunday the largest number of US vessels would be found at anchor in Pearl Harbour and they knew exactly where the ships would be, while their naval pilots had been trained in torpedo attacks in shallow water.

Japanese aircraft carriers were on their way to Pearl Harbor some few days before this. The Japanese Navy did not delay their operation even when it became apparent that, owing to slowness in decoding the Tokyo ultimatum, the Japanese Embassy in Washington had had to ask for a postponement of their 1300 hours meeting with the US authorities. No warning from the US Navy reached Pearl Harbor until the very moment that Japanese planes from the carriers were bombarding the base. Commander Mitsuo Fuchida, who led the attack, reported: 'I saw the main force of the United States Pacific Fleet were at anchor in the bay, so I ordered all squadrons into attack. We dropped fifty bombs. . . . From that moment the Pacific War was on.'

Pearl Harbor was the greatest disaster in American naval history. Apart from the damage done to the naval base, the USA lost 18 ships, 300 aeroplanes and 2,500 men. To sum up: the decipherers had done their job (for days and weeks ahead the vital intelligence had been intercepted); the analysts had, in the main, failed to decide that the evidence of this traffic pointed to war, though they had expressed their fears in a mild sort of way; the US Naval Command had merely passed the buck to the Government and the latter had dallied too long.[2]

Admiral Yamamoto had been delighted with Japan's success in attacking Pearl Harbor, but he felt that, devastating as it was, it was insufficient to ensure a quick victory. 'In a quick war Japan can always win,' he said, 'but whenever we are delayed, we face serious dangers. I am afraid that in our attack on Pearl Harbor all we have done is to wake up a sleeping giant and to prod him into action.'

Yamamoto was right in his prophecy, but this applied even more in the field of US naval intelligence than he could have anticipated. Rochefort's Combat Intelligence Unit almost immediately got to work to break the latest amendments and devices in the Japanese naval code. The real problem in achieving such a breakthrough in deciphering Japanese naval codes was that the Imperial Japanese Navy used a code within a code for added security. The major code might be broken, but this would still hide from enemy observers the fact that the inner code covered geographical locations. Thus a simple combination of letters in the inner code might hide from the enemy the information on whether the location was Corregidor or Midway Island. Rochefort had the answer to this problem: his lengthy service in the Navy and his knowledge of signalling and intelligence techniques, as well as the intricacies of wireless traffic, enabled him to think up a simple piece of deception designed to worm out of Tokyo the secret of the inner code. 'We must pinpoint one of our own bases in such a way that Japanese Naval Intelligence cannot fail to pick up our message and be forced to refer to that base in any message they refer back to their Fleet. If the locational symbol is one that we have come across before, we can be practically sure we are near to breaking their code.'

To simplify matters, it should be explained that US Naval Intelligence had isolated various inner codes symbols, but could not be sure to which locations they referred. All they knew was that the inner code directly referred to locations and that, if they could break the clue to one location, they could fairly soon establish the others. So a message was dispatched in a code which the Americans knew the Japanese would decipher, saying that Midway Island was desperately short of water supplies. Then came a prolonged round-the-clock wait for a Japanese follow-up. A few days later the Japanese passed this information to units of their Pacific Fleet and the Americans were able to establish that a certain symbol referred to Midway Island. From then onwards progress was rapid. But the Americans' problem in coping with the intricacies of Japanese naval communications was that there was an enormous volume of this traffic, but relatively few Americans cleared by the Security organization who could read Japanese. The code name of this code-breaking operation was 'Magic' and it enabled the US Navy to ascertain that the Roman letters 'A F' stood for Midway Island in the Japanese code. It was this discovery which paved the way for a brilliant recovery from the Pearl Harbor disaster by the American Naval Intelligence. In 1942 the Americans had every reason to believe that the Japanese would launch an attack either on Midway Island, the Aleutians, Hawaii or Australia. After it had been established that the message regarding lack of water at Midway had been taken seriously, the US Navy stepped up the defences of this sector. Mines were laid, torpedo boats were sent to Midway and the personnel of military and other shore forces increased.

Such preparations were soon justified when, on 3 June 1942, Admiral Nimitz at Pearl Harbor received news of an intercepted message which indicated that the Japanese Fleet was out to make an attack on Midway Island. He sent out a flying-boat patrol to check if the enemy was on the expected course and soon had confirmation. Rear-admiral T. S. Wilkinson, who had been DNI at the time of Pearl Harbor, had had no previous experience of intelligence work. Admiral Richmond K. Turner, who was head of the War Plans Division, had decreed that the ONI should make no estimate of enemy intentions prior to Pearl Harbor. Admiral Kirk had strongly criticized this ruling when he was DNI, but he had been overruled. All this was now put right. The lessons of Pearl Harbor were not only learned, but implemented with such alacrity that, in this theatre of the war at least, British Naval Intelligence was overtaken. Nimitz was thus able to benefit from the work not only of the Intelligence Combat Unit in Pearl Harbor, but of other sections of Naval Intelligence as well. The surprise attack by an American force on a much larger Japanese force at Midway was successful. The Japanese were certain that their messages had not been deciphered and that they would surprise the Americans. After the war, Lieutenant-commander Sesu Mitoya, communications officer of the Japanese ship *Kaga*, sunk off Midway, stated: 'We underestimated our opponents. They were waiting for us, and by an incredible effort they had broken our code while we failed to find out how they reinforced the island.'

The Japanese lost four carriers and a cruiser in this action as well as a large number of aircraft carrier pilots. But US Naval Intelligence never let up after this breakthrough. Combat Intelligence Unit picked up item after item of Japanese top secret messages. They deciphered a message from Admiral Yamamoto that he was proposing to make a trip to the Upper Solomon Islands. The more enthusiastic of the naval planners inside Intelligence suggested that this was the chance to send in fighter planes to shoot him down. There was opposition to this proposal on the grounds that assassination was an 'imperialist' tactic and something to be deplored in the brave new western world. The 'dirty tricks' of the 1950s and 1960s were still a long way off. The matter was referred to the President who passed the decision back to the Navy and only then was it decided to destroy the most brilliant strategist in the Japanese Imperial Fleet.

The whole operation was fraught with problems such as timing, wind strength, establishing contact at the right height and ensuring that Yamamoto was shot down before he landed, if possible. Captain John Mitchell, who was in charge of the operation, said: 'We didn't think we had the chance of a snowball in hell . . . but we had to go through the motions.'

Mitchell led the attack, mainly as a spotter, while Tom Lanphier, his number two, was detailed to deliver the attack. Mitchell first sighted the plane which he felt certain was the one containing Yamamoto, calling out to Lanphier: 'There's your meat, Tom. Don't miss him.'

But it was not until some weeks later that US Naval Intelligence could be sure that Yamamoto was dead. Then Tokyo Radio announced that the Admiral had, while engaged in combat, 'met his death gallantly in a war plane . . . an insupportable blow to Japan'.

It was a devastating blow to the Japanese from which they never recovered. Long afterwards Admiral Chester Nimitz told a press conference, in reply to a question as to how Yamamoto was shot down, 'we had broken the Japanese codes and ciphers and knew exactly where Admiral Yamamoto would be on that particular day. It was as simple as that'.

But before these revelations could be made there was an anxious time for US Naval Intelligence during the Presidential Election campaign of 1944. Roosevelt was being opposed by the Republican, Thomas Dewey. Few doubted that Roosevelt would win, but from the point of view of the military and naval hierarchy there was something like consternation when it was learned that Dewey had found out all about Operation Magic. A Chicago newspaper had carried a story that hinted at the operation and there had been a leakage of information by an indiscreet US naval officer to a Frenchman who was suspected of being in league with the Vichy regime in France. There was a distinct possibility that Dewey might try to capitalize on this information in the election campaign, either to show that he knew what was happening, or possibly to reveal that Roosevelt had passed the buck back to the Navy. General George Marshall undertook the task of informing Dewey that the interception of Japanese messages had not yet been realized by the enemy and begging him not to refer to it. Dewey agreed to comply.

The Congressional inquiry into the Pearl Harbor catastrophe revealed that it was at the highest administrative level that US naval intelligence was most disorganized. For example, at the time of the Japanese raid, Admiral Kimmel, then C-in-C of the US Pacific Fleet, had not been informed that there were indications, admittedly unconfirmed, that Japan might launch a surprise attack without declaring war. Thus no aerial reconnaissance had been ordered, though this should have been an obvious precaution if Kimmel had been given at least a summary of all up-to-date intelligence reports. This brought home to the Director of USNI that it was essential that Intelligence knew what Operations were planning and that the latter was completely in the picture as to what the former had to offer.

Lyman B. Kirkpatrick Jr writes that 'organization difficulties' on the intelligence side 'certainly contributed to the disaster at Hawaii . . . The intelligence staffs themselves were regarded as subordinate to the War Plans staff in both the Army and Navy, and this was reflected not only in the rank of the officers, but in the weight given the recommendations of the respective organizations. The Department of State carefully guarded cables and dispatches from its posts overseas and was reluctant to distribute them to other departments and agencies.'[3]

The fact that the dissemination of intelligence was drastically restricted inside the United States in itself demonstrates the obstacles to Anglo-American co-operation in the field of naval intelligence where it was more vital than elsewhere. From early 1942 co-operation between the two major navies steadily improved. Certainly British Naval Intelligence benefited indirectly from the spectacular improvement in the work done by the ONI, though there was a slowness to appreciate this. Nimitz stated that 'Midway was essentially a victory for intelligence' and General Marshal added that, as a result of cryptanalysis, the US were able to concentrate their forces on Midway, when otherwise 'we should have been 3,000 miles out of place'. Yet Rochefort was assigned to other duties after the war and it was not until 1966 that President Lyndon B. Johnson finally awarded a National Security Medal to Frank B. Rowlett, a retired civil servant who had played a tremendous role behind the scenes in furthering much of this work. The citation to the medal merely mentioned that it was for 'a profound contribution to the security of the United States'.

11

The Turning Point

One of the psychological barriers to Anglo-American understanding in naval intelligence in the early stages of the war had
been mutual mistrust and national prejudices. Blame can be
attributed almost equally to each side.

Up to the time of their entry into the war the Americans had
relied for a great deal of their naval intelligence on refugees
from Nazi-occupied countries of Europe—French, Dutch,
Belgians and especially Norwegians. From the last-named the
ONI had formed a poor opinion of certain senior officers in the
Admiralty and deep suspicion of the NID. There was the case of
'Operation Rubble' which became a success through the courage
and determination of a single naval officer and even then no
credit was due to the Admiralty or the NID. The latter had
merely tried to cover up the supine attitude of a British ambassador in wartime: perhaps this was the reason why Britain's
official naval historian, Captain S. W. Roskill, wrongly claims
that Operation Rubble was entirely a Norwegian affair.

The real hero of this enterprise was not a Norwegian, but
Commander George Binney RNVR (later Sir George Binney)
who, in peacetime, had been organizer and secretary of the
Oxford University Spitzbergen and Arctic expeditions and had
spent much time in the Arctic as a member of the Hudson's
Bay Company. In 1940 he was appointed assistant commercial
attaché in Stockholm. Early in January 1941, five Norwegian
ships sailed to Kirkwall in Orkney with a cargo of ball bearings, iron ore and steel from neutral Sweden. This was the
culmination of Operation Rubble for which George Binney,

then a civilian, was knighted that same year. Each master of the five ships was also awarded the OBE. Yet every time anyone attempted to tell this story of gallantry and individual endeavour in time of war, he was thwarted by the Admiralty and their subservience to the Foreign Office and the weapon of censorship. The reason for this was not far to seek: the cuckoo in the British diplomatic nest was the pro-German defeatist Victor Mallet, British Minister in Stockholm. He had not only disliked the operation; he had done his best to sabotage it. Yet even when his deplorable role was revealed for what it was, Mallet was, incredibly, rewarded after the war with ambassadorships in Spain and Italy.

Binney had been employed by the United Steel Company and it was the British Government's Iron and Steel organization which sent him to Stockholm to buy supplies when war broke out. Having found sympathizers to the Allied cause in Sweden, Binney secured vital war supplies and aimed to get these secretly to Britain by means of Norwegian ships which had been held in Swedish ports. The Skaggerak was controlled by the Germans, so their own intelligence would be on the alert for such smuggling. But Binney was determined to take the risk of trying to beat the blockade and he not only recruited a number of British merchant navy officers who had been interned, but Norwegian seamen as well. For good measure he indicated that he intended to sail with them. Yet Binney's plans were baulked at every turn by the defeatist attitude of Mallet who constantly warned the Admiralty to have nothing whatsoever to do with Binney's project. Binney replied to NID doubts with what was a masterly understatement: 'In my view, there is no justification for nervousness.'

Binney's plea for action was only reluctantly accepted by the NID. The five ships were loaded at Gothenberg and then sailed to an isolated fjiord with the intention of sailing under cover of the first fog that manifested itself. But the weather remained good and, in the end, Binney had to give the order to sail regardless of the hazards. Luck was with the tiny convoy and, several hours later, they rendezvoused with the cruiser *Aurora* and made for Orkney. As for Binney, he went back to Sweden and continued his blockade-running operations for four years, bringing more cargoes from Sweden with fast motor-torpedo boats. By 1942 a somewhat wiser Admiralty had made him a Commander RNVR.

Realizing that the American Navy was totally unprepared for a war in the Atlantic at the same time that it was so heavily committed in the Pacific, Admiral Doenitz ordered an immediate stepping-up of the U-boat campaign in US Atlantic waters when the USA entered the war. Yet even then, when the USA was on the side of the Allies, there was a reluctance at first for the US Navy Department to co-operate fully with the NID. There were long arguments between the senior officers of the NID and other sections of the British Admiralty on the one hand and the US Chief of Staff, Rear-admiral R. S. Edwards, the DNI, and COMINCH, the Operations organization of the Navy Department on the other. By the middle of 1942 the ONI had grown from being little more than an annexe of the Bureau of Navigation in the 1880s, with a strength of four officers, to a department with more than 300 officers. Yet it still suffered from a lack of feeling in the Navy as a whole for the vital role which intelligence played in losing and winning wars. As far as the Pacific theatre of the war was concerned, this was dramatically and positively corrected quickly enough, but in the Atlantic there was a sense of its being all right to learn from personal experience and no appreciation of the fact that the British NID could help to cut some corners.

This mentality can be summed up by the comment of Rear-admiral Edwards to Commander Rodger Winn RNVR of the NID, when the latter went to Washington for talks. 'Americans must learn by their own mistakes', he said, 'and we have plenty of ships to spare.' Winn bluntly replied: 'we are deeply concerned about your reluctance to co-operate and we are not prepared to sacrifice our men and ships to your incompetence and obstinacy'.

Unhappily, arrogance on the British side did not help to dispel suspicion on the American side where many still doubted whether Britain would hold out until victory was won. The US Navy Department was, as one Admiral put it, suspicious that the Royal Navy was 'dragging her anchors' in the Far East, while anxious to embroil the USA in the battle of the Atlantic. It was Doenitz's aim to foster this feeling and, for most of 1941, he had largely succeeded. Co-operation between the two navies was not particularly helped by the Dieppe raid on 19 August 1942, when a combined operations expedition of British and Canadian forces in 252 ships and small landing-craft set ashore on the French coast more than 6,000 men for what Churchill (then Prime Minister) guardedly called 'a reconnaissance in force', but which Colonel C. P. Stacey, in the Canadian official history of the war, described as 'tactically an almost complete failure, for we suffered extremely heavy losses and attained few of our objectives'.[1]

The Canadians had some reason for taking the view that the action was disastrous for, of the 4,384 Allied casualties, 3,367 were Canadians. Inevitably, the fact that theirs were the heavi-est casualties was exploited both by German propagandists and American isolationists as an excuse for asserting that the British were using North Americans to undertake their toughest assignments. The fact that the Canadians had long been clamouring for action of this kind was overlooked. Both the Americans and the Russians had been pressing for the opening of a Second Front in Europe and the operation across the English Channel was intended as a compromise on the part of the British who were still ill prepared for any major landings on enemy territory. Their commanders, both naval and military, had grave apprehensions about attempting too soon an invasion of the continent. What clinched the decision to go ahead was the urgent need by Intelligence for information on German radar and the view by Lord Louis Mountbatten (later Lord Mount-batten of Burma) that only a preliminary reconnaissance raid of this nature could provide the know-how and experience required before a successful invasion of the continent could be launched. There was the added urgent reason that 'Operation Torch' (the Allied invasion of North Africa) lay only a few months ahead and though the problems posed by that project were quite different from those of a cross-Channel expedition, opera-tional experience and intelligence on German defensive tactics were urgently needed.

Combined Operations had been the Cinderella of the Services in Britain. Started early in the war with the object of creating a force in which Army, Navy and RAF personnel would be blended, it had been viewed with some distaste by the Admir-alty, despite the fact that its first chief was Admiral Sir Roger

Keyes, chosen by Churchill because of his keenly aggressive spirit and fine World War I record. Until the Dieppe raid, Combined Operations had confined its actions to quick, small surprise attacks with a combination of destroyers and landing-craft in such places as the Lofoten Islands, Vaagso, St Nazaire and Bruneval. These had been carried out with relatively small loss of life, except at St Nazaire, and they had the advantage of forcing the Germans to spread their coastal defences from Norway in the north to the south-west of France, while also providing some useful intelligence. The NID had paid scant attention to Combined Operations' findings prior to the Dieppe Raid.

But disaster such as that encountered at Dieppe spotlighted the need both for improved intelligence from Combined Operations and, above all, the need for counter-intelligence to deceive the enemy as to intentions when such raids were planned. Security prior to the Dieppe raid had been appallingly bad. It is true that some attempt was made to devise a cover story that a raid was being planned for the Channel Islands and that a force was being assembled in south-coast ports to join the 10th Anti-Submarine Striking Force. Both cover stories were incredibly stupid: the fact that there might be a raid against the Channel Islands merely alerted the whole of the German defence organization along the northern coast of France, while the suggestion that groups of landing-craft in south-coast ports would be joining an Anti-Submarine force was unlikely to fool anyone. But rumours about the impending raid were circulating in Inverary, the Combined Operations base in Scotland, and around the Rothesay Bay–Glasgow area as early as the end of June 1942. MI5 reported indiscreet talk among Canadian troops in the Shoreham–Newhaven perimeter early in August, by which time leakages were widespread in the south of England. A Royal Navy lieutenant-commander left a copy of the naval operational orders in a bar and was arrested. There was no doubt that German Naval Intelligence had a fairly useful picture of what was likely to happen and the final blunder was that, on 4 July, all forces were embarked and told they were going to Dieppe. Three days later the raid was postponed. Thus there was the best part of two weeks before the operation took place, with consequent further opportunity for leakages.

In these circumstances it was not surprising that the ONI were inclined to believe that the British had deliberately allowed information to leak out to the enemy because they wanted the Dieppe operation to fail so that they could find adequate excuses for not launching a Second Front. The sources of intelligence for the raid ranged from aerial photography to somewhat amateurish collections of holiday snapshots and postcards of the terrain, from reports from the French underground movement and British agents, to a very meagre amount from the Admiralty itself. Little seems to have been done in the way of submarine reconnaissance and the first assault on the beaches revealed that there were inadequate details as to where pill-boxes had been set up, or of defences and gun emplacements on high land and at the approaches to the harbour. Colonel Stacey's view was that 'the planners underrated the influence of topography and of the enemy's strong defences in the Dieppe area'.[2] The Germans also noted that 'Allied intelligence generally lacked knowledge as to the location of regimental and battalion command posts'.

Admiral Lord Mountbatten made the point that 'for every soldier who died at Dieppe, ten were saved on D-Day': this was probably correct, but does not excuse the blunders which preceded the operation. The only justification for the raid was that great success was achieved in capturing enemy radar equipment. But this could have been carried out with a much smaller force just as effectively. The Germans learned enough from the raid, through captured documents, to delay the opening of a Second Front by anything from six months to a year. Yet, by the following year, vastly improved procedures for obtaining intelligence for the invasions of Sicily and Normandy had been put in hand. One member of the NID who actively helped to achieve this was Ian Fleming who had been an observer of the Dieppe raid from a warship. It was he who supervized and cosseted the No 30 Assault Unit, often nicknamed 'Fleming's Private Navy', or 'Fleming's Red Indians'. The idea of the need for an 'assault intelligence team' came partly from lessons learned from German activities in Crete in 1941 and the Dieppe raid. In the Crete campaign the Germans achieved great success with a special assault unit that penetrated British GHQ to make a swift appraisal of ciphers and technical equipment. No 30 AU was modelled on this, but improved and adapted in a more specialized way for intelligence-gathering.

The unit began to operate in the Middle East first under the dual command of Dunstan Curtis, a Coastal Forces officer, and Quentin Riley, a pre-war Polar explorer. The Admiralty regarded 30 AU with barely concealed, if not downright, disapproval at first and it required all Fleming's personal charm to jolly it along, win perks for his men and, to keep up their morale in what was highly dangerous work. By the time 30 AU reached North Africa, Sicily and Italy, it had begun to prove its worth. In beach reconnaissance, probing enemy territory, checking reports and bringing back intelligence from enemy shores, it was soon an astonishing success. It surpassed anything the Germans could contrive in this direction and maintained among its members a happy-go-lucky, piratical spirit, with a dislike of bureaucratic discipline and essentially the mood of enterprise and daredevilry such as one can only get from civilians turned into naval officers. One RNVR officer, for example, captured 300 Germans and their radar station with the aid of only half a dozen ratings. Another, during pre-Sicilian operations, altered his reconnaissance brief actually to go ashore during the night, three miles distant from the bay he was supposed to survey, solely to look up an old girlfriend and to obtain rather more information from her than he could have expected to get by sticking to naval orders!

The briefing, cajoling and cursing of 30 AU were all carried out by Fleming who had discovered in it a splendid excuse to escape from office routine from time to time. Robert Harling, himself a member of the NID team, writes that when preparations for 'Operation Overlord' (the invasion of Normandy) were being made,

> the unit [30 AU] was brought back to England and came within Fleming's close-range orbit . . . Fleming suggested that I should join the unit . . . By now Fleming was PA to the new DNI, Rear-Admiral Rushbrooke . . . I think that the new DNI occasionally wondered what kind of an outfit he had inherited in 30 AU. Certainly he saw us in training, which was more than Admiral Godfrey had been able to do. Fleming was unobtrusively in the background, casting a

wary and threatening eye over the brigands he had more or less created ... So D-Day came and the unit began its operations, a fierce and urgent quest for advanced German weapons and know-how, particularly in U-boat construction, torpedo performance and electronic devices. Casualties were suffered in the early landings, but the unit very soon began to show results and appreciative signals from the First Sea Lord were passed on by Fleming.[3]

Ultimately 30 AU was swallowed up in T-Force under General Eisenhower's SHAPE Command.

Astrology and the occult have down the centuries been linked in esoteric fashion with the intelligence game, but in World War II this became rather more pronounced because of the known predilection of some of the Nazi leaders for consulting astrologers. British interest in this had extended from the Foreign Office to both naval and military intelligence. The British aim was two-fold, first to counteract the Germans' own astrologers who had managed to obtain space in newspapers in neutral countries (in other words to use astrologers for propaganda purposes); secondly, to use astrologers to predict the predictions which the Nazi astrologers were likely to make for Hitler and his entourage. The idea was that from such horoscopes it would be possible to deduce what Hitler might or might not do.

In December 1940, a member of the NID was ordered to conduct an inquiry into the whole subject of astrologers and intelligence. A number of astrologers were interviewed and asked to provide horoscopes of various Nazi leaders, including one on Rudolf Hess. The result of the inquiry was not encouraging, as it had been left in the hands of someone who knew nothing about astrology. Fleming was personally convinced the idea was worth pursuing and that it had been mishandled. But, not wishing to get a reputation for crankiness, he kept his ideas to himself and by-passed the NID by dropping a few hints to an external branch of intelligence. Here the idea of working on horoscopes, and even of planting fake horoscopes on German leaders, was brilliantly worked out and, thanks to Fleming, played a useful role in luring Rudolf Hess into making his madcap trip to Britain in 1941. It was a gambit for which he, personally, never took any credit.

Only on one other occasion did Fleming bring up the subject of the occult again inside the NID. This was after Hess arrived in Britain and when his interrogators were finding it hard going to make much sense of what he told them. Fleming's idea was to get hold of the notorious Aleister Crowley, the black magician, and see if he could help either in interviewing Hess, or in making suggestions to the interrogators. Crowley was traced to an address at Barton Brow, Barton Cross, Torquay, and, on 14 May 1941, he replied as follows: 'If it is true that Herr Hess is much influenced by astrology and magick, my services might be of use to the Department [the NID], in case he should not be willing to do what you wish. Col. J. F. C. Carter, Scotland House, SW 1, Thos. N. Driberg, *Daily Express*, Karl J. Germer, 1007 Lexington Avenue, New York City, could testify to my status and reputation in these matters.'

But the NID do not appear to have agreed to Fleming proceeding any further with the plan, whatever it might have been. As I have said, Fleming liked to keep his colleagues in the dark as to what he really was planning on very many occasions. This was not the only private game which Fleming played where the occult and intelligence were concerned. One of his most successful gambits, again a cleverly worked operation in which he manipulated individuals into carrying out tasks quite subconsciously (nobody knew better than Ian when to plant a story on a potential enemy), was to pass on to the German Navy fake information about pendulum predictors. 'Pendulum prediction' had been used by certain occult practitioners before the war for finding hidden treasure, and even missing people, by swinging a pendulum over a map of the area where the treasure or the missing person was supposed to be. By studying the swing of the pendulum, or so it was suggested, the location of the object of the search could be defined. The Nazis employed a number of pendulum swingers, one of them, Herr Gohlis a member of the Nazi Party, and another, Dr W. Gutberlet, a Munich physician who had been a member of the Hitler circle in pre-war days.

News filtered through to Britain of the establishment in Berlin of a Pendulum Institute which had close links with

German Naval Intelligence. Sometimes after the round-up of astrologers in Germany, after the flight of Hess to Britain (the Deputy Fuhrer was surrounded by astrologers), officers from German Naval Intelligence were given the task of interrogating some of the detainees. As a result, a number of detainees were released and employed by German Naval Intelligence. They used to meet at what became known as the 'Naval Branch of the Pendulum Institute—Intelligence X 3', situated in an office in the Admiral von Schroederstrasse in Berlin. The detainees who gathered there included astrologers, radiesthetic experts and mathematicians. The head of the Pendulum Intelligence team was Kapitan Hans Roeder of German Naval Intelligence.

There is something farcical about this unworldly activity so seriously carried out in wartime by the German Naval Intelligence Service. Through detailed discussion and experiments with the astrologers and radiesthetists they sought to discover how pendulum detection could be used to pinpoint the positions and routes of enemy shipping with a view to their being sunk by U-boats! Somehow Fleming, operating outside the NID and through some of his contacts in the twilight world of the occult in which he always took an interest, had managed to plant information on the Germans that the NID were employing pendulum practitioners in the Admiralty where they would scan the charts with their pendulums and detect the positions of German U-boats. Very cleverly Fleming had managed to leak this information at a time when the British were actually sinking rather more submarines than usual. This success was therefore seen as proof of the pendulum practitioners story and the Germans decided that the information must be accurate. They actually believed that the pendulum practitioner fixed the position of the U-boats and reported to Operations who immediately sent a signal to a warship to proceed to a certain point and locate and sink submarines. Little did they know the slow processes of the British Admiralty where, even if all this had actually happened, by the time a signal filtered through to a warship, the submarines would almost certainly be elsewhere already.

Yet there was some excuse for the Germans, because they had been well aware of one of the most glaring failures of British

Naval Intelligence—that for the first three years of the war the NID upheld the view that no U-boat could dive below 600ft, as a result of which depth-charges were wrongly set and consequently often wasted. It was not until the second half of 1942 that the NID was eventually able to convince the Admiralty that U-boats could go much deeper. Even then many submarine captains, and also naval shipbuilders, remained unconvinced for a long time. When there were more U-boat sinkings, German Naval Intelligence believed they were due to pendulum swinging and not to better setting of depth charges. Kapitan Roeder himself was convinced that this was the case and he was determined to find out what it was and apply it to attacks on enemy shipping. Apparently German Naval Intelligence was impressed by the fact that a certain Herr Ludwig Straniak of Salzburg claimed to be able to locate the position of a ship by holding a pendulum over a photograph of it and then scanning charts with a pendulum. Straniak was invited to join the Pendulum Intelligence team in Berlin and it was apparently true that he had some successes with purely localized experiments, but the major task of applying the techniques of the large-scale spotting of shipping never succeeded. Nonetheless, German Naval Intelligence persisted in these experiments, later moving the Pendulum Institute to the island of Sylt, which location, it was hoped, would be removed from the disturbances of bombings and the bustle and noise of a capital city. So absorbed did they become in their own fruitless researches and experiments that it never dawned on them that the story of what the NID were doing might have been a fake.[4]

One of the ablest of the Royal Navy's informants overseas in World War II was Captain Henry Denham, the naval attaché in Stockholm, who performed miracles in obtaining information in a country where many of the natives in high places were markedly pro-German and there was a British Ambassador who was embarrassingly defeatist. Denham plied the NID with technical, political and all manner of intelligence information, often at great personal risk. He also organized a network of his own informants because, pre-war, the NID had shamefully neglected Sweden and allowed the Germans to establish far closer and friendlier relations with the Swedish Navy than themselves. Unfortunately, Denham not only had to suffer the tribulations of an uncooperative and sometimes hostile Ambassador, but dilatory appreciation of the value of some of his messages by the NID. An example of this was the message which Denham sent to the NID on 20 May 1941, to the effect that large warships escorted by destroyers had passed Marstrand on a north-westerly course. This was a tip-off which Denham had received from the Chief of Staff to the head of the Swedish Secret Service. This was only acted upon in very dilatory fashion and it is probable that, if the *Bismarck* had not sunk the *Hood*, the same fate might not have been so speedily meted out to the *Bismarck*. The truth is that, despite Denham's message, the British ships in the vicinity of the *Bismarck* at that time showed an almost incomprehensible lack of urgency even after the German battleship was sighted. German naval gunnery was trained for instant action on sighting an enemy; British naval gunnery was impeded by the sluggish reactions of the captain of the *Hood* who manoeuvred his ship into such a position that it became the perfect expanding target for the German gunners. Once the *Hood* was sunk, it was the equivalent in Royal Navy circles of a police operation when a policeman is shot dead: the whole of the Navy, from the Admiralty to the smallest ship in the area, concentrated on finding and destroying the *Bismarck*.

Much has been made on the British side of the failure of German Naval Intelligence to assist the *Bismarck* to escape from the relentless hunt operation mounted by the Royal Navy. But it is surely obvious that, once the *Hood* was sunk, the *Bismarck* could expect little help from German Naval Intelligence. Both the NID and the Germans depended equally upon a signal from the *Bismarck*, the former for fixing the *Bismarck*'s position and the latter to decide what disposition of ships, U-boats or planes could be made to help the German battleship. In fact the *Bismarck* sent a very long signal which enabled the British Admiralty to make the necessary dispositions, and German Naval Intelligence recorded that the 'wireless traffic lasted more than half an hour and seems to have enabled them [the British] to take exact bearings by D/F Gibraltar and Iceland to give a cross-bearing angle of approximately 90 degrees for the position'.

At this time *B Dienst* was unable to decipher quickly enough the high speed traffic in signals in great quantities being made between the British Admiralty and the Home Fleet. During the German inquiry into the whole sequence of events leading up to the sinking of the *Bismarck*, the reports from German listening stations and from those in charge of cryptanalysis were adamant on one point: there should be far stricter rules in future about the use of wireless at sea and long messages should be discouraged. It also became clear that the immaculately planned supply system and defensive cover provided for German battleship forays had become endangered through a speeding-up of the whole system of British naval intelligence.

But was it Admiral Canaris himself who supplied the vital intelligence concerning the ships passing Marstrand which was passed to Captain Denham? Or did he merely cause it to be supplemented in some way? In the German naval archives was a report from Canaris, dated the day after Denham made his report, stating that he had 'positive proof' that the British Admiralty had received a report of the outward passage of the *Bismarck* and the *Prinz Eugen*. Long afterwards when Canaris made one of his trips to Algeciras and he was dropping subtle hints that he might have secret talks with Royal Navy personnel, he mentioned very casually to a NID agent: 'If your people care to look up your records, you will find that you obtained some very important intelligence in Stockholm from a Hamburg source that led to the sinking of the *Bismarck* and you very nearly ignored the true purport of this.'

Canaris talked in riddles like so many intelligence officers: 'Today, in retrospect, it seems as though he must have been trying to warn us of a Soviet agent high up in the British Secret Service, but of course we never believed him,' said this same NID agent. Probably the gravest error the NID made regarding him was to consult with the Secret Service (MI6). It is not without significance that the head of the Iberian section of MI6 at that time was Kim Philby who, with an eye on his Soviet masters, would unquestionably sabotage any suggestion of talks with Canaris, or even of making a deal with the German admiral. General Sir Mason Macfarlane, the Governor of Gibraltar and himself an old hand in the intelligence game, had been anxious to kidnap Canaris when he visited Algeciras, being convinced that the Admiral would be a bonus for the Allies. Yet when, later in the war, Canaris planned once again to visit Spain *incognito* and actually set out on his journey, he learned that he was not allowed to cross the Spanish frontier. The refusal by the Spanish authorities was due mainly to some totally distorted information leaked to them by the British Secret Service. Yet on that occasion, when it was too late, an NID agent was waiting to meet Canaris.

Early in April 1945, Canaris was arrested and garrotted by the Gestapo on Hitler's orders. His diaries are now lost and so we may never discover how much he secretly wanted the Allies to win the war and what his devious aims really were.

A month after the Normandy landings *B Dienst* was reporting that, following a special inquiry conducted by a naval signals specialist, 'the present situation is characterised by disquiet in the U-boat command resulting from the pattern of operations, but without there being any concrete evidence of insufficient cipher security ... the cases of betrayal which have hitherto occurred and been discussed in the Navy have not been concerned with the principal cipher methods'.

This was a somewhat abstruse admission of failure, but it shows there was then a lack of confidence. German Naval Intelligence, which had started the war superlatively well in the interception and deciphering of enemy signals, had gradually lagged behind the British. One reason was that other cryptographic and monitoring agencies had achieved some spectacular results, notably the *Reichspost* Central Office, the *Forschungsamt* and *Personelle Z*. The first-named had brought off some splendid coups in telephone tapping, perhaps the most outstanding being in 1943 when, in breaking the scrambler code used on the radio-telephone link between Britain and the United States, it had intercepted a conversation between Churchill and Roosevelt which revealed that the Italians were secretly negotiating with Britain and the USA. There were almost certainly many other valuable interceptions which were not acted upon because of a foolish refusal to face facts in Berlin and the subservience of the able cryptographers to the Nazi leaders. An unpopular interpretation of an intercepted signal could easily bring dismissal.

But it was in direction-finding that the Germans lagged behind most at this time and where the Allies went ahead. In radar the British held an enormous lead and it was to prove of tremendous psychological advantage. The Royal Navy was helped not only by having a Fleet Air Arm and by being backed up by a Coastal Command of the Royal Air Force for reconnaissance and therefore intelligence purposes, but increasing intelligence reports from the Americans as well. Hermann Goering, the boastful and disastrous head of the Luftwaffe, frequently declined to give any worthwhile help to the German Navy. Admiral Doenitz bitterly commented: 'As we ourselves had no organised air reconnaissance at our disposal, my opposite number, Admiral Horton [Admiral Sir Max Horton] was able to take a look at my cards without my being able to do this.'[5]

Nevertheless, despite the cards being stacked against him in many respects, Doenitz was a resolute, determined and efficient commander who did his utmost to compensate for lack of long-range air reconnaissance by making the fullest use of intelligence reports. In his memoirs he states that, as a result of the work done by *B Dienst*, 'U-boat Command received not only the British signals and routing instructions sent to convoys, but also in January and February, 1943, the British U-Boat Situation Report, which was transmitted to Commanders of convoys at sea and which gave the known and presumed distribution of U-boats in the different areas'.[6]

In other words, Doenitz was able to obtain some indication of the kind of intelligence which the NID was providing for Operations and thus he could not merely take avoiding action, but check the security of U-Boat Command's signals system. Perhaps this knowledge gave the German over-confidence because, on this subject of naval intelligence, an extraordinarily paradoxical pattern emerged during the war. At the very beginning of the war German Naval Intelligence sometimes found it hard to believe their good luck; by 1941, when they were literally masters of Europe, they were disturbed about their own security, as Doenitz makes clear in his memoirs; yet, in the early days of 1944, when the U-boats had very nearly been totally mastered, they were inclined to doubt that their signal security was being broken to any great extent, but attributed any Allied success against U-boats to radar. Or, as Doenitz himself put it: 'Data regarding U-boats which are available to them [the British] on U-boat positions and on their own plotting of the boats' movements, combined with a quite feasible process of logical deduction. The most important result that has emerged from our investigation is the all-but-certain proof that, with the assistance of his air-borne radar, the enemy is able to discover U-boat dispositions with sufficient accuracy to enable his convoys to take evasive action.'[7]

Much of German Naval Intelligence thinking during the war only became clear when the Allies acquired the German archives. It should perhaps be stressed that, just as the German Navy had perhaps exaggerated respect for British intelligence generally, the British were equally determined to find out all they could about German naval intelligence methods, and when the Allied drive to the Baltic ports began in the spring of 1945, the NID gave instructions to its agents and units in operations in Germany to make the capture of *B Dienst* documents a prime objective. These documents revealed that the German deciphering system had been very much better than the Allies imagined in the early years of the war.

For the Allies the most dangerous year in the submarine war was in many respects 1943, at the very time when the overall war situation was swinging dramatically in their favour. In part this was because, in December 1942, following a change in German ciphers, the NID was guessing and calculating movements until the new ciphers were cracked. Patrick Beesly has drawn an accurate and fascinating picture of all this in *Very Special Intelligence*, revealing how Rodger Winn, the RNVR officer who later became Lord Justice Winn, was responsible for making intelligence forecasts of U-boat operations in this period of groping in the dark. Though described as 'damned black magic' by a sceptical First Sea Lord, Winn's disposition table of U-boats from the Atlantic to the Indian Ocean produced for the first month bore an almost uncanny similarity to that in the three subsequent weeks when the cipher had once more been cracked.[8]

The attack on the German battleships *Tirpitz* and *Scharnhorst* both involved intensive homework by the NID. Some hours before the *Scharnhorst* was sunk, on Boxing Day 1943, by HMS *Duke of York*, the junior officer at the head of the Operational Intelligence Centre in London calculated the time the two ships would meet off North Cape: his estimate was only twenty minutes out. This officer was Norman Denning (later Vice-admiral Sir Norman Denning). But the story of the *Tirpitz* was not such a happy one for the NID.

The *Tirpitz* had become a bogey image to the British Admiralty, sometimes frightening them into sacrificing convoys. Even Admiral of the Fleet Sir Dudley Pound, the First Sea Lord, had totally failed to realize how near the Royal Navy had been to knocking out the *Tirpitz* in an attack by the torpedo bombers of the *Victorious*. To make matters worse, the NID was, in the early part of the war, prejudiced against the Fleet Air Arm. It was not until 22 September 1943 that British midget submarines, as a direct result of NID reports, attacked the *Tirpitz* in Altenfjiord in the north of Norway, where she was lying in wait for British convoys en route to Russia.

Earlier reports on the *Tirpitz*'s movements from Madrid and Stockholm seem to have been ignored. Yet it was Captain Denham's messages which finally clinched the matter and he had every reason for being critical of the NID. Denham had gone to great trouble to pinpoint for the Admiralty the problems which the midget submarines would come up against in attacking the *Tirpitz*. He had supplied the NID with microfilms, dispatched across the borders into Norway and thence by Norwegian Resistance men to the small craft intelligence network that operated between Norway and the Shetlands. The midget submarines' attack was carried out while the *Tirpitz* was at anchor, but despite the fact that the mechanical gear of the battleship's main armament was put out of action and her main propeller shaft out of alignment, the operation was nearly jeopardized because no message was passed to the attacking craft about Denham's specific warning that there was an anti-torpedo net of double mesh lying across the entrance to the fjord. One of the midget submarines became entangled in this obstacle, but fortunately managed to free herself.

There was what looked suspiciously like an attempt to cover up this failure to transmit vital intelligence. The Admiralty decided, presumably on NID assessment, that only two of the three midget submarines had succeeded in their tasks. The captains of the two craft were awarded the Victoria Cross, but the fate of the third, X-5, was not disclosed, the excuse being that nothing definite was known about it. A few years ago an expedition was mounted to settle a naval controversy which has spanned more than thirty years. A team of sixteen British amateur sub-aqua divers sought the wreck of the X-5. Information from German officers aboard the *Tirpitz* after the war confirmed that the X-5 had certainly broken the minefield and anti-torpedo net defences as, thirty-one minutes after massive charges placed by her two sister craft, X-6 and X-7, exploded to cripple the *Tirpitz*, X-5 was seen to surface 700yd away and was heavily shelled. The Germans claimed her as sunk, and the family of Lieutenant Henty-Creer, the captain, have steadfastly refused to accept the Royal Navy's verdict that X-5 was destroyed before her attack could be pressed home. The wreck of the X-5 was duly located at a depth of 140ft close to where the *Tirpitz* had been at anchor, and it would now seem that there is proof that she did in fact carry out her assignment. It is to be hoped that the Admiralty will now reconsider the entire exploit and see that Lieutenant Henty-Creer and his crew receive posthumous decorations for this heroic wartime operation.

12

The Cold War

Immediately after the ending of the war in 1945 there was a feverish quest by all the Allied powers for German naval intelligence records. To check these records against their own was an urgent task for the NID, but both the Americans and the Russians were equally interested in this subject and so, to a lesser extent, were the French.

These naval archives included records of both world wars and, while the British Admiralty acquired a great number of these papers, many other German naval records were either destroyed in bombing, or confiscated by the Americans and Russians. Some of the papers taken by the Russians were returned to the *Deutsches Zentralarchiv* at Potsdam and Merseburg. On the German side it is generally admitted that Britain has important naval records from Berlin and Hamburg covering both world wars, but all too often what the British Admiralty has allowed to be revealed is material carefully tailored to fit in with the kind of pattern which the NID of the 1940s and 1950s preferred to preserve.

Rapid demobilization reduced the NID from its wartime strength of 4,000 to a mere eighty in 1951. This meant that the Admiralty could not possibly cope with a detailed research and analysis of what was contained in the German archives. Much was neglected through sheer lack of sufficient personnel to conduct the translation and analysis, while the limited amount that was dealt with was deliberately 'controlled' and released only to show the NID in the best possible light. It is significant that the best and most objective information available still comes from American sources, where tabulation of captured enemy material is far more efficiently carried out, but often this only reveals matters touching on naval intelligence through papers captured from other German Intelligence sources.

One of the most valuable of the British captures was that made in Capri in 1944 by 30 AU who discovered an important secret cipher which the Italians had failed to reveal as promised under the terms of their surrender in 1943. At this time, and especially in the weeks preceding the end of the war, a top priority for all Allied Naval Intelligence Services was to thwart the Russians from obtaining German naval intelligence documents, especially those which would reveal the extent to which the Germans had a knowledge of Royal Navy signalling procedures. For this reason naval forces spearheaded the drive to the Baltic ports. The battle for winning documents was on. The Russians had swiftly made the first move by proposing a three-power occupation of German Naval Headquarters in Berlin.

Soviet Naval Intelligence had been relatively quiet and dependent on the Allies up to the end of World War II. It was not unreasonable that the USSR should desire to have access to German naval secrets in 1945. Indeed, the attempts made by Britain and the USA to prevent this may be said to have been a contributory factor in precipitating the 'Cold War'. The Russians feared that this might be an attempt to encircle and isolate the Soviet Navy. On the other hand the American and British navies had a priority claim to such information if only on the grounds that both of them had borne the brunt of the war at sea.

One of the first lessons learned by all the major powers in this period was the importance of skilled interrogation of prisoners-of-war. The Russians, having had the experience of several years' intensive interrogation techniques in military and civil intelligence services, were the first to develop new techniques of interrogation as applied to naval prisoners. The British had often relied on interrogators with an excellent knowledge of German, but no experience of intelligence work. A great deal of this interrogation concerned the checking of captured naval archives. It was through his knowledge of languages that George Blake, subsequently unmasked as a Soviet agent, entered British Naval Intelligence. This young man, the son of Albert William Behar, an Egyptian Jew, married to a Dutchwoman, was born in Rotterdam in 1922. His father had a British passport and regarded himself as British. During World War II, when still a boy, George Behar joined the Dutch Resistance, escaped to Britain and eventually changed his name to Blake and joined the Royal Navy. As Lieutenant Blake RNVR he was posted to Hamburg as an intelligence officer when war ended. Put in charge of his own Naval Intelligence Unit, he installed himself in an office in the Flottbeker Chaussee in Hamburg which had previously been Doenitz's headquarters. Blake's task was to interrogate U-boat commanders and technicians as speedily as possible, as the NID had clearly laid down that a thorough investigation of the German submarine service was essential. Some of this work was required for the Admiralty lawyers preparing evidence for the Nuremberg trials, but by far the greater part was needed for checking on such specialized subjects as the German invention of the snorkel breathing system for submarines, the magnetic and pressure mines, torpedo developments and the lessons to be learned from German interception of Allied naval signals.

It was remarkable that Blake should have been given so much responsibility, not merely on account of his relative youth and junior rank, but because hitherto there had been a fairly rigid rule that intelligence work in the Royal Navy was only given to those who, by birth, were 100 per cent British. What seems to have weighed most in Blake's favour was that he was vouched for by Commander R. W. Child, who had been a British intelligence agent in Holland. His talents as an interrogator were formidable and it is significant that, at the age of twenty-three, he interviewed all the senior U-boat commanders personally. Any spare time he had in this period was spent in studying naval tactics, electronics and creating for himself the image of a highly specialized intelligence officer. Some found George Blake's professed anti-communism objectionable and cranky. He devised special security precautions and was for ever trying to catch out his colleagues for some breach of these, always reminding them that 'there are Soviet agents all round us'. This was the man who was sentenced in 1961 to forty-two years' imprisonment for spying for the Soviet Union, and who escaped from Wormwood Scrubs Prison in 1966 to reappear in Moscow.

The Royal Navy swiftly slipped back into the peacetime practice of changing the DNI every two or three years, Parry, Longley-Cook, Buzzard, Inglis and Denning all serving in this post between 1945 and 1960. The question naturally arises as to how much this was a factor in the total failure of the NID to detect not one of a number of traitors in the Royal Navy or among civilians in the Admiralty in the post-war period. Meanwhile the Russians gradually brought their own naval intelligence up to parity with the Americans and British in the immediate post-war years. Indeed, their impatience to achieve such parity was exemplified by the fact that they were not prepared to play a slow game by trying to break the codes of their rivals by cryptanalysis, but insisted on attempting the much more difficult, if possibly occasionally quicker, game of stealing codes.

Soviet ciphers are the best protected of those of all the great powers. David Kahn states that

> . . . complex-rotor-type cipher machines, well-designed in themselves and handled with a sophistication that changes keys after foreign cryptanalysts have reconstructed part of the wiring and the rotation pattern but before they can read any plain text, guard other high-level . . . messages of Soviet Russia . . . Whether this comprehension springs from the scientific ability that has enabled Russia to orbit great artificial satellites, or from the decades-long experience of cryptology that the Communist dictators have had to practice for their self-preservation . . . it has beyond question rocketed Red accomplishments in this black art to Sputnik height.[1]

Though the NID's numbers were drastically cut after the war, one enormously valuable asset was held—permanent co-operation with American Naval Intelligence—just as it had been enjoyed in the war. At last—almost entirely because of the development of the Cold War with Soviet Russia—the Western World became one and indivisible and, finally, from being allies to being part of an Atlantic Alliance such as Benjamin Franklin had dreamed about. It was the most important decision which was made and it was one which the Russians did everything possible to sabotage. By the end of the 1940s it was clear that the USSR gave top priority to naval intelligence and that they had engaged former German naval officers as advisers on submarine warfare.

The Navy Department of the United States had shown itself far more prepared to co-operate with the Royal Navy than had other sections of American Intelligence with their British counterparts. But, with the establishment of the North Atlantic Treaty Organization, the bureaucratic influence stifled a great many intelligence efforts. While Russia and her obedient satellites all agreed that Eastern bloc intelligence traffic should go through Moscow, NATO's Standing Group in Washington was responsible for providing 'analysed' intelligence to the various commanders in NATO. This was almost unavoidably a lukewarm version of intelligence: by the time it was ready to be consumed it was either out of date, or it had omitted from its brief many of the more succinct observations. For, in a conglomerate democracy such as NATO, the major problem for the suppliers of intelligence really often is that nobody wants to hear what is politically either unacceptable or unwelcome. In an organization such as NATO, where there are many different views as to what is politically unacceptable, this attitude on a subject such as intelligence can be, and usually is, disastrous. The Soviet Union, having no such inhibitions with her Eastern European allies, was not troubled with any such complications.

Soviet Russia was the first to appreciate that, in many respects, the nuclear revolution would affect the navies of the world more than the armies. But the ONI was determined to reap the benefits which electronics offered in the sphere of intelligence. The United States was soon to have the most efficient naval intelligence service in the world. This has been of vital importance in preserving the peace of the world since 1945. Yet, to achieve this dominance, the US Navy had to fight a great deal of opposition. It was far from easy for it to build up its own lobby in Congress. While the Royal Navy had, for more than a century, commended itself to the British people as one of the more beloved institutions of British life, the United States Navy had no such advantage. It was, in fact, regarded as a 'sub-culture', isolated, if not alienated from the American way of life. Its political influence was negligible.

The US Navy was outfought by the US Army Air Force. The

latter ruthlessly played down the role of the Navy and, by every 'dirty trick' in the book, aimed to reduce the Navy to impotence as far as policy-making was concerned. This caused great alarm inside the ONI. Given the politically organized structure of the Officer Corps, added to the orientation of Congress towards the Army, the political power of the Navy was hamstrung. Yet it was in these days of relative inferiority to the Army that the Naval Intelligence Service rapidly progressed. Professor Vincent Davis in his work, *The Admiral's Lobby*, poses the question of why the US Navy did not ally itself with any party or Navy-minded groups in Congress. The Navy, for example, allowed itself to be outwitted and misrepresented on the suggestion that the turning point in the Pacific War—the battle of Midway—was a victory for the USAF, when in fact it was entirely a naval achievement. One reason was the structure of Congress. The Navy, like the Army and the Air Force, had to deal with committee chairman, but, unlike the other forces, it lacked a political ally of any weight. In the end it was the Korean War which gave the US Navy a new kind of prestige and the realization that, ultimately, it would have a vital role to play in nuclear warfare and nuclear defence systems.

Meantime, Soviet Naval Intelligence made even fuller use of captured German technicians, U-boat commanders and wireless specialists than did the Americans. In many cases, former German naval officers were conscripted into Russian service, while teams of spies were sent into Germany to track down blue prints, plans and models from laboratories, factories and ministries. Many such plans were hidden away in safes, or buried in the ground and it took the Allied Intelligence Committee search parties several months to trace everything. The findings of such operations were, of course, made available to teams of Russian scientists and intelligence officers, but the latter never really trusted either the Americans or the British and the Russians rarely reciprocated this exchange of information. Much of the material they rounded up was sent straight back to Russia without the Allies being given a glimpse of it.

The Korean War and the stepping-up of the Cold War led to increased co-operation between the naval intelligence services of Britain and the United States, NATO itself involving much more naval intelligence work than had originally been anticipated. But now the Royal Navy's status was gradually reduced and in no sphere did this reveal itself so much as in that of naval intelligence. The apex of this NATO network was no longer London, but Norfolk, Virginia, and, to a lesser extent, Washington and Paris. At Norfolk, Virginia, the Supreme Allied Commander, North Atlantic (SACLANT) functioned, and from this centre naval intelligence was processed and passed to other naval formations in the Atlantic Command. Some naval intelligence was also made available from the Supreme Headquarters, then in Paris. From the early 1950s onwards, NATO became the prime target for Soviet naval intelligence as the Russians saw very clearly that the weakest link in the theory of the nuclear deterrent lay in the development of the nuclear submarine.

The brief honeymoon period between the Royal Navy and the Soviet Navy had ended. Commander Anthony Courtney RN, who had worked closely and amicably with Russian liaison officers during the war, noted the change on a return visit to Moscow: 'The barriers had come down and naval attachés were not given the same freedom.'[2] On the other hand, while depressed by the change in the atmosphere as between Britons and Russians, Courtney was equally critical of what seemed to him to be the American overreaction to the Cold War. On a visit to Washington in an official capacity, Commander Courtney said that 'the official American attitude towards the Russians, however, already diverged to some extent from our own. While in Washington I paid a courtesy call on the Soviet naval attaché and it was no time at all before a representative of the FBI [Federal Bureau of Investigation] was questioning our naval representatives about such an unheard of action by a visiting Britisher.'[3]

By 1952 the USA had tightened up its own security on account of the series of scandals involving the theft of nuclear secrets from America by Soviet agents, and Russia turned her attention to what had already become the Achilles heel of Western naval security—the Royal Navy. Indeed, the Russians realized the vulnerability of British naval security long before the Americans. They stepped up their espionage inside Britain, not merely to spy on RN establishments, but through contacts with Soviet sympathizers in Commonwealth-nation diplomatic offices in London to probe NATO secrets this way. By 1955 it was well known in Soviet circles that many NATO technical details were leaked through London to naval and military attachés of Commonwealth countries, not merely those of the old Commonwealth, such as Australia and Canada, but to those of the newly independent nations as well. Diplomats in London belonging to certain African members of the Commonwealth became a useful source of intelligence to the USSR.

Commander Courtney has thrown some light on the subject of laxity in British naval intelligence circles. He wrote:

> The NID, had a good deal to do with the Foreign Office, on the basis of what was presumed to be a full circulation of information available to brief our Director before meetings of the Joint Intelligence Committee and to draft appreciations for the Chiefs of Staff. The Foreign Office suffered then, and probably suffers still, from a chronic inability to separate information from policy-making, or, in military terms, intelligence from operations. In addition we had grave doubts about Foreign Office security, springing from the 'Cicero', King and other affairs, and from experience we had been unable to form a high opinion of its departmental efficiency.[4]

The NID had once more renewed its former relationship with the SIS and, indeed, history had almost repeated itself for, possibly recalling the Baltic operations of Agar and others at the end of World War I, the idea was mooted of using fast surface craft and submarines in co-operation with the SIS to obtain intelligence from the Black Sea area. Courtney was himself concerned in these projects, but he referred to

> . . . a kind of silken curtain of security which I had some difficulty in penetrating in order to have a meeting with an individual to whom I had been referred. The irony of this meeting did not become clear to me for nearly twenty years, when the man concerned, Kim Philby, was finally revealed as a Soviet Intelligence agent of many years' standing. Philby received me with courtesy and listened to my proposals with interest, for he had a wide knowledge of Turkish affairs and

his support was essential if Naval Intelligence was to make any contribution to the common effort in the Black Sea, where our information was deplorably scanty. But nothing whatsoever emerged from this meeting, a fact to which I gave no sinister significance at the time, as it was typical of SIS and Foreign Office resistance to any practical initiatives for the improvement of our intelligence effort.[5]

There can be little doubt that Philby also kept the Russians up to date on what the NID was thinking up. In 1949, when the Cold War was at its height, the NID once again re-opened the question of co-operation with the Secret Service, this time in the Baltic area. It was suggested that the NID should provide the SIS with detailed naval intelligence in the Baltic. The work involved an undercover arrangement with a naval construction firm in Germany and various contacts at Kiel, Lubeck, Flensburg, Eckerndorfe, Kappeln and other small harbours in the area. From these various points, under the control of the Staff Officers (Intelligence) in Hamburg and Kiel, espionage forays were mounted. All these were monitored by Soviet Naval Intelligence who had been kept informed of almost every move.

The Americans became increasingly perturbed about the laxity in security matters in the Royal Navy and especially about the lack of adequate communication on the subject between the Foreign Office and the Admiralty. The ONI had passed on several warnings to the NID, most of which appear to have been ignored. Two typical examples of the failures to carry out effective vetting were John Vassall and Harry Houghton. The former, an Admiralty civil servant and a practising homosexual, was attached to the British Embassy in Moscow where the Russians lost little time in exploiting this weakness by luring him to a party and having him photographed in compromising situations. Blackmailing threats followed and thereafter, for a period of eight years, Vassall passed on Admiralty secrets to the Russians. Houghton, a petty officer, was stationed in the British Embassy in Warsaw, despite the fact that he was a notorious womanizer (though married) and an habitual drinker. The Americans warned the Royal Navy about Houghton and insisted that he was a security risk. All that happened, however, was that Houghton was sacked from his Warsaw post because he had been mixed up in the black market there (his fraternization with the Poles should have been well known), and on his return to England he was, incredibly, posted to the secret Underwater Weapons Research Establishment at Portland.

The Foreign Office and the Admiralty were both to blame for these blunders which led to major espionage coups by the Soviet Union, but the Admiralty was more to blame in that they appear to have failed to acquaint MI5 with many of the facts about both men. In the end it was MI5 who eventually trapped Vassall and Houghton and brought about their arrest. But all this was long after the damage had been done. The Portland Spy Ring, as it became known, included not only Harry Houghton, but Ethel Gee who also worked there; Helen and Peter Kroger, two highly competent Soviet agents who were responsible for transmitting intelligence to Moscow; and Konon Molody who, under the name of Gordon Lonsdale, posed as a Canadian in London, but was also an intelligence officer attached to the Soviet Navy. He had been specially selected for naval intelligence work and his mission was to seek out the secrets of Britain's underwater defences, the new ASDICS which were being developed, the sonar buoys and homing torpedos.

Over a period of years traitors inside the Admiralty and the Royal Navy were able to help Russia to steal a march on many of the Western navies and there were bitter and, indeed justified, criticisms in the ONI that all this endangered the continuation of any close co-operation between the intelligence services of the two navies. As time passed and little seemed to be done to eradicate this weakness in security on the naval side, the Americans became even more concerned. There was the much more recent case of Sub-lieutenant Bingham, who also passed information to an assistant naval attaché in the Russian Embassy in London. Nobody seemed to recognize that here was another security risk. There have been attempts by complacent Ministerial and Service statements to try to minimize the enormity of the damage wrought by Vassall, Blake, Houghton, Gee and Philby and other suspected, but undiscovered, spies inside the Admiralty and the Royal Navy, but the truth is that this was a devastating blow to NATO. Not only was there slackness and incompetence among senior and junior ministers at the Admiralty, but really appalling mishandling of security questions. For example, an inquiry revealed that Vassall had not only worked in the office of the Deputy Director of Naval Intelligence at one time, but that he had twice been passed after positive vetting tests. On each occasion this was done by a two-man team and, though Vassall's homosexual tendencies had been noted by some of his colleagues in Moscow, this was either not revealed, or had been completely ignored by the vetting team. Nor did the latter heed the fact that Vassall was spending far in excess of his salary on his return to London from Moscow.

There were no other leakages of naval intelligence among the Western powers to compare with those occurring in Britain in this period. One remarkable factor which dismayed the ONI was that these happened mainly under Conservative governments in Britain. The laxity in security under the Churchill, Eden and Macmillan post-war administrations extended not merely to incursions by the USSR, but by the Americans too. During the abortive Suez operation by the Anglo-French forces, the Americans read all the British naval signals well in advance of the action, while the CIA knew more about the secret planning than some members of the British Cabinet.

The last traces of Britain's naval supremacy finally evaporated in 1956, the year in which the NOBSKA summer study school, organized by the US Navy and the National Academy of Science's Committee on Undersea Warfare, came up with the answer which paved the way for the nuclear-powered submarine as a deterrent force. As a result of this the Polaris missile was created, perfected and tested. Within a few years the US Navy had forty-one submarines armed with sixteen nuclear Polaris missiles each. From then on the Royal Navy depended to a large extent on the US Navy for its future development. Altogether 1956 was an unhappy year for Western naval intelligence, culminating in the recriminations voiced on both sides of the Atlantic following the disastrous plan secretly to examine the bottom of the Soviet cruiser *Ordzhonikidze* in Portsmouth harbour. This ship had brought the Soviet leaders, Bulganin and Khrushchev, on their goodwill tour of Britain which was supposed to mark a thaw in the Cold War. A peculiarly clumsy attempt at obtaining naval intelligence was quickly detected by the Russians when ex-Naval frogman, Commander Lionel Crabb RN, dived into Portsmouth harbour to carry out this mission. Crabb failed to return and his disappearance resulted in a Parliamentary row and outraged protests from the Russians. Fourteen months later a headless body was washed ashore near Chichester, Sussex, and, at an inquest, on the flimsiest of evidence, a verdict was recorded that it was the corpse of Crabb. The Crabb affair harmed both the Secret Service and the NID: there were also suspicions that this was a joint CIA-SIS plot to sabotage the Soviet goodwill visit. In any event the risks taken of employing a middle-aged, unstable, alcoholic, ex-naval diver to search for unspecified secret equipment attached to the cruiser's hull was, by any professional standards, a naval intelligence operation of imbecilic proportions.

While all this was happening moves were afoot both in the USA and Britain to integrate the intelligence services of Army, Navy and Air Force into an overall Defence Intelligence Agency. Throughout the late 1950s debates on this theme took place in the USA. When Macnamara became head of the Department of Defence he took the view that the three separate Service Intelligence Agencies were inefficient and gave the impression of wanting a merger. This was the rather brash opinion of a businessman suddenly coming into politics and it did not please the CIA, who were not at all happy at the idea of a competitive all-powerful DIA. They had come to rely on their own links with the separate Service Intelligence bodies. Finally, the DIA came into being in October 1961, and the emphasis was then on integration rather than a merger.

The prime advocate of the integration of the Service Intelligence bodies in Britain was Admiral of the Fleet Lord Mountbatten, who had been First Sea Lord from 1955–9 and then Chief of Defence Staff from 1959–65. The British plan differed from the American in that the political influence of the Royal Navy was drastically lessened by the proposal to bring all the fighting forces under the Ministry of Defence, with one senior minister in the Cabinet in control of all and with junior ministers responsible for the Army, Navy and Air Force. This meant that the post of First Lord of the Admiralty, who had always been a member of the Cabinet, disappeared. It was as chairman of the heads of the three services and their spokesman with the Defence Committee of the Cabinet that Mountbatten had great influence. In one sense his experience fitted him for the task of combining the three services under one Ministry, as he had for a short time been Chief of Combined Operations, while later, as Supreme Allied Commander, South-East Asia, he had been served by an integrated naval, military and air staff. But there are many senior naval officers on both sides of the Atlantic who feel that from an intelligence point of view—and especially that of naval intelligence—the integration was rushed through too quickly in Britain. Whereas, in the USA, the CIA and the FBI both had their say on integration proposals before they were implemented, in Britain neither the Secret Service, nor MI5 seem to have been consulted. Worse still, during the period immediately preceding the integration, the NID was allowed, to some extent, to run itself down.

Not surprisingly, while Mountbatten was First Sea Lord, the way was paved for a Director of Naval Intelligence who shared his views. As Mountbatten left the Admiralty to become Chief of Defence Staff, so Rear-admiral Norman Denning became DNI. Denning had been one of the most enthusiastic supporters of the idea of a Joint Intelligence Bureau and he proved to be the last DNI as, in 1965, the post was abolished. Technically, Rear-admiral Graham succeeded him, but with the new and subordinate title of Deputy Chief of Defence Staff (Intelligence). Few would deny that there was a need for the integration of air, naval, military, scientific and economic intelligence under the Ministry of Defence in Britain, but there, as in the USA, problems in connection with this have emerged and it cannot be said that the integration is yet 100 per cent effective. Under the British system the Chiefs of Staff receive their intelligence assessments from the DCDS (I) and this post goes, in rotation, to naval, military and air force officers. For practical purposes the Director of Naval Intelligence is as dead as the dodo. Nevertheless, some former US senior naval officers who worked with and appreciated the old NID regret its passing: 'the killing-off of your NID was a terrible blow to us,' said one. 'Whatever our differences, however much we may have felt the NID security left much to be desired, the fact remains that in two world wars the US Navy owed a great debt to NID and came to rely on it to a great degree. In the Mountbatten era we were sadly aware that the NID was running downhill and becoming increasingly negligible as far as we were concerned.'

Doubtless this view will be hotly contested by some British naval officers, but it must be admitted that, under the American system of integration, naval intelligence has preserved its identity much better. This has been achieved against enormous odds, largely because the dialogue on integration was conducted more fairly and less hastily. It was taken out of the heated atmosphere of party politics under which British integration was carried out. As to the importance still placed on naval intelligence by the Americans, it is not without significance that President Carter nominated Admiral Stansfield Turner as Director of the CIA in February 1977. Under the Defence Intelligence Agency the ONI has not been superseded, but its scope has been changed. The DNI is an Assistant Chief of Naval Operations who reports to the Vice-Chief of Naval Operations and also is responsible to the Secretary of the Navy (a more influential figure than his opposite number in Britain, the junior minister for the Navy). In addition there is an Assistant Chief of Naval Operations for Communications, under whom exists a Navy Security Group with special duties in cryptology. What is more the ONI is now also concerned with 'the development and recommendation of policies'.

Whereas the NID has been largely phased out in its traditional roles, and robbed of most of them, the ONI has gained in strength and, more important, in efficiency. It is true that much less is spent on naval intelligence than on that of the Army, but this is almost irrelevant because the modern navy has a much clearer idea of what kind of intelligence it is seeking than has the army. But the new heads of ONI are immeasurably better than in World War II when there were no less than seven of them in four years and when Ellis M. Zacharias could write: 'only one was qualified by previous training, intelligence interest and personal disposition to fill this job'.[6]

The ONI has, in fact, progressed rapidly since World War II while the NID has lapsed into a relative coma. Its security system is markedly more efficient than that of the Royal Navy, as ONI agents conduct all inquiries into criminal activities with the US Navy. Naval District Intelligence Officers, under the ONI, operate all over the USA and in outlying areas. Intelligence organizations with the US forces afloat come directly under ONI supervision, as do the naval attachés. In addition the ONI deals with counterespionage and all security matters and has contributed substantially to the National Intelligence Surveys with its detailed dossiers on the world's prime amphibious operations targets. As to how far it has progressed regarding the latter, one might note these words by Samuel Eliot Morison: 'we dearly wanted and never were able to obtain photographs of the Barbary coastline taken from sea level just offshore, in order to enable our forces readily to identify beaches and other landmarks at night [referring to the invasion of North Africa in 1942]'.[7]

So at last the Americans overtook the British in questions of naval intelligence. Smaller than the Army's budget that of the ONI may be, but today, with some 15,000 employees both Service and civilian, it is regarded by many experts as being an example of a high-growth industry within the intelligence community. Its annual budget is heading towards a figure of $1000 million and it is backed up by one of the most comprehensive, computerized electronic 'instant espionage' systems in the world, operating every conceivable listening device to cover the oceans. In the USA integration of intelligence has not cramped the activities of Service intelligence agencies, or reduced them to powerless departments, as has been the case in Britain. On the contrary, in America the ONI is actually larger than the CIA itself, even though not as large as the Army or Air Force intelligence services.

Not that the United States intelligence revolution was faultless on the naval side. In the early stages of integration it, too, suffered from the multiplicity of agencies linked to it and bureaucratic interference. The sheer weight of data and information which had to be processed and interpreted led to problems: it was essential to have an ever-increasing team of technical experts in cryptanalysis, radar, telemetry and photographic interpretation to transform the bleeps, radar images and other strange mechanical, esoteric raw material into something sufficiently comprehensible for the intelligence analysts. This, in its turn, led to a need for more personnel which meant far wider screening operations for security purposes.

Soon, too, the Navy Department and the ONI became targets for the growing environmental and ecological lobbies. The Pentagon had classified as 'secret' a naval programme designated 'Project Sanguine' which aimed at providing a means of instant, secure communications between naval commands and ships, bases and submarines anywhere in the world. This was to have been a vast underground system for sending emergency messages to missile-firing submarines and the project involved installing a grid of underground wires over some 8,000 square miles amidst the wooded lakes of North Wisconsin. But, in 1967, embarrassed Pentagon officials had to remove the 'secret' classification when it was realized that, though major newspapers had been debarred from writing on the subject, all Wisconsin's newspapers had been writing about Project Sanguine for some months and local politicians had been making speeches about the increase in employment which it would bring to the area. But the Navy Department was made to look somewhat foolish when Senator Gaylord Nelson of Wisconsin, ostensibly concerned at the possible effect of high energy transmissions on vegetation and soil in the area, asked for information and received in reply from the Navy a communication marked 'secret'. Later in 1974 the US Navy yielded to pressure from the environmentalists and suspended the development of Project Sanguine. It was not the first time that the US Navy Department had been in danger of being strangled in its own red tape. A few years previously, when the Navy stated solemnly that all details of Polaris submarines were rigidly classified as 'top secret', it was revealed that detailed scale model kits of the Polaris could be bought by any child in a toy shop!

When NATO headquarters was moved to Brussels in 1967, the Russians deliberately built the Skaldia-Volga motor assembly plant nearby and used it as a base for their agents. Naval intelligence was still given top priority by the Soviet Union which by now was firmly committed to building a navy to equal that of the other powers. Two important naval developments in the late 1960s were the stepping up of Soviet naval power in the Mediterranean and the Middle East and the decision of the Council of Western Europe to lift one of the main restrictions which West Germany accepted when joining the Western Alliance in 1954, allowing her to build submarines up to 1,800 tons. This was authorized to enable West Germany to build ocean-going submarines capable of taking over surveillance over the whole of the North Sea and part of the Atlantic. This move had long been urged by the USA whose Navy had been increasingly worried by the failure of the Royal Navy to measure up to its commitments under NATO. Paradoxically, while Britain somewhat tamely accepted the implied criticism of its own ineffectiveness in the field of submarine surveillance, opposition to the proposal came mainly from the French. It was General de Gaulle who overcame these prejudices on the French side. Having a global sense of naval and military strategy, and with a son who was a highly efficient naval officer, de Gaulle needed no Intelligence Department to tell him that if France and Germany were to co-operate in building up a European defence system, a new agreement with West Germany on submarines was essential. For, as de Gaulle appreciated, submarine surveillance meant improved intelligence and the latter meant a more solid safeguard against nuclear war.

13
Intelligence on the Seabed

An increasingly important subject in naval intelligence in the early 1960s was undersea research. While all navies were conscious of the need for this, it was the United States Navy which led the way, spending some $20 million in building underground chambers under the seabed. A sum of $10 million was paid out in investigating the geological possibilities of the extension of the Alaskan goldfield on to the continental shelf. Companies on both sides of the Atlantic were then researching into the mining not only of the continental shelf, but also of the deep ocean bed. Oil and gas under the sea had already attracted attention, but there was also a new theory that the seabed provided an enormous wealth of minerals and untapped food-stuffs.

A modernized, streamlined and powerful NID in Britain could have been used to explore such possibilities which presented themselves all over those very areas where the British flag still flew. But once the Royal Navy itself was reduced in status and the NID subordinate to a Joint Intelligence Organization, such initiative was stifled, despite the fact that in and around Malta and again in the area of Fiji there was tremendous scope for such exploration and untold benefits to be revealed. Such possibilities were totally neglected by the British, even though Dr Kingsley Dunham, who was then organizing an official survey of Britain's continental shelf, returned from the United States in 1967 with the firm impression that the dredging of the deeper ocean was a soluble problem. A report in the London *Times* of the period signified the slow realization of the world's navies, other than that of the United States, that undersea research was a prime function of naval intelligence.

At depths of 10,000 feet and more the Atlantic, Pacific and Indian Oceans are covered with deposits of phosphates and with manganese nodules. These nodules look like walnuts and apart from manganese contain copper and nickel. A company in Newport News, Virginia, is building a dredge to work at 4,000 feet. At present it is estimated that working at 10,000 feet might cost three or four times as much as would make the operation commercial. But research might bring the cost down to an economic level. The claim that more minerals have been in use so far this century than in the whole of the previous civilization indicated the need to find new sources. Oil and gas under the sea have attracted a lot of attention. Dr. Dunham found that American experts are forecasting that by 1980 the world will get more oil from under the sea than from the land.[1]

This statement, it should be noted, came years before any serious attention had been paid to the discovery of oil in the North and Celtic Seas around Britain. The importance of all this had been stressed in a confidential report to the NID in 1960, but it had been shelved and forgotten. Yet had the NID been in a position to help to guide Britain's destiny at that time, considerable economic problems could have been overcome and the balance of payments situation changed overnight.

The Russian Navy, though belatedly, recognized the importance of the unexplored world under the seas and appreciated more than the Western nations how expertise on this subject could be exploited politically. It was this realization which helped to speed up Soviet naval developments in the late 1960s when, having established a presence in the Mediterranean, the USSR expanded its naval influence southwards into the Indian Ocean and the Pacific. Soviet deployment in the Indian Ocean dated from early in 1968, by which time it had been quick to sense that the British were pulling out of all bases east of Suez and that, regardless of whether any future government was Labour or Tory, this contracting out would continue. Within a year the USSR had not only managed to expand extensively in this area, but to disguise its motives. In the Indian Ocean Russia had, by the end of 1970, a force which included one cruiser, three destroyers, five submarines (one of which was nuclear), a submarine depot ship and various supporting vessels. Much of this expansion was for political purposes, but overall it resulted in great gains for Soviet naval intelligence. Since about 1960 the aim of Soviet naval intelligence has been two-fold; firstly, that political influence and the showing of the flag should go hand in hand with naval intelligence, and secondly, that the target for such intelligence should be for the years 1980 onwards. Thus, already in 1970 the Russians super-vized the use of deep-water facilities at Hodeida in the Yemen and Berbera in Somalia, while there was a Soviet harbour mas-ter at Aden and indications that the Russians were developing facilities on the island of Socotra. The London *Times* duly recorded, under the by-line of its diplomatic correspondent, A. M. Rendel, on 30 December 1970, that 'the Russians appear to be developing facilities on the island of Socotra'.

Now, though the USSR undoubtedly had increased its influence in the Indian Ocean in this period, there were signs, not always correctly read by Western Intelligence, that Russia was deliberately exaggerating such influence. The 'disinforma-tion' department of the KGB, no doubt enforced by USSR Naval Intelligence, was planting material in the latter part of 1970 and the early part of 1971 to suggest that the Russians were planning to achieve dominance in the Indian Ocean. Stories—all traceable to the KGB or Soviet Naval Intelligence —were put out that the Russians intended to set up a base on the island of Socotra, to obtain a base in Mauritius, to acquire special facilities in Singapore and to direct certain African navies. This was so cunningly done that, for a long time, Western intelligence services and, more important, Western newspapers, regarded this as propaganda by right-wing, old fashioned Imperialists, and much time was spent knocking down the stories. In fact, almost every one of these rumours was planted by the KGB. This epoch merely marked the passing of the 'disinformation' game from Britain to Russia. What the British had brilliantly achieved in World War II, the Russians were now developing in times of peace. It might at first seem incredible that the Russians would put out such items of disinformation, but if one considers them together with the fact that Russia has increasingly been making her presence felt in the Indian Ocean, the incredible becomes plausible. Russian ships steamed past Singapore while the Commonwealth prime ministers' conference was in session. Then other Russian ships arrived off Diego Garcia, an uninhabited British possession in the Indian Ocean. These moves were not made accidentally; they were quite deliberate. When one weighs this ostentatious display of naval might against the chief topic of discussion at the Singapore Conference—whether Britain should sell arms to South Africa—the link between the KGB stories and the movements of Russian ships becomes clear. By showing the Russian flag in the Indian Ocean at this time, the USSR was, in effect, bolstering the British Prime Minister's (Edward Heath) case for wanting to sell arms to South Africa and, by doing so, ruining Britain's future relationships with black Africa. Thus the Russians believed they could strike two blows at once: disrupt British influence in black Africa and at the same time achieve a naval presence in the Indian Ocean which would counter Chinese influence.

But, while their Intelligence Service was anxious to play up some of these bogus stories, the Soviet Navy steadily, slowly and without any bombast, achieved greater gains in the Indian Ocean in this period. The Russians established an embassy on Mauritius and made a fisheries agreement with that island which gave a certain amount of scope to the Soviet Navy. Over all this hung the problem of the reopening of the Suez Canal. The economic advantages of the opening of the Canal as far as Russia was concerned were more questionable. At the time it was closed, in June 1967, about one-tenth of Soviet sea-borne foreign trade passed through the canal, or about 1,800 Soviet, or Soviet-controlled, ships a year. But the Russians had no reason to reckon that their oil interests were seriously harmed by continued closure of the canal. They bore in mind the fact that the continued closure of the canal was a greater economic disadvantage to the West than to themselves, especially as it increased the costs for Western oil companies. Though these arguments have long since ceased to be valid, this has in no way changed the Russians' decision to maintain a naval force in the Indian Ocean and to take a keen interest in seabed intelligence in this area, notably around the Seychelles.

In the 1950s and 1960s the Russians were still attempting to infiltrate US Naval Intelligence, though with nothing like the success they achieved against the British. The Americans' National Security Agency, which was created after Pearl Harbor, was an example of a vast, amorphous intelligence agency aimed at integrating military, naval and air intelligence which, like all such large organizations, was vulnerable to penetration. The intention was to make it 100 per cent security-minded, but, despite this, it was breached more than once during the Cold War and afterwards. Bernard Michell, whose father had a law practice in California, enlisted in the US Navy and was sent to the Yokohama naval base where he met William Martin, a chess champion, and both were engaged in cryptographical work which was linked with that of the NSA. They became friends, associated with Communists and, in 1959, against all the rules, went to Cuba. When they returned, they applied for leave, went to Mexico City and then on to Havana, where they took passage in a Russian trawler for the USSR. On arrival in Moscow they announced at a press conference that they had defected because 'in the Soviet Union our main values and interests appear to be shared by a greater number of the people. Consequently we feel we will be better accepted and able to carry out our professional activities . . . We were disenchanted by the US Government's practice of intercepting and deciphering the secret communications of its own allies'. The reason for the publicity which the Russians eagerly granted them is not far to seek: to expose the USA as spying on their allies and so creating mistrust.

Sonar technology has the advantage of not only being vital to the problem of anti-nuclear submarine warfare, but of being applicable to peacetime programmes, for example the exploration of the seabeds, marine biology, oceanography, the tracking and identification of fish and, of course, the underwater search for food for starving Asians and Africans and the quest for oil and minerals. It is the fourth dimension of all underwater territory which now becomes the supreme challenge for the world's navies. It is a challenge that is not entirely a question of destruction and defence, of pollution and discord, but also one that, in the long run, can vastly benefit mankind and a rising world population. This is a fact which is appreciated just as much by the Russians as the Western World, though the former's approach is essentially secretive.

More than 70 per cent of the world is covered by seawater and it includes some 165 million tons of solid material in every cubic mile of ocean. Some of this material contains valuable substitute foodstuffs apart from fish, but there is also untold wealth of oil, gold, silver, manganese, vanadium and other minerals. The siting of this material, its exploration and development could raise the standard of living for future generations and, even more important, as the cost of nuclear energy becomes less, so it will be cheaper to desalinate water and convert it into a useful commodity. To this extent naval intelligence, if carried out on a global-sharing basis by all the world's navies, could improve the standard of living for countless millions within a very short period. Western socialism might decree that this is a proper and idealistic course to take: Soviet communism will have none of it.

It is now clear that both the Russians and the Americans aim at achieving naval supremacy through nuclear submarines which can dive to the deepest part of the ocean, through missile silos on the ocean beds and anti-ballistic missile systems in such areas as the Arctic and Antarctic, the Pacific and mid-Atlantic ridge. A great deal of the underwater research of today, including expeditions which, superficially, seem to be aimed merely at photographing marine life beneath the sea, has been undertaken as a cover for naval intelligence in the game of anti-submarine warfare. Courageous divers have become highly skilled in underwater photography. It is fairly easy to speculate on which areas have been surveyed by NATO powers, but less easy to know just what the Russians have been doing in this respect. One suspects from what evidence is available that they are keenly interested in both the Indian and the Pacific Oceans from the particular aspect of exploitation of the seabed, while in more recent years there has been a tendency on all sides to explore the possibilities of the Arctic and Antarctic.

'Our knowledge of the ocean environment is being accumulated in a lop-sided way,' writes Robin Clarke. 'Today it is easier to get funds to work on the noises fish make than it is to work on methods of catching fish. The motivation is not to provide more food, but to improve methods of detecting enemy submarines. . . . It is the prospect of the oceans becoming a three-dimensional battlefield which has dictated the form of most of our oceanographic research.'[2]

Yet, despite all this, it may well be that, if and when saner counsels prevail in the world, the shared knowledge of all this research will provide an impetus to the further progress of mankind. The US Navy has made great strides in this type of research, ably supported by its intelligence agency. It is estimated that the USN pays for more than a half of all the marine research conducted around American waters, and if proof of this is wanted there is surely a hint of it in a statement made as long ago as 1956 by Mr Robert H. Baldwin, the Under-secretary of the Navy, when he declared that 'our oceanographic and ocean engineering programmes are specifically and directly responsive to military requirements ... we are not in the business of exploiting the ocean's abundant mineral or living resources'.

Nevertheless, this narrow outlook has changed and it has been belatedly realized in Washington that the Russians have paid as much attention to the peaceful uses of underwater research as to anti-submarine warfare. US Naval Intelligence was the first to warn of the Arab states' moves to push up the price of oil. This enabled the US Navy to experiment in replacing oil with liquid coal in November 1973 when the USS *Johnston*, a World War II destroyer, left Philadelphia as the first ship to use liquefied coal to power its engines. The US Navy worked for one and a half years on this project, as it was consuming oil at the rate of 42 million gallons a year and the aim was to re-place oil fuels to a substantial extent by 1976. Encouraged by its own naval intelligence research teams, the US Navy has set up such organizations as the Naval Electronics Laboratory, the Radiological Defence Laboratory, the Undersea Weapons System and various other research departments aimed at probing underwater problems.

Nationalism has reared its ugly head underwater on the most trivial issues. It was fatuous as well as thoroughly undigni-fied for the Royal Navy to be trapped in an untenable and stupid situation over the Cod War entirely through the pos-tures of a few influential Icelandic Communists. Here again, naval intelligence is to blame for not pointing out the disad-vantages of this futile and parochial bickering, matched only by that other undignified 'bully-boy' operation when the Royal Navy played a farcical part in the 'invasion' of Anguilla. Such blunders are extremely damaging to the Western World, more especially when they affect relations in the Arctic area where the USSR is slowly establishing dominance. Far more important than these nationalistic fishing disputes is the question of the law of the sea wrangle on underwater minerals. After years of futile dallying with the problem by the United Nations Law of the Sea Conference, the United States has decided unilaterally to extend her national jurisdiction over mining and fishing in the open sea. The potential profits which await any nation or company which develops a practical method of mining the manganese nodules found in such large quantities on the seabed are alluring. These nodules, containing nickel, copper, cobalt, iron and molybdenum as well as manganese, appear to be increasing as a result of some unknown process which is forcing them up from the core of the earth. One American study suggests that the Pacific Ocean alone contains 358,000 million tons of manganese, equivalent to nearly half a million years' supply at current rates of consumption; 14,700 million tons of nickel that would last 150,000 years and 7,800 million tons of copper, enough to last 6,000 years. Apart from all this US oil experts are convinced that from 1980 onwards more oil will be found under the seabeds than on land. But what poses the major problem of obtaining this, apart from the colossal costs, is the defence of such installations from sabotage.

In the Arctic Ocean the naval intelligence services of both the NATO powers and the Russians are constantly engaged in watching one another. Several islands of ice in the Arctic have, for the past decade, been manned by American and Soviet specialists engaged in Polar research, especially beneath the ocean. The ice islands have served as bases for both sides in the Arctic 'intelligence war'. Canada's main Arctic military base is at Alert, on the northern tip of Ellesmere Island; it is manned by some 200 men and is a communications centre in NATO's global defence network. One of the tasks of Western naval intelligence in this area is to keep a watch on Soviet-occupied ice islands.

One such ice island close to the North Pole was observed to be occupied by Russian naval personnel in 1973. It was then assumed that the Soviet party was merely there to conduct meteorological and ice research. In recent years this ice island drifted steadily in a south-easterly direction until, late in 1976, it was no more than 250 miles from Canada's Alert base. Reports by Canadian Air Force pilots, backed up by photographic evidence, suggested that, by this period, North Pole 22, as it was designated, was something rather larger than the temporary headquarters of a meteorological team. The Canadians believed that the Russians had set up a military base with a runway for planes to land on. Naval Intelligence in Washington, however, consider that the evidence added up to the fact that the USSR had created an advance observation post with electronic equipment capable of monitoring the movements of NATO nuclear submarines on their voyages beneath Polar ice.

14

The Spy-Ship as an Aid to Political Strategy

Despite the advent of such sophisticated equipment as satellite reconnaissance and the high-flying, high-speed espionage plane, the most practical intelligence aid for the formulation of instant decision-making and creating a political strategy under war conditions has been the spy-ship.

Such ships, as used by the Americans, have not always been conventional warships, but more usually converted civilian freighters, or similar vessels, but capable of speeds of 18–20 knots and armed with a system of radio antennae, including a 'big ear' sonar-radio listening device with a range of up to 600 miles. They are strictly known as 'communications vessels', or, in the language of the lower deck, 'ferrets'. So secret is the equipment in these ships that, at one time, certain sections of them were ruled out of bounds to the entire crew, including the captain: that is to say, the only personnel allowed in these sections were naval intelligence specialists.

The value of the spy-ship as an aid to political strategy has been proved on various occasions in the past twenty years, most of which must remain closely guarded secrets. While such vessels have not been so useful in a conflict such as that in Vietnam, they proved of the utmost value to the United States in both the Arab-Israeli wars, that of 1967 and again in 1973. It is not putting too fine a point on it to assert that the peace of the rest of the world was then that much safer because of it. The great advantage of a spy-ship is that it is mobile, it can get close to the scene of hostilities without too much risk of being involved in them and can much more easily monitor the communications of the combatants than any other intelligence unit.

It is true there have been a few unfortunate failures, the most notable being the capture, in 1968, of the spy-ship, *Pueblo*, by the North Koreans who, allegedly, seized valuable cryptological equipment. Victor Marchetti, author of *The CIA and the Cult of Intelligence*, has written that 'the [US] Navy formerly sent surface ships, like the *Liberty* and the *Pueblo*, on similar [spy] missions, but since the attack on the former and the capture of the latter, these missions have largely been discontinued.' But this statement is misleading. By and large both American and the rather more cautious Russian spy-ships have operated in the Mediterranean and Indian Oceans, listening in on communications and other electronic signals with great success over a period lasting into the middle 1970s.

Marchetti mentions the case of the USS *Liberty*, a converted freighter built in the early 1940s. The inside story of the tragedy which befell this ship is rather different from what Marchetti suggests. On 8 June 1967, the Arab-Israeli Six-Day War was in its fourth day and Israel was well on the way to victory. Yet, surprisingly, and at the time seemingly inexplicably, on the afternoon of that day there was a co-ordinated raid by Israeli planes and torpedo-boats on the *Liberty* when that ship was sailing close to Gaza. Some thirty-four Americans were killed and 164 injured. Officially, the Israelis claimed this was an error and that the *Liberty* had been mistaken for an Egyptian vessel. In fact, as both the US and Israeli governments learned quickly enough, this was a deliberate attack because the Israelis had discovered that the *Liberty* had been listening in to their communications. The order had gone out that the *Liberty* must be put out of action as speedily as possible because what the Americans had begun to learn from their eavesdropping was that the Israelis had intercepted and 'cooked' messages passing between the Egyptians, Jordanians and Syrians. Cleverly, the Israelis had thrown a spanner into the whole communications system of the enemy, rerouting enemy signals to convince the Jordanians in particular that the war was going well for the Arabs and to make them keep on fighting so that Israel could establish a clear-cut, 100 per cent victory. This trick of 'cooked' messages enabled the Israelis completely to bewilder their enemies. But in doing this Israel was technically violating a plan worked out secretly with the Americans that Israel would only fight a strictly defensive war and not seek to extend her boundaries. But if the uss *Liberty* had been able to transmit back to the USA the Israeli plan to attack the Syrian Golan Heights, then not only could this attack have been thwarted but the Israelis could have found themselves violating a United Nations-negotiated cease-fire.

However, the best example in recent times of the value of spy-ships in assisting super-power naval diplomacy was in the 1973 Arab-Israeli War. Neither the USSR, nor the USA participated directly in the war, but both were not only vitally concerned as to its outcome, but actively involved in supporting their respective allies. The lesson of this war was a classic reminder of the supreme importance of modern 'instant' naval intelligence in that each side relied on this. Both the USA and the USSR were concentrating on monitoring not only the combatants' signals, but those of each other, and, by so doing, trying to influence each other's actions. The Americans wanted to minimize the Russians' involvement in the war and the latter were anxious to persuade the Americans to withhold support from the Israelis. It could be said that throughout this war naval intelligence played a tremendous role. Each side used this intelligence in a political-strategist sense to try to influence the other through signals they sent and, equally important, signals they intended the other side to read. Spy-ships on both sides were the vehicles which provided the data on which political-strategic decisions were taken.

On the Russian side there had been considerable naval activity prior to the war—enough to show that they had prior knowledge of Egyptian intentions. A Moroccan expeditionary force had been sent to Syria in Soviet amphibious warships, while a contingent of Russian submarines was entering the Mediterranean just as the war began. American naval intelligence processing techniques were by this time able to produce graphs and charts showing movements and locations of Soviet ships in the whole Mediterranean area, in particular plotting the concentration of ships in any particular sector. These were produced at great speed by the Centre for Naval Analyses. The initial impact of these reports and charts was enough to show that restraint by the United States was not being reciprocated by the USSR. Therefore it provided sound reasons why the Americans should react to this with precautionary measures of their own. The substantial and massive airlift and sealift of supplies and planes to Israel were only made in time to be effective because of naval intelligence.

As a result, from 25 October to 17 November 1973, when the US 6th Fleet in the Mediterranean was put on the alert, the USA indicated its intention of reacting to Soviet naval moves by strengthening its own forces in the vicinity of the war zone. Signals unmistakeably giving this impression were allowed to be leaked to the *V Eskadra* (Soviet Mediterranean Squadron). Until this autumn of 1973 it had always been the policy of the USSR to move their own ships away from the scene of activities in the event of war. They had done this in 1967, but in 1973 their pressurizing tactics were obviously based on their own naval intelligence which had indicated to them that Israel would not attack their transport ships and that the Americans would maintain a low profile at least for the first few days of the conflict. But, though the Russians obviously had been receiving instant naval intelligence from their spy-vessels during this period, it is by no means certain that all this was obtained by conventional means. In trying to assess how their monitoring of American and Israeli signals was being carried out, one has to weigh the following facts: (1) that the Soviet 'intelligence collector' (AGI) ship, normally located off the Israeli coast at regular periods, was not at sea throughout the whole of the war period, though she may have been for some of the time; (2) when the war started, Soviet submarines in the Mediterranean were twice as many as usual; (3) one US battleship reported that it was not even under Soviet surveillance by what is called a 'tattle-tale' ship during the whole of the war period. The overall impression is that the Russians were playing a somewhat devious game by engaging in escalatory tactics by their navy in making their presence in the area felt and in keeping the Arabs supplied, but at the same time avoiding 'aggressive monitoring' by sending their spy-ships away from the vicinity of the US Sixth Fleet and the Israeli coast.

The Soviet Naval Intelligence had been worried in 1960 by a report from Dr Leonid Vasiliev, a leading physiologist, that the

US Navy was 'testing telepathy in their atomic submarines . . . we must again plunge into the exploration of this vital field'.[1] This report may have been provoked by a story in a French newspaper in 1959 that the US Navy had conducted ship to shore telepathy experiments from the uss *Nautilus*.[2] Though the US Navy Department denied this story at the time, experiments by the Soviet Navy were ordered at the behest of Naval Intelligence. The object was to ascertain whether telepathic codes could be devised so that there could be telepathic communication and monitoring from ship to shore. Independent intelligence reports from some Western European nations suggest that the Russians had made some progress in this direction and that further experiments under war conditions were carried out by *V Eskadra* submarines during the Arab-Israeli war of 1973.

Once the Suez Canal was reopened the Russians took full advantage of this to expand their naval forces in the Indian Ocean. The build-up of the Soviet Indian Ocean squadron has continued, and the missile-armed, helicopter cruiser *Leningrad* has made regular visits to Somalia, Mauritius and other ports in the western part of this ocean. Apart from Diego Garcia, the British-owned island in the central Indian Ocean, where the American Navy is building a large air-field and anchorage, there are no ports and airbases now readily available to the Western powers in that area. The British naval radio station in Mauritius closed in 1975. The need for spy-ships became greater, especially when the Russian Navy set up a ground communication station on the former British-owned island of Socotra at the mouth of the Red Sea.

Some indication of the very real need for a strong, integrated Western naval intelligence system may be provided by some simple comparisons of naval strengths. On the one hand there is the evidence of a CIA analysis, made in May 1976, which showed that in the previous five years the US had outspent the USSR by 2 : 1 in construction of warships; on the other hand there is the fact that, as regards conventional warships, the US had fallen behind the Soviet Union because of the Rickover policy which had concentrated on building nuclear submarines. On the British side there is the indisputable fact that in 1939 the Royal Navy entered the war with 15 battleships and battle cruisers, 6 aircraft carriers, 60 cruisers, 168 destroyers, 69 submarines and numerous smaller vessels, all manned by 119,000 men. Yet, despite this preponderance of strength, with several oceans to police, the opposition to the Royal Navy never totalled more than 7 battleships and pocket battleships, 6 cruisers, 31 destroyers and 57 submarines. And it was not until the last two years of the war that the Battle of the Atlantic was decisively won. Compare this with the strength of the modern Soviet Navy which, early in 1976, possessed 36 cruisers and helicopter cruisers, 215 destroyers and frigates, 196 corvettes, 320 submarines (of which probably 120 are nuclear-powered) and various smaller fast craft. The Royal Navy, now committed solely to NATO, has no secure bases beyond Gibraltar other than Hong Kong. The Soviet Navy has facilities for bases, fuelling supplies and intelligence-gathering in the Angolan ports, Guinea, Cuba, Somalia, Mauritius, the Seychelles, Algeria, Libya, the Yemen and many other areas of Africa and the Middle East.

It has been the swift decline of the Royal Navy which has caused all the intelligence services of NATO to concentrate on checking and watching Soviet submarine tactics. It resulted in a drive by the RAF to start a major refit of its hunter-killer anti-submarine Nimrods to include new surveillance radar coupled with acoustic processors and sono-buoys, allowing positive detection at longer ranges with a new ability to identify submarines lying beneath the surface. To this extent, in Britain at least, a vital part of anti-submarine warfare has passed from the Royal Navy to the RAF. The latter's new radar can detect the smallest object on the surface at substantial ranges and a magnetic innovation can detect the smallest change in the ocean's magnetic field caused by the movement of the submarine. In this respect the RAF took on a major part of the work that used to belong to Naval Intelligence. Extremely sensitive infra-red sensors will note the tiniest changes in water temperature, indicating the track of a deeply submerged submarine which has mixed up the water on its passage.

It is still mainly in the Mediterranean where the task of assessing Soviet naval strength and its changing patterns demands the most comprehensive, round-the-clock intelligence system. One useful aid to this system is the restrictions imposed on the Soviet Union by the Montreux Convention which regulates the passage of ships through the Turkish Straits. The USSR must give eight days' notice of any proposed movement of ships before any transit can be carried out. By making declarations for many more transits than they propose to carry out, and by modifying the apparent identities of individual units to match these 'extra' declarations, the Russians have been able to minimize the effects of this restriction. It is true that they have not been able totally to circumvent it, but they have created confusion among Western naval intelligence services.

However, in more recent years it has been the Russian threat in the far north which has attracted increased attention in NATO intelligence circles. The theory, held by some strategists in the West, is that if the Russians ever attack the West it will not be through Central Europe, but in the Arctic Circle. The key area here is the Kola Peninsula between the White Sea and the Barents Sea which lies to the east of Murmansk, but also reaches westwards as far as the vicinity of Sweden, Finland and Norway. On this peninsula are no fewer than forty strategic airfields, of which between fifteen and twenty are kept permanently operational all round the year. Stationed at these are some 600 aircraft, while at the Soviet naval base at Murmansk the largest fleet of nuclear missile submarines to be found in one place at one time is maintained. From the Barents Sea these submarines can fire their missiles at any target in the USA east of the Mississippi River.

General Sir Walter Walker, former NATO commander, concisely summed up the situation as follows: 'Why bother with an attack on Norway when the continuous extension westwards of the Soviet naval "line" to Iceland and the Faroes is turning the Norwegian Sea into a Soviet lake? ... This is a greater danger than NATO's present chronic weakness in the Mediterranean.'[3]

General Walker's theories have sometimes been criticized as unduly alarmist, but the ONI has long been concerned about the 'Arctic back-door threat', as they call it. During the summer of 1976 serious interference was experienced over most of the western hemisphere, and particularly in the northern part, from high-pulsed signals, originating from the USSR, which especially interfered with radio hams operating on the 20-metre band. Indeed, it was a North American radio ham who first drew the attention of the naval authorities to this phenomenon. An exhaustive examination and monitoring of these signals was conducted when protests to the Russians were ignored and no explanation was offered. Because analysis of the signals revealed that they consisted of a sequence of varying higher-frequency square waves repeated every ten seconds, it was eventually deduced that Russia was on the way to perfecting a system of long-range radar to pick up signals and images over the horizon, that is, beyond the curvature of the earth. This would be particularly effective in the Arctic.

Much of the gathering of naval intelligence in the post-war period has been carried out by ships at sea, though very many of these have not been what are technically called 'spy-ships'. Shadowing of rival navies has become all-important and the contestants have used every conceivable device to camouflage it on some occasions, while also utilizing the open method of ship shadowing without any attempt at concealment. Both the American and Soviet navies indulged in this and the former gave it the name of 'chicken of the sea'. This referred to the US Navy's practice of shadowing and buzzing Soviet ships and planes which led to some near misses and even some 'grazes' between ships. Such incidents are rarely discussed publicly (often they are covered up by both sides much as the attack on the *Liberty* was played down by the US and Israel), but it is known, for instance, that a Soviet aircrew were lost a few years ago when their plane crashed into the sea after making a very low pass over an American ship. The 'Incidents at Sea' agreement which was signed in Moscow in May 1972, one of many to come off the Brezhnev-Nixon production line, laid down the rules to be observed by both sides in future. There were to be no simultaneous attacks with guns, missile launchers, or torpedo tubes and no aerobatics over ships.

Nevertheless the buzzing of ships has continued, though more discreetly and at greater distances. Possibly what has given the Soviet Union and her allies even greater scope for intelligence-gathering has been partly the relatively easy treatment of spies in Western Europe, as well as the fact that her ships, both naval and non-naval, can, with impunity, buzz NATO shipping

(European perhaps more than American), not to mention spying on oil-rigs in the North Sea developments. Even Dr Joseph Luns, the Secretary-General of NATO and himself a specialist in naval affairs, admits that 'a vast amount of espionage is going on' and he attributed this to the 'mild punishments meted out to spies in our part of the world'.[4]

Aggressive espionage is, however, conducted by both sides, despite the Brezhnev-Nixon agreement. There was the incident in 1974 when a Russian naval intelligence-gathering trawler broke international regulations by approaching to within 30ft of a North Sea gas-rig to take photographs. It also came within 200yd of another rig, despite radio calls, on the international distress frequency, from the rigs, begging it to keep clear. An attempt by a safety boat to warn off the trawler was also ignored. The name of the trawler had been painted out, but its number was seen to be GS 242 and the crew wore Russian naval uniforms. The Royal Navy, through its intelligence advisers, has for a long time been urging the need to provide much greater security for rigs, not only in respect of the Russians, but of terrorists and hijackers of all nations.

On 16 July 1974, it was reported that the Russian Navy was assembling a comprehensive task force in the Red Sea, which was clearly intended to do much more than sweep mines for the Egyptians in the Strait of Gubal, 150 miles south of Suez. The naval correspondent of the London *Daily Telegraph* stated that

... the composition of the Russian force indicates that it has an intelligence and probably a salvage as well as a minesweeping role. The most interesting vessel from the point of view of Western naval intelligence is undoubtedly the intelligence-gathering ship, *Primorye*, 5,000 tons. This ship, unlike the more commonplace intelligence-gathering trawlers, is one of a class of ships specially built for the task. She is believed to be capable of analysing electronic and other data and is described as one of 'the most modern intelligence collectors in the world'.

A month earlier a Russian 'research' vessel arrived and docked on Clydeside. Described officially by the USSR as the *Eisberg*, a weather-research ship, it was believed to be a spy-vessel packed with electronic devices and, without demur from the British Government, she tied up within twenty miles of the Polaris submarine base at Holy Loch. There have also been two or three instances of Soviet submarines penetrating Norwegian fjords, and one such craft, detected in December 1972, was stated to have been a Soviet W-Class submarine which had been tracked by NATO air and naval surveillance from the Baltic into the North Sea shortly before the first sighting in Sognefjiord. The submarine, it was said, disappeared from electronic sight and sound, but later there were reports of a periscope breaking surface of the 3,000ft deep, 120 mile long fjord. It would be reasonable to deduce that a ship of this type was on a spying mission, probably specifically sent to discover how easy or difficult it would be to enter the fjord without being detected.

In various periods of 1975–6 there was concern that Russian submarines were using the Irish Sea at regular intervals on passage to and from a patrol area off Northern Ireland. These again were intelligence-gathering missions, aimed at keeping a watch on NATO submarines in the Clyde area, or off the west coast of Scotland, any new developments in oil exploration under the sea, the missile tests in Cardigan Bay, the torpedo and underwater weapons testing establishment on the Clyde, the US Navy's oceanographic research conducted at Brawdy in Pembrokeshire, while they are even suspected of taking a keen interest in the Scottish Marine Biological Station at Keppel on the island of Great Cumbrae. Russia's reluctance to accept an increase in the 12 mile territorial limit, demanded about this time by some countries at the Law of the Sea Conference, is said to have been partly based on the fact that this could prevent Soviet submarines from using the Irish Sea route. Paradoxically, wrangles about fishing and other sea limits by the Common Market countries can be said to have helped the USSR while increasing the problems of NATO.

Collisions between American and Russian submarines have presented a sufficiently big problem for the US Navy for the subject to be referred to the President himself during the Ford administration. Early in 1976 the President, supported by Congress, was demanding more details be supplied to him of reported 'underwater bumps', including one which involved a nuclear-armed vessel off the coast of Britain. On 16 February that year the House Intelligence Committee issued a report which stated that there had been 'at least nine collisions with hostile vessels in the last ten years'. The report added that the Soviet Union had made '110 possible detections' of American submarines operating in Soviet waters. An aide of Senator William Proxmire said: 'we want to get from the Pentagon an assurance that this dangerous game will be stopped immediately'. He was referring to confirmed information in diplomatic circles that American nuclear submarines were invading Russian waters for espionage purposes. The House Intelligence Report added: 'the programme clearly produces useful information on our adversaries, training, exercises, weapons-testing and general naval capabilities. It is also clear that the programme is inherently risky'.

Since the capture of the *Pueblo* electronic spy-ship 13 miles off the coast of North Korea in 1968, the ONI had lent strong support to proposals for extending and developing underwater spy-craft, partly to monitor Soviet nuclear submarines, but for various other intelligence-gathering missions also. Some scanty details of this were leaked to the press early in 1976, appearing in the *Washington Post* of 4 January, when this newspaper revealed that, since the late 1960s, the US had deployed a fleet of electronic spy-submarines close to the coastline of the Soviet Union, dubbing them 'underwater U2s'. Clearly, what had prompted this story was confirmation of the fact that, on 3 November 1974, the US nuclear submarine *Madison*, armed with sixteen nuclear missiles, bumped or was bumped by a Soviet submarine in the North Sea.

The underwater espionage programme was code-named 'Holy Stone' and it is still one of the most closely guarded of all US naval intelligence operations. Nevertheless, as a result of mishaps during operations, critics of these espionage tactics during a period of so-called *détente* have been able to piece together certain facts which make a coherent picture. Seymour Hersh in a *New York Times* article declared that for nearly fifteen years the US Navy had been 'using the specially equipped electronic submarine to spy at times inside the 3-mile limits of various nations'.[5] A senior admiral spokesman in the Pentagon conceded that the Navy had used such craft to spy on the Soviet Union, but added: 'no submarines have been closer than three miles'.

One can only speculate as to how many of such craft have been used on either side. The Americans have had at least four such submarines in operation during the 1970s. It has been suggested that the Russians' eavesdropping operations are conducted mainly by surface trawlers and that Soviet submarines have not the same electronic capability of the US craft: this is wishful thinking, as, during 1977, there has been ample evidence of Soviet countermeasures. Critics of this form of underwater spying stress the constant danger of major catastrophes resulting from such a policy. There have probably been as many near misses under the water as there have been on the surface and it is certain that the USSR knew all about Operation Holy Stone at the time of the Brezhnev-Nixon agreement. There have been two known collisions between US and USSR submarines; there was the accidental sinking of a North Vietnamese mine-sweeper by a submarine on patrol in the Gulf of Tonkin during the Vietnam War, while one Holy Stone submarine was grounded, but eventually escaped from within the three mile limit off the east coast of the Soviet Union. Yet another Holy Stone submarine damaged herself while trying to surface from underneath a Soviet ship in the midst of Russian Fleet manoeuvres. Once again the submarine escaped after suffering damage to her conning-tower, despite a search by the Soviet Navy.

Holy Stone was officially authorized in the early 1960s, long before the *Pueblo* incident or that of the *Liberty*. The method of its implementation was, from an administrative point of view, admirably carried out. The then Secretary of Defence, Robert McNamara, gave control of the whole operation to the Chief of Naval Operations. It is perhaps remarkable that Holy Stone remained a secret for so many years, especially as in more recent years its missions had to be approved each month by the 40 Committee, an intelligence panel headed by the former Secretary of State, Henry Kissinger. But by this time the element of surprise had disappeared. Not only were the Russians aware of what was going on and taking countermeasures, but the Chinese as well had used radar to track the American spy-craft.

It has been argued that a safer and less provocative means of getting intelligence would be via aerial satellites or other methods, but naval experts insist that no other method would obtain the kind of intelligence they are seeking and that Holy Stone is simpler and cheaper. Any scientifically objective investigation must come to the same conclusion, even if political considerations might suggest otherwise. The US Navy employs nuclear-powered basic attack submarines of the Sturgeon or 637 class, merely adding more electronic gear and a special unit from the National Security Agency to convert the vessel into a spy-ship. As to the argument that it provoked the Soviet Union, perhaps the best reply to this was that of a naval spokesman who said that the Holy Stone operation was vital to the USA-USSR Strategic Arms Limitations Talks which led, in 1972, to an interim five-year accord: 'One reason we can have a SALT agreement', he added, 'is because we know what the Russians are doing, and Holy Stone is an important factor in what we learn about the Soviet submarine force.'

Both the Russians and the Americans have employed various methods of plugging into communications cables across the seabed and intercepting top-secret messages transmitted by this route rather than by the less secure radio routes. Between 1976 and 1977 there was a suspected campaign of harassment by the Russians concerning the seabed cable which carries South Africa's main communications link with Europe. During January 1977, a Russian trawler, the *Belemorsk*, put the cable out of action for sixty hours. On other occasions Soviet trawlers had been observed sailing slowly close to the track of the cable. There was, however, no evidence on any of these occasions as to whether or not the cables had been tapped. It is possible that something of this sort has been carried out, as the Russians claim that there have been attempts by the US Navy to use submarines to plug into cables on the seabed.

An interesting aside on all this underwater espionage is that the Russian submarines using the Irish Sea route around Britain appear to be of the older diesel-electric type and not nuclear-powered vessels. One deduces from this that the object is to reduce the chances of American or British aircraft, helicopters or surface ships obtaining a fix or a check on the underwater noise 'signatures', known as hydrophonic effect, of their latest submarines.

Even that most attractive and fascinating of all sea mammals—the dolphin—has not been overlooked by the ingenious planners of naval intelligence. Scientists have observed that the dolphin is almost a 'bionic fish', being able to dive to incredible depths, swim at speeds which baffle mathematicians and, when it is necessary, can be as aggressive and more deadly than a shark. Experiments were carried out by the US Navy's Department of Biological Weapons to see what uses dolphins could be put to in the sphere of espionage. So successful were these that one Navy-trained dolphin actually placed a detection device in a foreign harbour to find out what kind of atomic fuel is used in Russian nuclear submarines. The dolphin which actually delivered the device went back a few weeks later and retrieved it for American intelligence analysis. In the Vietnam War dolphins were also used to guard craft against enemy frogmen.

In charge of a $30 million sea-mammal programme is Harris Stone, special assistant for intelligence in the Bureau of Naval Operations. Since 1972 dolphins have been trained to place explosives, as well as monitoring devices, on ships and to attack enemy divers and are able to be kept under control for distances up to several miles.[6]

15

Chess Under the Oceans

By 1970 naval intelligence had acquired a new and vital role in the world. From that date onwards it was in the forefront of all secret service work, the front line and ubiquitous force which, for twenty-four hours of every day, unremittingly, had to spearhead all its battles by constant vigilance. In terms of national defence naval intelligence became the *élan vital* of the whole system and, as a common denominator, the ultimate deterrent to nuclear attack.

To simplify this somewhat all-embracing statement: nuclear attack had tended to depend much more on the mobile nuclear submarine, safe in the depths of the ocean, than on the well defended, even underground, static nuclear launching bases on land. As new and sophisticated weapons were able to counter-attack nuclear aggression from fixed points on land, so the tendency had grown to deploy nuclear weapons more widely in submarine craft. Thus, gradually, the nuclear submarine, armed with the latest missiles, came to be deployed by all the major naval powers over an increasingly larger area of the world. Parallel with this development, the main duty of naval intelligence came to be the tracking and pinpointing of the movements of all such craft. Indeed, to those who were only concerned with the possibility of nuclear attack, this had become the prime function of naval intelligence, so that all else was of a secondary nature. The essential task was to convince an adversary that one had the power to track down its nuclear submarines. Once again anti-submarine warfare dominated naval intelligence thinking and planning, as it had done in two world wars. Yet, just as it was not until the end of these wars—almost, in fact, the last six months of each—that intelligence services became fully apprised of all aspects of war under the seas, so it was only slowly that the full implications of what intelligence had to do in the age of the nuclear submarine dawned on the respective navies.

While it was relatively easy to pinpoint a nuclear weapon base on land, the whole question of tracking, plotting and fixing the ever-changing positions of nuclear submarines was one which called for a highly specialized form of 'instant' naval intelligence. The new thinking was that the nuclear submarine, in view of its wide range as an underwater craft and its ability to move from one ocean to another fairly swiftly, was, compared with a missile base, relatively safe from reciprocal attack. It was, of course, even safer from an unexpected attack except when it was at base. The psychological effect of the nuclear submarine was to make populations feel safer than if their own territory was dotted with rocket bases. This latter argument weighed considerably with a small nation such as Britain and it is probably true to say that the advent of the Polaris submarine for Britain marked the beginning of the dwindling support for nuclear disarmament which had been so vociferous in the 1950s.

Thus the safety, not merely of a single nation, but of most of the world, depended upon finding a new system of speedy, round-the-clock naval intelligence which would reduce the invulnerability of the nuclear submarine and gradually develop methods by which such craft could be fixed in any part of the globe. This problem has by no means been solved, though great strides have been made. To a large extent the role of the intelligence agencies in tracking down submarines and keeping tabs on them is still in the experimental stage, but it will be of enormous significance in the coming decade as the super-powers come to rely more and more on the submarine-based nuclear deterrent.

Nevertheless, this is naval intelligence of a totally different type from that which concerned itself with anti-submarine warfare in either of the last two wars. It is essentially a job for experts, scientists and technicians and not until they have mastered the intricacies of their new role will the use of deception tactics once again be adopted in anti-submarine warfare. There is, of course, one great temptation to employ such tactics now because of the one great weakness of the deterrent missile submarine—that of maintaining communications with strategic submarines without giving away their positions. Probably— it would be exceedingly incautious not to qualify the statement —the NATO powers still have a slight edge over the Soviet Union and its allies in anti-submarine naval intelligence. But it is a very narrow gap indeed and, by the time this is written, may have narrowed still further. What is certainly true is that, in the early 1970s, American superiority in nuclear weapons had rapidly diminished and, by the mid 1970s, the numbers of submarines capable of firing nuclear missiles on both sides roughly balanced out, though actual ranges tended to vary. In that period it was calculated that Russia had upwards of seventy of the largest type of submarines capable of delivering long-range missiles and most of these were of nuclear propulsion. More recently the US nuclear submarine force has been undergoing change. While planning to leave ten of the submarines with their A-3 Polaris missiles, the aim was that, by the end of 1977, the remainder would be equipped with the completely new Poseidon missile. Capable of carrying a warhead of more than two megatons, the Poseidon should have the advantages of a longer range and much greater accuracy. If it is equipped with multiple warheads, each of which can be targeted independently, then the striking force of the US nuclear submarine fleet will be immensely enhanced. The Poseidon makes a major challenge to the Russian Naval Intelligence Service and its technical advisers, for it means that one submarine can fire as many as 224 warheads within four and a half minutes, while all of this time staying on the surface.

In 1975 the Stockholm International Peace Research Institute stated, in its sixth annual report, that Britain's Polaris nuclear submarine fleet was already highly vulnerable to a concentrated Russian attack. At this time Britain had four nuclear-armed submarines, each carrying sixteen missiles with a range of 2,800 miles. In addition the Royal Navy operated seven nuclear hunter-killer submarines and four more were under construction. The Stockholm report took the view that in one sense the British submarine force was substantial in that there were only about 100 urban and industrial targets in the USSR large enough to justify the use of nuclear warheads and that the British force was capable of delivering 192 nuclear bombs of 200 kilotons. Then came the warning: '. . . the small size, limited missile range and geographic basing of the British force makes it vulnerable to Soviet anti-submarine forces, particularly nuclear hunter-killer submarines of various types and an additional 40 nuclear submarines capable of anti-submarine warfare. A concentrated attack by Soviet anti-submarine forces could not be effectively repelled by this small British force.'

It should be borne in mind that the Stockholm report is, in effect, an important item of neutral naval intelligence. As the Institute is devoted to the cause of world peace, its indictment of the shortcomings of British naval nuclear forces is a powerful argument against the left-wingers in Britain who have been clamouring for the abolition of the Polaris submarine. The truth is they are merely spitting in the wind: the Polaris is already making itself obsolete and, by 1980, the Royal Navy will have to replace it, possibly by the American Cruise missile, or cease to have a deterrent.

Nuclear deterrents consume an enormous amount of the money raised by taxation and the intelligence needed to counter them a far larger sum than was even thought possible World War II. It was reported by Drew Middleton in the *New York Times* that, between 1974 and 1978, the US Navy would spend an average of $3·6 billion a year on anti-submarine warfare and that there were more than 140 research programmes relating to ASW.

The cost of maintaining the Polaris fleet by Britain was, up to 1976, only about £40 million a year, less than 1 per cent of the defence budget. It was a deterrent on the cheap—at least for a few years. But meanwhile the United States was developing Under-Sea Long-Range Missile systems with a range o 4,500 miles, enabling targets to be reached from home waters. It is against this background of mutual deterrents that the SALT conferences continue in an effort to stabilize the stalemate of balanced terror and at the same time to keep the rapidly rising costs of such defence within bounds. Increasingly, those who take part in the SALT talks have to depend on the effectiveness of the advice they are given by their intelligence analysers. It is naval intelligence more than any other single factor which will from now on tend to dominate such talks. For this is a complex game of chess played under the ocean by long-distance spotting and the longer the game continues the less the statesmen and politicians will be able to understand it. Very few people understand what goes on at SALT conferences, even including the journalists who write about them: to make the findings of such conferences intelligible to the public is sometimes almost an impossible task. Briefly, what so far the SALT talks have achieved is to agree to limit the numbers of certain types of missiles allowed to each super-power. Then both sides promptly expand their production of other weapons—for example, the USA's MIRV rockets, each of which carries several nuclear warheads, have now been copied by the USSR. So the talks have to start all over again to cope with the new problem. For example, the Soviet Union were able to argue quite logically that the Poseidon was a first-strike weapon and therefore wholly aggressive and not a nuclear deterrent. While this argument was logical, it was also somewhat specious, for the American reply to this was that because of its greater accuracy the Poseidon missile could be directed against enemy missile silos and therefore was, in effect, a deterrent.

Naval intelligence has developed infra-red photography as an aid to submarine spotting and experience has shown that the reactors of the nuclear submarine give off such an enormous amount of heat that this enables the craft to be detected. But communications are what make the nuclear submarine most vulnerable, though there are a variety of ways in which these can now be detected. In the arts of submarine detection the Western powers would still appear to have a slight lead. The Americans claim they are able to get a fix on Soviet submarines because the latter have to surface to communicate. Once such craft have been fixed in this manner, it is possible to plot the course they are likely to take, as nearly all nuclear submarines have definite patterns of movement. But so fast-developing are the systems of detection and counterdetection that it is highly probable at this very moment of writing that the Russians have remedied this situation. There is evidence that they are experimenting with new deception devices which are designed to baffle the trackers and so frustrate an enemy's sensing and detecting system.

Russian submarines have been more easily detectable than those of the West because they make more noise than their NATO counterparts. Another disadvantage for them has been that their submarines cannot stay at sea as long as American underwater craft, mainly because the Russians do not carry a second crew, as do the Americans. Yet the Soviet submarine force is impressive. According to calculations made by the International Institute of Strategic Studies, less than a third of the Russians' nuclear-powered submarines can fire ballistic missiles, but it is probable that about thirty-five to forty of their conventionally powered submarines can do so. Their missiles, which can be launched under water, are the Sark and the Serb, with maximum ranges of 300 and 650 miles respectively. But by now it is probable that their other missile has a range of 1,700–2,200 miles. This makes nonsense of Henry Kissinger's theory of six years ago that the US has a trump bargaining card with the Cruise Missile, which, it is claimed, should be able to travel 2,000 miles and land within 30yd of its target by the early 1980s.

The final Nixon-Brezhnev summit meeting in Moscow agreed to work towards a ten-year agreement to replace the 1972 interim five-year 'freeze' on land-based and submarine-launched intercontinental ballistic missiles. Restriction then theoretically kept the Russians down to 1,410 land-based and 650 sea-based missiles as against 1,054 and 656 on the part of the USA. While the US had an advantage in MIRVs, the Russians were catching up in multiple warheads and testing their latest submarine-launched type in the Pacific. But, to project this picture into the future, technical experts predict that, by the mid-1980s, Russia could be deploying as many as 17,000 multiple nuclear warheads, and when either the USSR or the USA, or both together, reach these kind of figures, it would be exceedingly difficult to say exactly where superiority lies.

The invulnerability—temporary as it might be in the light of even slow advances in detection techniques and naval intelligence—of the nuclear submarine has depended upon its keeping below the surface. Once it surfaces it risks identification and the possibility that an enemy submarine is dispatched to tail it when it submerges again. The sending out of messages while on patrol is also inviting detection. But, of course, such a submarine must always be able to take orders from base while on patrol and so far it has not been easy to do this without breaking radio silence or surfacing. Communications problems involving security have been the major bugbear of the rival submarine forces, and this has only been partially overcome by communications with very low-frequency radio waves, which entails a high-cost communications system, and even then the submarine must travel only a few feet below the surface to receive radio signals from its aerial which floats on the surface.

Yet in this game of chess under the oceans everything is changing all the time, though this may be far from obvious to the general public, or even, perhaps, to some naval commanders. Indeed, the game is changing so fast that soon only the naval intelligence services will really know the score and it might then be a sound policy for future SALT conferences to be conducted solely by naval intelligence experts on both sides. That is a revolutionary concept and one which would no doubt be as rigorously challenged by the military and air force commanders as the politicians who seek kudos for themselves out of the results (or non-results) of the talks. Yet, at this stage, and perhaps for the next decade, such a plan would probably enable greater progress to be made than is now possible. For it is in this no man's land of underwater warfare that the talks on arms limitation are most likely to break down. The Russians themselves have realized this, for their own Naval Intelligence actually monitors discussions at SALT talks while the latter are going on.

In the next ten years, which will be vital to the peace of the world in many respects, these problems have got to be resolved. It is true that by resolving them even bigger problems could be posed; for example, the removal of the underwater nuclear threat could be replaced by one or both super-powers putting the deterrent into outer space, that is, by having launching platforms in outer space. But, because of the cost and manpower which would need to be expended in such a cause, there would be easier opportunities for resolving the deterrent problem than there are now: sheer cost alone might make SALT work at last. One thing is certain, the naval intelligence officer and planner of the next ten years ought to be regarded as supremely important. It would be wise to give relatively high senior rank to all such officers. Meanwhile development goes on and testing follows and it will be increasingly difficult to decide where the one ends and the other begins. For example, when one considers the American deployment of ABMs—the US installation of multiple independently targetable re-entry vehicles (MIRV) in the Minuteman and Polaris missile system—and the Russian testing and (presumably) deployment of fractional orbital bombardment systems (FOBs), each of these has provoked reactions from the other side and both developments are not only speeding up the arms race, but decreasing the relative security of both sides.

'Land-based missiles are no longer crucial for deterrence owing to the existence of Russian and American missile-carrying nuclear submarine fleets which remain completely invulnerable by virtue of their unknown positions in the vast oceans and which carry a sufficient number of deliverable missiles (even without MIRV) to ensure retaliation against any aggression,' wrote Bernard T. Feld, the secretary-general of Pugwash.[1]

Though there have been some optimistic reports of progress towards solving the various problems of anti-submarine warfare today, naval intelligence circles generally agree that, to be really effective, the anti-submarine warfare system of any power must not simply be able to track down and plot the course of a given nuclear submarine, but be in a position to do this so reliably that a large fraction of the opposing nuclear submarine fleet could be suddenly and simultaneously eliminated without any prior warning. In this way the world has passed from the anti-ballistic missile problem of the 1960s to the anti-submarine warfare posers of the 1970s. ASW is far more difficult than the AB techniques because the seas, unlike the atmosphere, are relatively an opaque medium. Electromagnetic radiations are very strongly absorbed, but really efficient sound-generating systems are not only enormous and unwieldy, but present problems in deployment and maintenance and are almost impossible to disguise. The oceans also differ from one another markedly in a sonar sense and each has a wide range of distinctive noises, so the sonar systems are all subject to a multiplicity of spoofing, jamming, simulated signalling and other countermeasures.

Under the ocean exploration has increasingly become a prime task of naval intelligence. There are so many adequate 'covers' for it that it is relatively simple, if costly, to carry out. Sometimes the work is disguised as a marine biological exploration project; more often than not the cost can be 'lost' in some ostensibly commercial enterprise such as oil research.

In June 1973, it was the assessment of objective opinion inside NATO that there was a new Soviet capability of hitting any part of the NATO land mass with underwater missiles launched from submarines in their own well protected home waters. This thesis was expounded in a top-level intelligence report presented to the NATO defence ministers. In effect this report attributed to the Soviet Union the kind of capability which the United States had been striving for with its Trident submarines which were then still in a research and development stage. Detailing the growth of the Warsaw Pact armed forces over the previous five years, reference was also made to the advent of Russia's new Delta Class submarine as 'a most striking and strategically significant highlight of the period'. The Delta is capable of launching missiles from a range of about 4,000 nautical miles. With the introduction of this new factor to submarine warfare, the Russians had achieved the capability virtually to cover the whole of the NATO territories, thus enabling them to fire strategic missiles from submarines submerged in well protected home waters. From the same report it was also clear that almost all Soviet development in the naval sphere was prompted by its own naval intelligence directors.

As long ago as October 1971, the then Defence Secretary of the USA, Mr Melvin Laird, warned that the Soviet Union would catch up with the United States in the number of missile-carrying submarines in service by 1973, stating in support of of this that the Soviet progress 'far outdistances the estimates I gave to Congress in March in my defence report. *I believe we would be placed at a political disadvantage if the Soviet Union was able to ring the United States with missile-carrying submarines in a vastly superior fleet off all our coasts'*.

The italics are mine, but they underline the realization by

Melvin Laird as to where the real threat lay. Prior to this statement, Leonid Brezhnev of Russia had suggested that the USSR and the USA could make 'an equal bargain' about the presence of their Fleets in the world's oceans. 'We do not think it an ideal situation that the navies of the great powers should sail to the other end of the world away from their native shores,' was his observation. But this was double-talk: Russia was already building up a formidable ring of naval strength all round the world. One has only to consider the statement of Admiral Gorshkov on 28 July 1967:

The Soviet Navy has been converted, in the full sense of the word, into an offensive type of long-ranged armed force . . . which could exert a decisive influence on the course of an armed struggle in theatres of military operations of vast extent. . . . and which is also able to support state interests at sea in peacetime.

This statement could be applied equally to the Indian Ocean and the Suez Canal. At that time the Indians and the Russians were protesting about American plans to develop facilities for the US naval craft on Diego Garcia atoll. The atoll about which so much fuss seemed to be made, is a mere 13 miles long and 4 wide, situated 1,000 miles south west of the southernmost tip of India. It is strategic in the sense that it commands the approaches to the Red Sea and the Persian Gulf, the US Navy had been using it since 1969 for minor repairs, and it had the facilities for an airstrip and harbour and fuel storage. The US plan was simply to improve Diego Garcia's harbour, extend the airstrip and increase storage facilities. As a matter of comparison, the US Navy had only about 8 to 10 ships operating in the area, while the Soviet Navy had averaged between 18 and 22 warships in this part of the Indian Ocean, including submarines. That number was swiftly stepped up, within the next year, to between 22 and 30.

Naval intelligence now has a more accurate method of measuring 'naval presence' by a rival. According to the tests applied by the US Navy, the vital factor is 'ship days'. To work this out the basis is that one ship operating at sea for one day equals one ship day, which is a much more accurate method of assessing a rival's potentialities than the number of craft it may have in a given area. In comparing the US and USSR navies, statistics show that the number of Russian 'ship days' has increased from 1,985 in 1968 to more than 8,600 in April 1976. The significance of this figure, carefully checked and counterchecked by naval intelligence, is that it exceeds the 'ship days' of the US Navy by more than 3 : 1. Even more significant, not least in assessing Soviet naval intelligence, is that, as regards hours spent in various ports, Russian ships put in four times as many days as American ships.

Such statistics are a tribute to the Russians' ability to acquire additional port and other facilities for their ships in return for military and economic aid. In the Middle East and Africa such port facilities have been built up and from them have accrued considerable benefits in the field of intelligence. Now the Suez Canal route is once again open, the major oil-producing countries of the Middle East will be effectively ringed by the Soviet Navy so that, in the long-term, it could be that the problem of oil for the NATO powers is not so much one of the ever higher price being demanded by the Arab countries holding it as the fact that it could, to a large extent, be cut off by the Soviet Navy.

Despite the setback which the US Navy suffered from the antagonism of the Wisconsin preservationists to Project Sanguine, which was suspended in 1974, this has not prevented its planners from turning their attention elsewhere. This time they have concentrated on the lonely upper peninsula of Michigan and the project has been modified and changed to the title of 'Seafarer'—an acronym for Surface Extremely Low Frequency Antennae for Addressing Remotely Employed Receivers. This is, perhaps, the most all-comprehensive communications project for defence purposes ever embarked on, entailing a vast network of radio transmitters that would take up 360 square miles of forest land, would consume as much electrical power by day and night as would be used by a township of a population of 35,000, and have, as its prime purpose, the means of safe communication with America's fleet of nuclear submarines.

This plan originated as far back as 1959, but has met with constant setbacks owing to hostile criticism by preservationists. The US Navy's concern was to make the nuclear underwater fleet less liable to detection. These craft were easiest to detect when, once a day or so, they came up to the surface, or lay around just below the waves to pick up their transmission of orders from land-based commanders. Only by conducting communications while they were deeply submerged and travelling at high speeds could detection be assuredly avoided. Ordinary radio waves cannot penetrate more than 6ft or so below the surface of the sea, so the only answer was low frequency radio transmissions adapted to naval requirements. Messages can be transmitted by this means to vessels deep below the surface, but the disadvantages are the high cost of the whole system, the huge construction problem involved and the fact that transmission can be slow. Critics of the project also alleged that the ecological consequences of Project Seafarer are fraught with the most dreadful hazards to the population, insisting that it would expose some twenty small towns to intense radiation and have dire effects on landstock, agriculture and forestry. The US Navy, on the other hand, is equally emphatic that there are no serious environmental problems.

One of the greatest brains in developing Britain's anti-submarine warfare tactics was the late Lord Blackett, a former naval cadet who fought at Jutland, then left the Navy in 1919 to take up a scientific career which was to win for him a Nobel Prize. It was Blackett who suggested using the turret rack of a battleship to steer the Jodrell Bank radio-telescope. In 1932 Blackett was investigating cosmic rays and had perfected the cloud-chamber so that it could be used to photograph cosmic rays as well as ordinary radioactive particles. He set up part of his laboratory on an unused platform of Holborn underground railway station in London, where he measured the penetrative powers of cosmic rays. Later he became scientific adviser at the British Admiralty where he developed improved tactics in submarine and anti-submarine warfare. His Nobel Prize was awarded for his improvement of the Wilson cloud-chamber and his work on cosmic radiation in 1948, when he established a hypothesis that 'magnetism is a property of rotating bodies', which in some circles was regarded as being as important as Einstein's theory of relativity. In the same year he published a controversial book entitled *Military and Political Consequences of Atomic Energy*.

Blackett was one of many examples of men of genius who used to be advisers to British Naval Intelligence. He once spent a night in a submarine, making notes and furiously scribbling out a brief thesis on *The Vital Importance of Ensuring that all Naval Intelligence Reports are Scientifically Checked*, arguing that 'a computerised analysis and checking of reports would save hundreds of thousands of pounds and hundreds of lives'. It is a tragedy that, today, the brain drain has robbed Britain of so many splendid technical experts and inventive minds.

16

Ocean Surveillance Above and Below

Never before in history have the naval intelligence services of the world had to cover every ocean, every sea and, in effect, every inlet and creek. This applies as much in the Arctic and Antarctic as in the Atlantic, Pacific and Mediterranean, the Baltic and the North Sea. There has been a long, silent and largely unpublicized struggle between the super-powers for supremacy and influence in the Antarctic just as much as in the Arctic.

One aspect of this global watch is that of weather-watching which now concerns the navies of the world as much as it has for the past twelve years been a subject of lively interest for the CIA. To some extent this has been stimulated by the theories of some American meteorological experts that the world's climate is changing and that a new ice age is on the way. This may be a subtle war of nerves by some intelligence men, but it has scared the Russians as much as it has fascinated the CIA. For several years now the Soviet Union has suffered from severe setbacks because of poor wheat and other crops; one weather theory is that this situation may worsen drastically because an ice-belt will appear across large areas of Russia and, to some extent, of Europe, too. As poor harvests can affect the political situation—as Nikita Khrushchev learned to his cost—so there is a need for anticipating drastic weather changes from an intelligence viewpoint. But quite often 'meteorological research' is simply a cover for ASW intelligence-gathering. For example, the Royal Navy still requires data on submarines travelling around the western approaches to Britain and some few years ago it embarked on a project for setting up a line of some 300 'weather buoys' from Iceland to the vicinity of the Azores. This was essentially an operation for monitoring submarine movements.

All manner of subterfuges have been adopted in the cause of underwater detection systems which, in terms of naval intelligence, remain the most highly secretive of all such operations. Even NATO has turned its attention to the seemingly innocuous work of oceanography, having set up a committee and charged it with supporting research in this sphere. In 1960 NATO officially reported that Professor Haken Mosby of Bergen University had been engaged to conduct oceanographic research around the Faroes and the Straits of Gibraltar. This was simply an attempt to lay down underwater hydrophones in both areas. Similarly the United States Navy has lent active support to studies of the sounds made by some few hundreds of species of fish. The aim of this operation was not to distinguish fish noises from submarine noises, but to ensure that they did not interfere with signals.

Japan, who for years clung closely to the Western alliance, has recently been forced to a reappraisal of foreign policy and towards better relations with China solely because of the information flowing in from her own naval intelligence. She has been forced to keep an anti-submarine watch around her coasts. The American Seventh Fleet takes care of this problem outside Japanese territorial waters, while Japan's own Intelligence Service, in close collaboration with the USA, maintains an inshore watch. As a result of this round-the-clock check Mr Michita Sakata, Director-general of the Japanese Defence Agency, stated that the Soviet Navy had, at the end of 1975, about 750 ships, totalling 1,200,000 tons, in the sea of Japan, based on the ice-free port of Vladivostok. This Russian force comprised 10 cruisers, 80 destroyers and 120 submarines. But what concerned the Japanese even more were the facts that, firstly, more than 40 of these submarines were nuclear-powered and equally divided between strategic (long-range) missile carriers and the 'hunter-killer' type. The Russians had further advantages in that the average age of their vessels was ten years or so younger, while the American Fleet confronting them was much older. The Soviet fleet had been under the command of one highly experienced, intelligence-minded commanding officer, Admiral Sergei Gorshkov, for all of twenty years. There was the added warning for the Japanese that the Soviet Navy had no intention of relying only on Vladivostok as a base, but that they were developing bases at Korsakov in Sakhalin Island, and the submarine base at Sovetskaia on the mainland, to enable the fleet to disperse. There was also evidence of the creation of a summer base for the Soviet Navy at Petropavlovsk Kamchatsky on the Kamchatka Peninsula.

Undoubtedly a thorough Soviet naval intelligence probe is being carried out in Japanese waters and on the mainland itself. In the spring of 1976 there was a probe by Russian Naval Intelligence into the efficiency of the 'scrambling system' of the Japanese home defence forces and at the same time the Soviet Navy mounted a submarine exercise just south of Tokyo Bay. This last exercise took place on the same day that the Japanese detained the Russian correspondent of the Novesti News Agency, Alexandre Matchekhine, on suspicion of trying to obtain secret information about American naval radar and coding systems. Matchekhine was arrested after he had been found trying to bribe an American sailor to supply information on the naval electronic systems and secret codes of the United States.

Both the great super-powers of the world will have to come to terms with the development of the Nuclear Depth Bomb, the existence of which was denied for so long by spokesmen for Britain's Ministry of Defence. This denial was fatuous and unnecessary from an intelligence point of view, because knowledge of this weapon has long been a matter of considerable controversy behind closed doors at east-west discussions. The public has a right to know what this new and, in many respects, revolutionary bomb involves. From a political point of view this weapon of sea warfare makes an all-out nuclear war less likely than, for example, the existence of tactical nuclear weapons used on land. NATO now has this new weapon which is essentially a super depth-charge for attacking submarines from the air, being the equivalent of many thousands of tons of TNT. It has been made necessary because the higher speed now attainable by submarines under water has meant that the conventional torpedo has less chance of scoring a hit, whereas the nuclear depth-bomb can destroy anything within a wide range.

Admiral Elmo R. Zumwalt USN, former Chief of Naval Operations, has been one of the severest critics of the credibility of the deterrent missile submarine force of the West on the grounds that communications make these craft vulnerable. 'The most persuasive criticism made of the effectiveness of the Polaris-Poseidon system is that sometimes it is difficult to stay in touch with the boats', he has said, and also 'that, in a nuclear exchange situation, a breakdown in communications would have major consequences indeed'.[1]

This somewhat unduly apprehensive view of the system is based on Zumwalt's pessimistic assessment that the Russians have a lead over the Americans in the development of deception devices designed to frustrate an enemy's sensing and detection system. Moreover, the Admiral believes his own efforts to strengthen American means of gathering naval intelligence were overruled by the Pentagon. But some of Zumwalt's fears on this subject have been allayed in the last few years and technical developments have overcome some at least of his criticisms. He has complained that nuclear-propulsion systems are so big and heavy that they make for bigger and more expensive ships, but a vital factor in a nuclear-powered submarine is the fact that it can steam at high speed without refuelling for very long periods.

It was not the ONI, but the CIA which, recollecting how the Russians had located and salvaged the British submarine L-55 in 1928, decided to spend £152 million in salvage operations on a Soviet nuclear missile submarine which sank in more than 16,000ft of water about 750 miles north west of Hawaii in 1968. The Americans had taken a special interest in the earlier operation by the Russians and had decided that the Soviet Union had obtained valuable intelligence as a result which greatly helped their own submarine-building programme. This salvage operation, which, of course, had the co-operation of the US Navy, though many senior officers questioned the wisdom of it, was code-named 'Project Jennifer': it was certainly one of the most bizarre and expensive intelligence-gathering operation ever devised.

The story started when, late in 1968, sonar rays (or 'sonar arrays' as they are more often described), planted in the seabed, picked up the track of a submarine steaming out of Vladivostok towards Hawaii. It was quickly identified as a Soviet craft of what, in NATO naval circles, was called a 'Golf Class ship'. Suddenly the sonar rays picked up the sound of an explosion, after which there was total silence. US Naval Intelligence kept a close watch on the area for some months afterwards by surface craft, submarines and sonar detection devices. It was soon apparent that the USSR had mounted a large-scale search for their submarine with planes and spy trawlers, but that they had not found the craft and that it must be presumed sunk.

With future SALT talks in mind and the need to know the full capabilities of the Golf Class submarine, somebody in US Naval Intelligence raised the question of a salvage operation. The exact position of the sinking had been pinpointed; the only problem was the cost of the operation and it was because this would inevitably be so phenomenally high that the CIA was asked to take over. The only other initial problem was that absolute secrecy was essential: if the Russians had discovered what was afoot, any future SALT talks could have been wrecked before they began. So the CIA needed a 'cover' for Project Jennifer. It was at this stage that the whole affair began to be wrapped up in an aura of pure fantasy. For the man they turned to for assistance was none other than that mysterious millionaire, the late Howard Hughes. In 1969 the CIA offered Hughes the contract for the job of salvaging the Soviet submarine not only because of his interest in deep-sea mining, which would, it was felt, provide an excuse for a cover, but as a tribute to Hughes' own obsessive secrecy, his paranoic sense of security and aid to the CIA on previous occasions. A Hughes subsidiary company, Global Marine, prepared two vessels for Jennifer—*Glomar Explorer*, built in Pennsylvania, and the *Glomar Challenger*, built in San Diego. In the summer of 1974 the two ships headed for the site in the Pacific where the submarine had been sunk. The cover story for the operation was that Howard Hughes' two ships were employed in deep-sea mining for manganese nodules and, in part, this story was true.

Two unfortunate incidents contributed to a leakage on the story behind Project Jennifer. In October 1973, a trade union took Global Marine to court for the dismissal of ten men. The company had to refuse to let its senior executives appear in court in case they would be compelled under oath to reveal the ships' real objective. Then in June 1974, the Hughes headquarters on Romaine Street, Los Angeles, were burgled by armed men who made off with a large quantity of documents. Somebody shortly afterwards telephoned a Hughes agent anonymously and demanded $500,000 for the return of the documents, hinting that otherwise he could prove links between the CIA and Hughes' Summa Corporation. But it was only when the FBI intervened and tried to buy back the papers on behalf of the US Government that the press began to suspect there was a major story behind the whole affair. Then, on 8 February 1975, the *Los Angeles Times* reported that the stolen documents from Summa referred to a joint CIA-Summa operation to raise a sunken Russian submarine.

Full details of the salvage operation have not been made public, but, despite some reports of setbacks, it seems certain that part of the wrecked craft was lifted from the ocean bed. The aim, of course, was to retrieve the submarine's code-books and top secret equipment. Eventually, after they had made strenuous efforts to persuade newspapers not to publish the story (there is no Official Secrets Act in the USA) the CIA gave their own account of Project Jennifer. In this they claimed that they had partially recovered the wreckage, the implication being that it would require a further attempt to bring up the rest of the submarine and the code-books. The official account added that seventy Soviet sailors' bodies had been recovered and that they were formally buried at sea, the ceremony being conducted in Russian and English and the whole proceedings filmed. Naturally, when it was stated that the operation had only been partially successful, the inevitable clamour went up in Congress and the press about a gross waste of public money. But this was countered to some extent by stories in the press that it would be in the United States' interest to let the Russians think the operation was a failure and that the code-books and the entire missile system were not yet in American hands.

The Kremlin maintained a discreet silence throughout this controversial period. Curiously, shortly before the main story on Project Jennifer broke, but when some scant details were already known by the press, the Secretary-general of the United Nations, Kurt Waldheim, sent this message to the UN Committee on Disarmament in Geneva:

> Environmental warfare might soon pass from the realm of imagination to terrifying reality unless preventive action is taken promptly. The technology might soon exist to trigger earthquakes, steer hurricanes or release tidal waves. The General Assembly [of the UN] has recently gone on record in favour of a convention prohibiting the uses of nature as an instrument of war . . .

To this statement by Waldheim, James Reston added his own comment in the *International Herald Tribune*:

> The main point is the struggle for the mastery of the seas and the economic and military exploitation of the bottom of the waters of the earth. Back of all this Buck Rogers and scientific fiction stuff about broken Soviet submarines, dead sailors and the efforts of the CIA to recover the Soviet missiles and codes, there is the much larger strategic question of who can operate effectively on the bed of the oceans. The salt-water seas and oceans cover 72 per cent of the globe. They contain not only oil, but precious metals and food—nobody knows how much —but maybe enough to drive the machines and feed the recklessly fertile human family in the last quarter of the twentieth century.[2]

On 13 April 1975, it was reported that the CIA was preparing to send back the *Glomar Explorer* to lift up the remaining sections of the sunken submarine and its code-books. No word of complaint came from Moscow, possibly because it had never acknowledged the loss of the submarine and its crew. The new operation was code-named 'Matador' and a certain amount of information on the project was forthcoming. It was said that a new claw was being designed to fit the wreck so exactly that it could be lifted without harming the conning tower where nuclear missiles were housed. The aim of the return mission, it was said, was to recover the missiles and torpedoes and secure the code-books. By this time the code-books would be almost an irrelevance and it is more than likely that the second mission was just a cover-up for the fact that the CIA already had obtained what they set out to get originally.

About the same time that the Project Jennifer story broke, the National Broadcasting Company in the USA reported joint Anglo-American operations to recover electronic gear from a Soviet aircraft which crashed in the North Sea in 1972. NBC mentioned that this was one of at least four such operations in which Soviet military equipment had been recovered after mishaps at sea. The NBC correspondent, Ford Rowan, quoted a former CIA official and a US naval officer as confirming these operations. The Ministry of Defence in London refused either to confirm or deny these reports.[3]

Further strong criticism of the American recovery plans was voiced later in 1975 when it was learned that the budget of £152 million of Navy research funds had been increased to £275 million. Afterwards it was reported from Honolulu that a Russian tug had been in the area for several days and that not only were two large Soviet oceanographic ships heading for Hawaii, but that a third ship was shortly expected. A mask of silence has been drawn over the silent and supposedly secret battle between the two navies. But the magazine *Sea Technology* reported in March 1976 that the US Navy had opposed the project in the first place, but had had salt rubbed in its wounds when it was decided, above its head, that most of the money for the project should come from its own research funds. The magazine, which has its own 'Navy lobby', alleged that as a result of this some of the US Navy's anti-submarine warfare research activities had had to be cut. Whether or not these criticisms were justifiable, the real danger to modern naval intelligence is that, in certain circumstances, it tends to be taken away from the very organization which, professionally and otherwise, is best equipped to tackle it. In an operation such as Project Jennifer only the ONI ought to be able to assess whether the expense or the political and other risks involved were justified.

The same query applies to another of the many unsolved naval intelligence mysteries which the anti-submarine warfare battle is now producing. This was the case of the 1,100-ton British trawler *Gaul*, which vanished in a gale 70 miles off

North Cape in the Arctic Circle on 8 February 1974. The *Gaul* was nicknamed the 'Unsinkable' in her home port of Hull, because of her special construction and the sophisticated equipment she carried. She was one of the safest and best of all modern trawlers, especially built to withstand all the hazards of fishing in the Arctic Circle. A steel-strengthened hull and other devices made her more stable, and special heating systems to prevent her from icing-up were provided. There was more than £12,000 worth of radio equipment alone, and lifeboats fitted with distress beacons and walkie-talkie-type radios with a range of 7 miles were part of her emergency kit.

Yet none of the crew of thirty-six survived and there was no positive trace of the wreckage. To the general public it must have seemed as though the *Gaul* was just an unlucky victim of a freak sea. But there were whispers that something strange, something out of the ordinary had happened to the ship, that she was a sdy-ship for the Royal Navy, fitted out with the latest devices for anti-submarine warfare. Belatedly, on 21 February 1974, some thirteen days after she had been presumed sunk, the British Prime Minister ordered a new search for the vessel or its wreckage.

One trawler skipper claimed he had signed the Official Secrets Act and that he had secret equipment aboard his ship, but trawler owners denied that their vessels carried secret 'spy equipment' or that any of them had been asked to sign the OSA. Mr William Rodgers of the Defence Ministry said categorically that the *Gaul* was not a spy-ship, that there was no naval equipment or personnel aboard and that the ship was not involved in intelligence work.

Later, however, there was this statement from a spokesman for the British Trawlers' Federation which put a slightly different emphasis on the subject: 'In the early days of the development of satellite navigation some trawlers took equipment aboard for test purposes and for calibration in Arctic waters, but there was nothing secret or sinister about it. If a skipper was asked to sign the OSA, it could only have been a bit of bureaucratic formality. Satellite navigation equipment is now in common use in merchant ships.'

One theory was that the *Gaul* may have been sunk in collision with a Soviet or even a NATO submarine. The gale could have swept a submarine to the surface to cause the collision, though this would have been an exceptional occurrence. Repeatedly, despite denials, it was alleged that the *Gaul* was fitted with an intercept receiver for naval intelligence work. The theory that the *Gaul* might have been tipped over by a Soviet or friendly submarine coming up from below in a gale was put forward in a Thames Television investigation of the whole story, producing some surprising new evidence. Their research team showed that the vessel's lifebuoy, picked up three months later 18 miles off North Cape, was almost certainly deliberately planted there. It was also made clear that British trawlers had carried intelligence electronics at various times. Obviously, somebody in Whitehall had very wisely said (even if not for publication) that 'what the Russians can do with their trawlers, we can do just as well'. While not solving the mystery of the *Gaul*, the television programme totally undermined the findings of the official court of investigation into the loss of the ship, an inquiry which was even less convincing than that made half a century before into the sinking of the *Hampshire*.

Another theory was that the *Gaul* had been arrested for spying by the Soviet Navy and that she might still be held in some Arctic port. When the lifebuoy was brought ashore by the Norwegian skipper who picked it up, he was puzzled by its location and the cleanliness and lack of marine weed growth. Structural tests showed that the buoy had never been submerged in more than 60 or 70ft, although the *Gaul* had been assumed to have sunk in 900ft of water.[4]

At the time of the *Gaul*'s disappearance *détente* talks between the West and the Soviet Union were continuing and there was great anxiety among the American delegation to avoid any incidents involving the sea or air forces of either side. Incidents at sea already far too numerous, were in themselves likely to sabotage the talks. While the Russians had never made much attempt to disguise the fact that they used their own merchant trawlers on spying missions, the West had always been vociferous in denying that they used such methods and were eager to hide all evidence of such tactics. The Soviet Union knew full well that the Western powers, and especially the British, had often made use of the trawler skipper for secret missions; after all, many trawler fishing skippers had served in the Royal Naval Reserve in World War II and some of these were still technically on the Reserve and working under the Official Secrets Act, even though they became fewer each year. One sinister story that was mooted was that the *Gaul* was not captured or sunk by the Soviet Navy, but had been deliberately sunk by a NATO warship or submarine to prevent her from falling into Russian hands, thus providing the Russians with the kind of evidence they would need to call off the SALT talks.

A NATO exercise involving British and Norwegian naval forces was being held off Norway at this time and some of the units were detached to search for the vanished *Gaul*. Aircraft carrying electronic devices for detecting submarines covered a wide area, yet there was no indication of the site of the wreck. Plotters knew exactly the direction in which the *Gaul* had been heading at the time radar contact with her was lost, yet neither by 'sonar arrays' nor any other ASW techniques could they pinpoint a sunken craft that might have been the missing trawler. It is this lack of evidence that lends credence to the possibility that the *Gaul* was not just sunk by freak waves in a fierce gale.

The Russians were known to be closely watching the NATO exercise and to be employing spy-ships for this purpose. It seemed almost impossible that any Russian vessel could have captured the *Gaul* in such a gale. It is true that they had 'arrested' British trawlers on other occasions for alleged breaches of fishing limits rules. But the incident of the floating life-buoy made the whole affair even more mysterious. One theory was that the life-buoy might have been a copy of one belonging to the *Gaul*, thrown into the sea to give the impression that the trawler had been sunk. But tests by the Royal Navy proved that it undoubtedly was one of the ship's life-buoys. But why just one life-buoy? Why was other material from the wreck not floating on the surface? Was the life-buoy released on the surface by a submarine?

There have been fewer answers to the mystery of the *Gaul* than there were to that of the Soviet submarine sunk off Hawaii. But one American naval intelligence officer posed this solution of the affair:

We have no doubt that there was a definite link between the attempt to salvage the Soviet submarine in the Pacific with the loss of the *Gaul*. We believe that the Russians learned all about our salvage efforts some long time before the *Gaul* was sunk. They were certainly worried about reports that the British and American navies had co-operated in rescuing electronic gear from one of their aircraft. The incident of the *Gaul* was a warning by the Soviet Union to the NATO powers generally. It was, if you like, a low-key response to our own intelligence-gathering. But when the USSR makes a low-key response it is often ambiguous and you are left trying to guess the meaning. You know it's a keep 'off' warning all right, but that's all. But one must assume that if the Russians had captured the ship and they wished to convince NATO that she had been sunk, they would have provided more evidence than a single life-buoy. What is much more likely is that they wanted to convince us that they had actually captured the trawler when in fact they had attempted to do so and failed, possibly causing the *Gaul* to sink in the process.

In the history of anti-submarine warfare nothing is impossible and any one of these theories may to a certain extent be correct. Apart from the suppositions put forward, it cannot be ruled out that the *Gaul* was damaged in the gale, was heading for the shelter of land—her last signal said 'we're going to dodge more into land'—and that a NATO plane or ship sank her to prevent her from falling into Soviet hands. If this had happened, the Russians would certainly have had confirmation of what they had long suspected—that British trawlers were often used as spy-ships just as much as their own.

This is where the Official Secrets Act's very existence can be a highly dangerous weapon in peacetime. If the USA suffers from not having such an act, Britain has probably been damaged as much as she has ever been aided by its existence. The Ministry of Defence will no doubt continue to deny that trawlers are used as spy-ships and will cite the Official Secrets Act to defend its suspect denials. But the truth is that, whatever official spokesmen may say, all NATO powers employ civilian craft as spy-ships as much as the Soviet Union. In the near future the silent intelligence battle under and on the oceans will be stepped up and more ruthless and revolutionary tactics may be employed. These tactics may ultimately involve a navy sinking and destroying one of its own ships to preserve vital secrets. The Soviet Navy has actually indulged in such ruthless tactics on a least two occasions and there is no reason to doubt that NATO forces have acted in similar fashion. *Détente* may well encourage rather than discourage such tactics and even tolerate their perpetration by either side.

17
Glimpse Into the 1980s

From now on the naval intelligence of any major power must not be merely three-dimensional, but four-dimensional, or even five-dimensional, as some would express it. This will take in land masses, the surface of the oceans, the depths of the ocean, air space around the earth and, not least, outer space. The four (or five) will be indivisible when it comes to waging war.

A very serious argument for the policy of *détente* and in favour of the seemingly largely abortive SALT talks is one which is never officially admitted. This is the concern by both the super-powers about the battle for winning knowledge and power by probing outer space. There are some in both the USA and Russia who abhor the waste of vast sums of money on such research programmes and the inherent danger of one of them being able to gain an advantage in this sphere and so blackmail the other. These people urge a secret policy of collaboration on all outer space projects, thus sharing the costs, and an agreement to exploit their findings jointly. But probably only when the Europeans and the Chinese have caught up with the Russians and Americans in outer space technology will such a programme be openly mooted.

Whatever may come out of this secret debate in the inner counsels of the US Government and the USSR, there will increasingly be efforts by both sides to exploit the opportunities for blackmail which outer space seems to offer. Remarkably, but understandably, because of the importance of the submarine nuclear deterrent, the navies of both powers seem to regard a truce in outer space rather more seriously than the respective airforces. The *Baltimore Sun* of 18 January 1974, carried a news story about the United States planning 'a global satellite system', while, on 27 April 1974, the *Herald-Tribune* of New York reported how Soviet radar was being used to track ships on our oceans from outer space. There have even been suggestions that the Soviet Union has launched naval intelligence deception tactics to lure the USA into wasting time and money on moon explorations rather than on probing the sea-beds of the world. It is certainly arguable that concentrating on ocean probing can—at least in the short run—be more profitable than sending men to the moon. Then there is the counterstory that the CIA has embarked on its weather investigations partly to frighten the Soviet Union into some kind of an agreement on the exploration of outer space, the idea being that the earth is not only faced with the disaster of a new ice age and climatic upheavals, but with ecological hazards through which the atmosphere round the world will be destroyed and this planet made uninhabitable. Presumably, the intention would be for the USA and the USSR to band together in a programme to ensure that plans could be made to evacuate some of the population of Mother Earth.

It is easy to read too much or too little into any such speculations, but truth and science fiction, deception tactics and imaginative development are often so mixed up that it is almost impossible to arrive at the truth quickly. But to neglect studying the future of naval intelligence without taking into account the dimension of outer space would be to ignore developments that are almost certain to take place in the late 1980s. In July 1974, experts at a US Army missile base at Huntsville, Alabama, were perplexed about strange 'ghost ships' picked up by powerful radar scanners in the Pacific Ocean during a tracking exercise. Some of these had been observed as long ago as August 1973. A US Naval Intelligence expert told me that, while he was always sceptical of anything in the nature of an unidentified flying object,

> . . . these ghost ships were clearly in the sky and they compared with nothing we had seen before. When we launched a Minuteman ICBM [intercontinental ballistic missile] towards the Pacific test site, it began its descent on a normal

ballistic trajectory. The nose cone had separated from the third stage of the missile and was entering the atmosphere at 22,000 feet per second. Radar scanners were tracking the nose cone routinely when they found they were also tracking an unidentified flying object next to the ICBMs nose cone. Radar picked up an inverted saucer-shaped object to the right and above the descending nose cone and watched it cross the warhead's trajectory to a point where it was below and to the left of it before the 'ghost ship' disappeared.

The 'ghost ship' was described as being 10ft high and 40ft long. On this so far unexplained incident one might usefully pose the question as to whether air and naval intelligence should not be much more closely co-ordinated. Guiseppe Cocconi and Philip Morrison raised the question in 1961 whether superior civilizations in outer space might be trying to contact us.[1] 'We expect that the signal [from outer space] will be pulse-modulated with a speed not very fast, or very slow compared to a second, on grounds of bandwidth and of rotations,' they added later. The immediate moral of all this is that such signals could easily come not from distant civilizations on other planets, but from Soviet spy-stations in outer space. No doubt the Russians have an equal fear of such a development from the Americans. Our naval intelligence expert's comment on this is: 'Once again we need to know as much about any possible deception tactics by signal from outer space as we do about signals directed to or from underwater craft.'

British Ministry of Defence spokesmen have continued to deny the use of non-naval vessels for electronic or any other form of espionage. After the *Gaul* affair, however, Mr Derek Oswald of British United Trawlers admitted to one of the relatives of the lost trawlermen that 'naval officials or members of the Navy' had been carried on their trawlers. Yet he, too, denied this was the case with the *Gaul*.[2] Whenever naval personnel have been identified as being aboard trawlers, the excuse has always been that they were there as observers during the fishing dispute with Iceland, or for training purposes.

Probably it has been because of these belated and ambiguous admissions that the Royal Navy's policy has changed somewhat.

For sometime past, instead of using naval officers aboard trawlers, Naval Intelligence has secretly recruited trawler skippers, mainly Scottish, or those operating in Scottish waters, to spy on Russian shipping. This has been part of 'Operation Hornbeam', conducted mainly by Intelligence officers at the Portreavie naval centre near Rosyth, from which operations against suspected Soviet trawlers and for the protection of North Sea oil installations are directed.

Early in 1977 carefully selected trawler skippers were issued with special handbooks to decipher Russian ship-markings. They were asked to plot the movements of, and classify, all USSR shipping which they sighted and to supply photographs of them. The Ministry of Defence in London had belatedly responded to criticisms from both inside Britain and in NATO circles that not enough was being done to protect seabed installations against sabotage and destruction by hostile forces. Some in NATO had long felt that this should be a major task for all NATO forces. It was not merely a question of Soviet espionage (the USSR has, to some extent, been most unfairly made the bogey on this issue), but of the very real threat of international terrorism, including Palestinian blackmail gangs with quite considerable technical know-how. So the watch was to be extended to North Sea oil-rigs. There was some evidence that international terrorist organizations might well pose as Soviet agents operating in craft purporting to be under the Russian flag. The theory would be that, if they did this, they would be treated with much more respect and caution.

There is considerable justification for these tactics in that, in an area some 5–10 miles east of the Shetlands, there is an almost permanent presence of Soviet ships, both of the Russian Navy and their merchant fleet. The USSR nearly always has a rescue tug and tanker within sight of the Shetlands and Desmond Wettern, the naval correspondent of the London *Daily Telegraph*, reported, on 29 July 1977, that:

> . . . often there are more Russian than British ships to be seen. Yesterday *Orkney*, 1,250 tons, passed three Russian ships within the space of an hour. One, the rescue tug, *Oktenskiy*, of about 800–900 tons, is believed to have the task of going to the rescue of any Russian ships, and particularly submarines,

that may get into difficulties in the North Atlantic and Norwegian Sea. The Russians have kept a tug or salvage ship permanently on station, usually at anchor off the Shetlands, for several years . . .'.

The Shetlands are a focal point for the Russians on their routes to Cuba, West Africa and the Mediterranean. Soviet mine-sweepers keep a close watch on North Sea oil-rigs.

But it was the two-way threat—Soviet espionage and international terrorist aggression—which caused the British to adopt tactics which had been employed by the Soviet Union for more than twenty years. Inevitably this had to be launched without the Minister involved—ie, the now junior-rank Minister for the Navy—being consulted. The post of Minister for the Navy was passed so rapidly from one MP to another that there was barely time to have the new Minister cleared for security purposes before he was moved to another post.

Because of the two-way threat, of espionage by the Russians and sabotage by international terrorists, a hot-line was installed to the Joint Intelligence Section at Portreavie so that trawlermen could phone in their information. The truth was that, though Nimrod aircraft were making daily sorties to keep a watch on Soviet shipping, the Ministry of Defence had been forced to admit that their intelligence was far from complete. The average trawler skipper is a far better judge of what an intelligence organization requires than any RAF pilot. This may seem a sweeping statement, but it has been proved an accurate judgement by countless reports from trawlermen. All the new intelligence gained from the trawler skippers is to be passed back to NATO; the handbook given to the skippers translates the cyrillic alphabet, used by Soviet ships, into English characters.

By April 1977, there was an intensification of the campaign to keep Soviet spy-ships out of British waters. A Russian trawler skipper was fined £10,000 and had his £4,000 gear and catch confiscated at Lerwick Sheriff Court. It was the first time a foreigner had been sentenced for poaching since the 200-mile limit came into operation. Even then there was a curious plea put forward by the defence. Soviet skipper Anatoly Kremensky claimed he had received a message from his mother ship 'saying he was authorised to take the place of a Russian boat which had a license to fish within the limit'. The sheriff refused to accept this explanation, but the procurator fiscal made the astonishing admission that 'certain Russian ships had been granted licenses to fish within our waters'.[3]

The facts which emerged from this case were that the Russians had a quota of no less than twenty-seven licenses to fish within British waters, while the East Germans had six and the Poles five. What kind of sense does this make? And who made the rules?

There has since been abundant evidence of Soviet espionage around the North Sea oil-rigs, but it would seem that the message of the British trawlers' counterespionage operation has been learned and that, recently, they have switched the spying to their aircraft. In May 1977, a Soviet Tupolev bomber was nosing around the Brent oilfield when a British Phantom forced it to turn away. Later twenty TU 16 bombers—code-named 'Badgers' by NATO—were intercepted some 45 miles from Aberdeen, once again closely surveying the oil-rigs. The employment of the TU 16 for these missions has sinister undertones: there is an implied threat, as this aircraft, while highly effective from a reconnaissance viewpoint, is also a ship-strike aircraft. However, this may be to counter the fact that the British Phantom carries eight air-to-air missiles.

The increased accuracy of nuclear weapons threatens to produce a potentially destabilized relationship between the two major nuclear powers in land-based strategic nuclear missiles, but not in sea-based systems, by the 1980s. Sea-launched ballistic missiles (SLBMs) have a number of long-run advantages as deterrent systems. Apart from their mobility, which makes them difficult to destroy before they are launched, their capabilities seem likely to be increased by the 1980s. At present the Undersea Long-Range Missile System has a range of 5,000 miles, thus increasing the area of ocean within which it can patrol. Meanwhile certain progress is being made in reducing the noise which nuclear submarines make so that major advances in submarine detection and tracking are required to produce an answer to this. Equally, destruction techniques will require further development. Sonic nuclear submarines receive, but rarely send, radio messages, and it is almost impossible to detect them by RDF. The use of satellites, equipped with infra-red and magnetic anomaly systems make detection of such craft possible, but as yet such experiments are not altogether promising. There is much more hope of success for effective detection measures and localization of submarines in the use of active or passive fixed 'sonar arrays'. The United States has a number of these systems in the experimental stage—'Sea Spider' and 'Project Caesar'.

The device known as 'MAD', or Magnetic Anomaly Detector, works on the principle that the presence of a submarine influences and changes the readings of the earth's magnetic field. Thus the submarine appears as a 'magnetic anomaly'. But this is far from being a perfect system, as certain formations of rock jutting up from the ocean bed can appear on the MAD system as the outline of a submarine. Much research still needs to be done into the distribution of magnetic anomalies across the seabed. Project Caesar was launched back in 1965 with a survey of the oceanbed and it was followed by SONUS, or Sound System for Underwater Surveillance. The latter system employed listening devices anchored at the depth of the sound channel and not on the ocean bed. Presumably some progress on research was made, as the Navy was given nearly £15 million for further work in this field in 1968. But effective development of passive systems of detection will depend mainly upon the improvement of computer programmes which can separate the background acoustic noises of the submarine environment from those made by submarines or surface ships. When this can be done, detection can be much more accurately conducted by using highly sensitive directional hydrophone arrays and normal triangular techniques.

Development of all ASW techniques is essentially slower than that of detection devices which operate above the ocean. 'Oyster' mines, for example, one of the last of the Nazis' secret weapons, remained invincible for the greater part of forty years. The Royal Navy never found an adequate answer to them. Eventually, in the mid-1970s, experiments conducted by a cross-Channel Mountbatten Class hovercraft revealed that the oyster mine, so called because it operates on a principle similar to that of an oyster opening and closing its shell, could not be detonated by a hovercraft passing over it. In the normal way oyster mines are detonated by the decrease in water pressure caused by a passing ship. There had been one way only to tackle this type of mine: first, to detect it by sonar apparatus well ahead of any ship searching for it, and then to send down a frogman to lay a controlled demolition charge. Now the hovercraft mine-sweeper will be a new ally in the fight against oyster and similar mines laid on the seabed. Thus, in 1977, has an idea been brought to fruition which was mooted by a naval intelligence officer at Algiers in World War II. In that period German and Italian submarines laid oyster mines close in to the coast of North Africa, often at depths at which normal mines would not be expected.

The ONI has long been keenly interested in analysing the results of a system of ship and submarine detection by identifying them by comparison with their 'sound memory tapes and noise signatures'. By the late 1980s, submarine detection systems will have been revolutionized if, and only if, sufficient funds for research have been provided. The research is so costly that it is exceedingly doubtful if such a system could ever be produced on a national basis and, apart from finance, for it to succeed there would need to be the co-operation of several nations. In this respect NATO has a positive advantage and would, indeed, have more if CENTO and SEATO were still allied to it. If fixed 'sonar arrays' are used, some of the NATO countries can provide geographical bonuses in that their coastlines are admirably situated for providing detection coverage over the whole of the North Atlantic. The Russians, on the other hand, can only counter this system by the method of a semi-permanent, deep-sea buoyage system or permanent ocean bed installations.

Certainly there will be a concentration on the submarine as a deterrent force for sometime to come and there will also be an increasing use of non-missile submarines to track down missile submarines. Indeed, the nation which foolishly concentrates on the latter and ignores the former will swiftly be at a disadvantage. The Americans' Anti-Submarine Warfare Environmental Prediction System (ANSWEPS) and the Royal Navy's Oceanographic Forecasting Service (OFS) are both working hard on developing new detection systems. At the same time the planners of nuclear destruction are devoting much time to improving their destruction systems. Much importance is now attached to a revised method of what the navies call SINS (ship's inertial navigation systems). Each submarine equipped with SINS is, claim the exponents of this system, able to deliver a missile to its target with an accuracy to within a few hundred feet. The system can work at any depth, but over a period errors can creep into it so that, after a long submerged journey, during which these errors accumulate, the submarine could not possibly fire its missiles with anything like this degree of accuracy. This defect in the system has been counteracted to some extent by updating the SIN's readings daily, but even this is by no means foolproof, relying as it does on the 'Omega' transmitting station network system. Greater accuracy can only be obtained at present by obtaining surface fixes.

New types of submarine are being experimented with all the time. British engineers have perfected a plastic submarine which has the advantage of being cheaper, easier to produce and highly adaptable for use by companies engaged in underwater oil prospection. The Russians have established a considerable lead in their own research into the use of the Lorentz force for propulsion and super-conductors for magnetic fields. This is a force which is developed when a current intersects a magnetic field; acting at right angles to both current and field it is capable of propelling a physical object. In 1966 Dr Stewart Way of Westinghouse built an electromagnetic submarine on these principles. In a letter to the author he writes: 'a 10-foot model was built while I served as Professor of Mechanical Engineering at the University of California in 1966. The US Navy was mildly interested, but was always so concerned with problems of the moment that they did not see fit to undertake an extensive development. . . . It was my hope that the idea of electromagnetic propulsion might take hold, either for small research submarines, large cargo submarines or submarine tankers.'

The Russians, always anxious to steal a march, have, according to the latest intelligence reports, taken the project of the electromagnetic submarine away from the oceans and are said to be applying it to outer space. An American naval intelligence expert says:

We are now convinced that some of the unidentified flying objects reported these days are in fact Soviet spacecraft based on the Lorentz principles. We know that they have experimented successfully with underwater craft propelled in this fashion, that is, by electromagnetic propulsion and superconductivity. Our own information more than ten years ago was that they based their underwater craft of this description on the blueprints of Berkhardt Heim, a German scientist, who was developing models of this back in the early 1940s. Some of these plans came into our own hands, but others were seized by the Russians. Such craft developed for the air can hover and accelerate from 10 mph to 20,000 mph.

With all these dramatic experiments heralding the dawn of the 1980s, it is not surprising that some NATO senior officers are recommending computerized war games as a necessary part of the intelligence officer's training. Certainly the intelligence officer who is not constantly brought up to date with the development of scientific ideas is going to be sadly out of touch in the next decade. The US Naval War College replaced its traditional table-top method of war games three years ago with computers and cinematic projectors. Captain Don Henderson USN stated that 'wargames are the cheapest way of discovering and demonstrating faulty combat decisions and the new methods being tried here make the college's War Gaming Centre a trailblazer in that area'.[4] In a dark room at the War Gaming Centre, combat situations are plotted on a large cinema screen using forty-eight projectors, along with hand drawings and paste-on cutouts. A computer keeps count of the damage done and the strengths, courses and speeds in ships and aircraft involved. The games include combat situations, ranging from a single aircraft against a submarine, to a major conflict between nations involving decisions by fleet commands and the joint Chiefs of Staff.

A British naval intelligence officer who has seen something of the American war-gaming training makes this comment: 'The centre has been greatly developed by its digital computer system and those of us who have studied war gaming from an intelligence point of view now realise that use of this system for testing out theories of detection and counter-detection in anti-submarine warfare could be of inestimable value to all NATO intelligence officers. It provides a chance of testing out methods of counteracting the seeming invulnerability of the underwater nuclear missile.'

In peering into the future one can say that naval intelligence has come to be a combination of chess and computer science, and that on its development over the next ten vital years will largely depend the safety of the world from nuclear war. Perhaps a stalemate is the best we can hope for, but that may well be much safer than a checkmate.

Supplementary Notes to Chapters

CHAPTER I

1   *A History of the Royal Navy*, Sir Nicholas Harris Nicholas, Richard Bentley (London, 1887)

2   Camden *Annals* (1635), p 394. Walsingham's will is published in full in *History of Chislehurst*, Webb, p 383

3   No copies of these invisible ink letters are in existence today, as far as is known, but those reaching their destination were copied by Alexander Hamilton and members of General Washington's staff, and have been preserved in the Washington Papers.

4   *The Two Spies*, Morton Pennypacker, a member of the New York State Historical Society

5   See article entitled 'The Origin of the Franklin-Lee Imbroglio', in the *North Carolina Historical Review*, XV (January 1938), 41

6   See also *The Hell-Fire Club*, Donald McCormick (Jarrolds, London, 1958)

7   Correspondence of Mlle Yvette Perrault with the author

8   'Observations of my Reading History in Library', 9 May 1731, in Leonard W. Labaree's *The Papers of Benjamin Franklin*, 11 vols to date (New Haven, 1959–69) I, 192

9   For this and also for succeeding paragraphs see Lord Stormont to Lord Eden, Auckland Correspondence, British Museum, Additional Mss, 2138–2249

10   *The Published Letters of King George III*, revised edition, 1932. See also Paul Wentworth to William Eden, Auckland Correspondence, British Museum, Add Mss, 2241, f 119

11   Franklin Papers, APSL, XIX, 22

12   Cited from Papers in the Public Records Office, London

13   Ibid

14   Franklin to J. Galloway, Passy (14 August 1777) Franklin Papers, APSL, XXV, 10a

15   *Published Letters of King George III*

16   Joseph Vardill to John Hynson (1 December 1777) British Museum, Add Mss, 1505, f 3

17   Correspondence, undated, from Rachel Antonina Lee to Thomas de Quincey
18   Arthur Lee to Richard Henry Lee, Paris (12 September 1778) Lee Papers, Alderman Library, University of Virginia, Charlottesville

CHAPTER 2

1   *Les Grands Espions*, Paul and Suzanne Lanoir, Paris
2   *Narrative of a Secret Mission in 1808*, by James Robertson, edited by A. C. Fraser (London, 1863). Also *DNB*, XLVIII, p 410
3   Cited in *Nelson the Commander*, Geoffrey Bennett (Batsford, London, 1972)
4   Ibid
5   Letter from Robert Fulton to a friend [Stephen] (3 February 1805)
6   *Anecdotes of the Life of the Right Honourable William Pitt, Earl of Chatham and of the Principal Events of his Times*, J. Almon (London, 1793) vol I, p 307
7   Naval Records Collection of the Office of Naval Records & Library (Records Group 54), National Archives, Washington; *Letters to Officers, Ships of War*, vol 25, p 303
8   *A History of the Russian Secret Service*, Richard Deacon, Frederick Muller (London, 1969)
9   *Twenty-five Years in the Secret Service: the Recollections of a Spy*, Henri Le Caron (Heinemann, London, 1892)

CHAPTER 3

1   *Eyes of the Navy*, Admiral Sir William James
2   *Annual Report of the Secretary of the Navy (1883)*, US Department of the Navy archives
3   Cited in *Room 39*, Donald McLachlan
4   Letter from Admiral Sir Francis Beaufort to Captain R. P. Cator RN (14 July 1868)
5   *Dictionary of National Biography*
6   A letter from Morrison in the files of the Mercurii, undated other than the words 'Tuesday the 5th'
7   *Pall Mall Gazette* (13 October 1886)
8   Cited by Admiral Sir William James in *Eyes of the Navy*
9   The Playfair Cipher was based on a key-word which was placed in the first position of a square containing the alphabet (from which J was omitted). Suppose the key-word to be Edinburgh, the alphabet square was made up in the following manner, letters not in the key-word being written after those in it:

EDINB
URGHA
CFKLM
VWXYZ

10   An amusing sidelight on the arrival of the USS *Charleston* in the Philippines is that when this ship sailed into the harbour at Guam, in June 1898, she opened fire on fort installations there. The Spanish Governor, who had received no communication by post for some months and therefore did not know that Spain and the USA were at war, sent a message to the warship, apologizing for not answering the 'friendly salute' on the grounds that his gunpowder was spoiled.

11   *Annual Report of the Chief of the Bureau of Navigation* (1898): see CIO's report included therein

CHAPTER 4

1   In the 1903 edition of Erskine Childers' book, *The Riddle of the Sands*, there is the following note on page ix: 'the fragment of charts [Charts A and B] are reproductions, on a slightly reduced scale, and omitting some confusing and irrelevant details, of British and German Admiralty charts. Space precludes the insertion of those bulky engravings in full; but the reader who wishes for fuller information is referred to Charts Nos. 406 and 407 of the British series and No. 64 of the German series. The maps are necessarily on a very small scale, but can be supplemented by reference to standard publications.' It is, of course, astonishing that the Royal Navy was so unaware of the charting of this area by both the British and German navies that it took Childers' book to make them realize it. All Childers had done was to 'marry' the two sets of charts; this the NID had failed to do.

2   Capt W. R. (later Admiral) Hall made amends to both these officers when he became DNI in 1914. Not only were they reimbursed, but Brandon became Assistant DNI with the rank of Commander, and Trench worked under him.

3   Attempts to establish intelligence systems in Germany: letter from Sir Basil Zaharoff to Sir Vincent Caillard in *Documents Politiques de la Guerre*

CHAPTER 5

1   *The Man of Room 40*, A. W. Ewing
2   Ibid
3   *The Dark Invader*, Rintelen
4   Ibid
5   *New York Times* (14 May 1913)
6   *40 OB*, Hoy
7   *The Dark Invader*, Rintelen
8   Ibid
9   Ibid
10   Ibid
11   *40 OB*, Hoy
12   *The Dark Invader*, Rintelen

13 *The Life & Letters of Walter H. Page*, B. J. Hendrick (Heinemann, London)
14 *40 OB*, Hoy
15 Ibid
16 *The Autobiography of an Adventurer*, J. T. Trebitsch Lincoln

CHAPTER 6
1 *40 OB*, Hoy
2 *Eyes of the Navy*, James
3 Personal letter from Admiral Preston to the author. See also *The Mystery of Lord Kitchener's Death*, McCormick
4 Ibid. It was normal practice for the Germans to inscribe torpedoes, bombs and mines with messages to the enemy; *Kurfels* was probably a misreading of the word *Teufels*, meaning 'Devils'.
5 Ibid
6 *Admiralty White Paper Cmd. 2710 (concerning the loss of HMS Hampshire)* (HMSO, London, 1926)
7 The first transcript of the Zimmermann telegram as cited by Hoy
8 *40 OB*, Hoy

CHAPTER 7
1 *Eyes of the Navy*, James
2 Jules Crawford Silber wrote an account of his wartime espionage in a most unassuming manner in his book, *Invisible Weapons*
3 *The Code-Breakers*, David Kahn
4 *U-boat Intelligence 1914–18*, Robert M. Grant
5 Letter from Rear-admiral Welles to the Chairman of the Board of Awards (20 January 1920): reference Welles Papers, Box 203, Item 11
6 *Danger Zone*, E. K. Chatterton (Boston, 1934)
7 'Scapa Flow to the Dover Straits' in *Naval Memoirs*, vol ii, Admiral of the Fleet Sir Roger Keyes
8 Article entitled 'A War Secret' in the *Saturday Evening Post* (23 October 1926)
9 Letter from Rear-admiral Welles to Lieutenant-general Sir John Maxwell (12 February 1919): reference Welles Papers, Box 203, Item 11
10 *Baltic Episode: A Classic of Secret Service in Russian Waters*, Captain Augustus Agar
11 Ibid

CHAPTER 8
1 *The American Black Chamber*, Herbert O. Yardley, the Bobbs-Merrill Co, Indianapolis, 1931
2 *Secret & Urgent*, Fletcher Pratt

3　*Secret Missions: the Story of an Intelligence Officer*, Ellis M. Zacharias (G. P. Putnam, New York, 1946)
4　*The Double Cross System*, Masterman
5　In a letter to the author (June 1974)

CHAPTER 9

1　Cited by David Irving in *Breach of Security*
2　*Schellenberg Memoirs*, Walter Schellenberg, edited and translated by Louis Hagen (André Deutsch, London, 1956)
3　*The Game of the Foxes*, Ladislas Farago
4　In a letter to the author (July 1976)
5　*Zehn Jahre und Zwanzig Tage*, Admiral Karl Doenitz (Bonn, 1958)
6　*The Game of the Foxes*, Farago
7　The actual title of *B-Dienst* was not introduced until later in the war, though it had been operating since the day hostilities broke out and in a slightly different form from that date.
8　*The Ultra Secret*, F. W. Winterbotham (Weidenfeld & Nicolson, London, 1974)
9　Comments by Marshal of the RAF Sir John Slessor in his introduction to *The Ultra Secret*
10　This was the code-name for the XX, or Double-Cross Committee which drew up the briefing plans for the operation of 'turning' German agents to work for the Allied side.
11　*The Double-Cross System*, Masterman
12　*Coroner: a biography of William Bentley Purchase*, Robert Jackson
13　Cited by David Irving in *Breach of Security*
14　*Guilt-Edged*, Merlin Minshall (Bachman & Turner, London, 1975)
15　'Will the Real James Bond please stand up?': an article in the London *Sunday Times* (28 September 1975)
16　Letter from Sir Alexander Glen to the *Sunday Times* (5 October 1975)
17　*Room 39*, Donald McLachlan

CHAPTER 10

1　*The Rising Sun in the Pacific: History of United States Naval Operations in World War II*, vol iii, Samuel E. Morison (Little, Brown & Co, Boston, 1950)
2　For further technical information on the development of US code-tapping in the Pacific see *The Code-Breakers*, Kahn
3　*Captains Without Eyes*, Lyman Kirkpatrick, Jr

CHAPTER 11

1　*Official History of the Canadian Army in the Second World War*, Colonel C. P. Stacey (Ottawa, 1955)
2　Ibid

3 'An Unwritten Chapter in the Life of Ian Fleming,' by Robert Harling, London *Sunday Times* (16 August 1964)

4 See German Intelligence Personnel Records. For further information on the pendulum operations and the Pendulum Institute see *Zum anderen Ufer*, Dr Gerda Walther (1960) and 3 articles entitled '*Der Okkultismus in Dritten Reich*', also by Dr Walther in Neue Wissenschaft (1950–1)

5 *Zehn Jahre und Zwanzig Tage*, Admiral Karl Doenitz (Bonn, 1958)

6 Ibid

7 Ibid

8 *Very Special Intelligence*, Patrick Beesly (Hamish Hamilton, London, 1977)

CHAPTER 12

1 *The Code-Breakers*, David Kahn
2 *Sailor in a Russian Frame*, Commander Courtney
3 Ibid
4 Ibid
5 Ibid
6 *Secret Missions*, Ellis M. Zacharias
7 *History of the US Naval Operations in World War II*, vol ii, Samuel E. Morison

CHAPTER 13

1 Article entitled 'The Pace Quickens in Undersea Research', by Richard Casement, in the London *Times* (16 June 1967)
2 *Science of Peace & War*, Robin Clarke

CHAPTER 14

1 *Soviet Review*, vol II, no 6 (June 1961)
2 Article entitled 'Du Nautilus', in *Science et Vie*, no 509 (Paris, February 1960)
3 Statement in a letter to the London *Daily Telegraph* (1977)
4 Cited in an article by Anthony Mann, entitled 'How Secure is our Collective Security?' in the *Daily Telegraph Magazine* (12 July 1974)
5 *New York Times* (25 May 1974)
6 *International Herald Tribune* (20 February 1973)

CHAPTER 15

1 Article by Bernard T. Feld in the *Stamford Journal of International Studies*

CHAPTER 16

1 Cited in the *US Naval Institute Proceedings* (1976)

2 Article entitled 'Battle for the Oceans' by James Reston, *International Herald Tribune* (22 March 1975)
3 News story of Defence Correspondent Henry Stanhope in the London *Times* (21 March 1975)
4 Television programme *This Week* featured on Thames Television (London, 16 October 1975)

CHAPTER 17
1 Article entitled 'Searching for Interstellar Communications', by G. Cocconi and P. Morrison, in *Nature* (19 September 1961). See also *The Code Breakers*, p 952, where Kahn cites Cocconi and Morrison
2 Cited in article entitled 'We Heard the Gaul's SOS', by Ralph Barker, London *Sunday Express* (16 January 1977)
3 *Scottish Daily Record* (12 April 1977)
4 *International Herald-Tribune* (29 May 1974)

Bibliography

Abshagen, Karl Heinz. *Canaris* (Union Verlag, Stuttgart)

Agar, Captain Augustus, RN. *Baltic Episode: A Classic of Secret Service in Russian Waters* (Hodder & Stoughton, London, 1963)

Beesly, Patrick. *Very Special Intelligence* (Hamish Hamilton, London, 1977)

Bennett, Geoffrey. *Nelson The Commander* (Batsford, London, 1972)

Bywater, H. C. *Their Secret Purposes* (London, 1932)

Carnegie endowment for International Peace: Official Documents Relating to the World War (New York, 1923)

Chatelle, A. *Le Base Navale du Havre* (Paris, 1949)

Clarke, Robin. *Science of Peace & War* (Jonathan Cape, London, 1971)

Colvin, Ian. *Chief of Intelligence: Was Canaris, Hitler's Chief of Intelligence, A British Agent?* (Gollancz, London, 1951)

Courtney, Cdr Anthony, RN. *Sailor in a Russian Frame* (Johnson, London, 1968)

Davis, Vincent. *The Admirals' Lobby* (North Carolina University Press and Oxford University Press, London, 1968)

Dinklage, L. *U-Boat-Fahrer Under Kamelsreiter: Kriegsfahrten Eienes Deutschen Unterseebootes* (Stuttgart, 1939)

Doenitz, Admiral Karl. *Zehn Jahre und Zwanzig Tage* (Bonn, 1958)

Ewing, A. W. *The Man of Room 40: The Life of Sir Alfred Ewing* (Hutchinson, London, 1939),

Farago, Ladislas. *The Game of the Foxes: British and German Intelligence Operations & Personalities Which Changed the Course of the Second World War* (Hodder & Stoughton, London, 1972)

Grant, Robert M. *U-Boat Intelligence 1914–18* (Putnam, London, 1969)

Green, James Robert. *The First Sixty Years of the Office of Naval Intelligence* (American University, Washington, 1963) (available from University Microfilms, Inc, Ann Arbor, Michigan, microfilms catalogue no M–534)

Hoy, Hugh Cleland. *40 OB or How the War Was Won* (Hutchinson, London, 1932)

Ireland, Dr John de Courcy. *The Sea & The Easter Rising*

Irving, David. *Breach of Security: The German Secret Intelligence File on Events Leading to the Second World War* (William Kimber, London, 1968)

James, Admiral Sir William. *The British Navy in Adversity* (Longman, London)

———. *The Eyes of the Navy: A Biographical Study of Admiral Sir Reginald Hall* (Methuen, London, 1955)

Kahn, David. *The Code-Breakers: The Story of Secret Writing* (Weidenfeld & Nicolson, London, 1968)

Kittredge, Tracy Barrett. *Naval Lessons of the Great War* (Doubleday & Page, New York, 1921)

Knox, Captain Dudley. *A History of the United States Navy* (G. P. Putnam, New York, 1936)

Keyes, Admiral of the Fleet, Sir Roger. *Scapa Flow to the Dover Straits* (London, 1935)

Kirkpatrick, Lyman B., Jr. *Captains Without Eyes: Intelligence Failures in World War II* (Rupert Hart-Davies, London, 1970)

Masterman, Sir John C. *The Double-Cross System in the War of 1939–45* (Yale University Press, 1972)

McCormick, Donald. *The Mystery of Lord Kitchener's Death* (Putnam, London, 1959)

McLachlan, Donald. *Room 39: Naval Intelligence in Action 1939–45* (Weidenfeld & Nicolson, London, 1968)

Newhouse, John. *Cold Dawn* (Holt, Rinehart & Winston, New York, 1972)

Norman, Bruce. *Secret Warfare: The Battle of Codes and Cyphers* (David & Charles, Newton Abbot, 1973)

Packard, W. H. 'Intelligence & the Navy', *Naval Review* (Annapolis, Md, Naval Institute, 1968)

Paullin, Charles O. *Paullin's History of Naval Administration 1775–1911* (Annapolis, Md, Naval Institute, 1968)

Pratt, Fletcher. *Secret & Urgent: The Story of Codes & Ciphers* (Robert Hale, London, 1939)

Read, Conyers. *Mr. Secretary Walsingham & the Policy of Queen Elizabeth*, 3 vols (Oxford University Press, 1925)

Rintelen, Captain Franz von Kleist. *The Dark Invader: Wartime Reminiscences of a German Naval Intelligence Officer* (Lovat Dickson, London, 1933)

Rowan, Richard Wolmer and Deindorfer, Robert G. *Secret Service: Thirty-three Centuries of Espionage* (Hawthorn Books, New York, 1967)

Sachse, William L. 'Our Naval Attaché System: Its Origins and Development to 1917' *United States Naval Institute Proceedings*, vol 72, no 5 (May, 1946)

Scheer, Admiral. *Germany's High Seas Fleet in the World War*

Schellenberg, Walter. *The Schellenberg Memoirs* (Deutsch, London, 1956)

Scott, J. D. *Vickers: A History* (Weidenfeld & Nicolson, London, 1962)

Simpson, Colin. *Lusitania* (Longman, London, 1972)

Stacey, Colonel C. P. *Official History of the Canadian Army in the Second World War* (Ottawa, 1955)

Thompson, J. W. and Padover, S. K. *A Record of Espionage & Double-Dealing 1500–1815* (Jarrolds, London, 1937)

United States Government Printing Office. *Pearl Harbor Attack: United States Congress Joint Committee on the Investigation of the Pearl Harbor Attack* (Washington, 1946)

United States Navy Department. *United States Naval History: A Bibliography*, 6th edition (1972)

Winterbotham, F. W. *The Ultra Secret* (Weidenfeld & Nicolson, London, 1974)

Yardley, Herbert O. *The American Black Chamber* (The Bobbs-Merrill Co, Indianapolis, 1931)

Zacharias, Captain Ellis M. *Secret Missions: The Story of an Intelligence Officer* (G. P. Putnam, New York, 1946)

Acknowledgements

I should like to pay tribute to the US Navy's *United States Naval History: A Bibliography*, which is frequently brought up to date and contains an enormously helpful guide to the by-paths of which a researcher in this field must take cognisance. It is a pity that other navies have not followed suit in this respect.

I should also like to express my appreciation of the help given to me by the International Institute of Strategic Studies in London; the Public Records Office in London; the Department of US Navy Naval Historical Research Centre in Washington, and especially to Mr W. J. Morgan, Head of its Historical Research Branch; to Mr Lawrence Freedman, of Nuffield College, Oxford, whose advice on the latest trends in anti-submarine warfare was invaluable; to Dr John de Courcy Ireland, of the Maritime Institute of Ireland; to the late Admiral Sir Lionel Preston RN, whose memory for the details of events in World War I remained impeccable to the end of his life; to various former shipmates and friends in the Royal Navy past and present, and officers of the US and German navies who have helped unobtrusively and anonymously but with total selflessness.

Index

Adams, John, 14, 24, 27
Agar, Capt Augustus, RN, 131, 205, 278
Alan, A. J., 76
Amberger, Kapitan Gustav, 106–9
American Civil War, 13, 38, 43–4
American War of Independence, 11–14, 21, 33–4, 38
Anderson, Adml W. S., USN, 166
ANSWEPS, 271
Arab-Israeli War, 1967, 224–5
Arab-Israeli War, 1973, 224, 226–7
Aspinall, W. H., 38
Assault Unit No 30, 185–7, 199
Aston, Sir George, 96
Atlantic, Battle of 1939–45, 182–3, 190–5
Auckland, Lord, see Eden, Hon Wm, 20, 275
Audacious, HMS, 103
Aurora, HMS, 181

Backhouse, Adml Sir Roger, 146
Baldwin, Robert H., 221
Balfour, Lord, 98, 112, 116
Bancroft, Edward, 20–1, 24, 26–7
Barclay, Capt Robert, RN, 34
Barnaby de Pedrosa, 10
Bartlett, Capt John R., USN, 58
Battenberg, Adml Prince Louis of, 60–1
Bauer, Wilhelm, 37–9, 40
Beach, Thomas, 40–1, 46, 59
Beatty, Adml Sir David (later Adml of the Fleet Lord Beatty), 104
Beaufort, Adml Sir Francis, RN, 46, 276
Beaumont, Adml Sir Lewis, RN, 49, 59
Beitzen, Ober-Leutnant Kurt, 106–9
Bell, Edward, 86, 99, 112
Beresford, Adml Lord Charles, 48–9, 59
Bethell, Capt, RN, 65
Binney, Cdr George, RNVR (later Sir George), 180–1
Bismarck, 191–2
Blackett, Lord, 250

Blake, George, 199–200
Blake, Adml Robert, 11
Boy-Ed, Capt Karl, 78, 80, 83
Brandon, Lt, RN (later Cdr), 64–5
Bridge, Capt (afterwards Adml Sir Cyprian), 49
Buck, Ensign Wm H., 58
Burchard, Adolf, 77
Bushnell, David, 13, 38
Buzzard, Capt (later Rear-Adml Sir Anthony), 201

Camara, Admiral, 58
Campbell, Rear-Admiral Donald, 31
Canaris, Adml Wilhelm, 88–90, 137–9, 149, 151–3, 192–4
Carranza, President of Mexico, 112
Carranza, Lt Ramon, 52–3, 55
Carver, Lt Clifford N., USN, 129
Casement, Sir Roger, 80, 114–15
Cator, Lt R. P., RN (later Capt), 46–8, 276
Cervera, Adml, 58
Chaco War, 55
Chadwick, Lt-Cdr F. E., USN, 52
Chandler, Wm E., 44
Chatterton, E. K., 124, 278
Childers, Erskine, 64, 277
Churchill, Winston (later Sir), 96, 101, 142–3, 148, 153, 155, 183–4, 193, 208
CIA links with naval intelligence, 208–11, 228, 251, 254–6, 265
Clarke, Russell, 70
Clemenceau, Georges, 58
Combat Intelligence Unit, USN, 170, 174, 176
Cornwallis, Lord, 13
Courtney, Cdr Anthony, RN, 204–5, 280
Cromie, Capt Francis, RN, 132
Cumming, Cdr, RN (later Capt Sir Mansfield Cumming), 131–2
Curtis, Lt-Cdr Dunstan, RN, 165, 186
Custance, Adml, RN, 59–60

Davis, Professor Vincent, 203
Deane, Silas, 14, 21–2, 26
de Gaulle, General, 214
del Campo, Fernandez, 57
Denham, Capt Henry, RN, 190–2, 196
Denning, Rear-Adml Norman, RN, 196, 201, 210
Denniston, Cdr A. G., RN, 70, 79, 155
Despard, Capt Max, 165
Dewey, Commodore George, USN, 56–7
Dieppe Raid, 158, 183–5
Doenitz, Admiral Karl, 149–51, 153, 156, 182, 194, 200, 279
Dolphins, use of for intelligence purposes, 237
Domville, Adml Sir Barry, 139
Downing, George, 56–7
Dukes, Sir Paul, 131
Dulles, Allen, 173
Dumba, Count Constantin, 85

Eden, Hon Wm, 20–1, 275
Edwards, Rear-Adml R. S., USN, 182
Eisberg, spy-weather-research ship, 232
Emden, 78
Enver Pasha, 97
Erie, Battle of Lake, 33
Ernst, Karl Gustav, 63
Ewing, Sir Alfred, 67–9, 74–5, 78, 84, 111
Ewing, A. W., 74

Falkland Islands, Battle of, 147
Fenian Ram, 41
Fisher, Adml of the Fleet, Lord Fisher, 96–8
Fitzmaurice, Gerald, 91
Fitzpatrick, Dr, 27
Fleming, Lt-Cdr Ian, RNVR, 162–3, 165–6, 185–9, 280
Forbes, John M., 38
Ford, President Gerald, 233
Franklin, Benjamin, 14–28, 201, 275
Friedman, William, 137
Fuchida, Cdr Mitsuo, 174
Fuji, Admiral, 67
Fulton, Robert, 31–2, 276

Galloway, Joseph, 24, 275
Gaul, British trawler, loss of, 258–62, 266, 281
Gaunt, Capt (afterwards Commodore and Adml Sir Guy), 85–6, 102, 130
Glen, Lt-Cdr, RNVR (later Sir Alan), 164–5, 279
Glomar Challenger, 255
Glomar Explorer, 255, 257
Godfrey, Capt (later Adml Sir John), 146, 155–6, 162, 166, 186
Goering, Marshal Hermann, 194
Golst, Horst von der, 78
Gomez-Beare, Lt-Cdr Don, RNVR, 139, 160–1

Gordon, Col Chas (later General), 45–6
Gorshkov, Admiral, 247, 253
Graves, Dr Armgaard, 70
Grenfell, Cdr Hubert, RN, 45

Hall, Capt W. H., RN, 46, 48–9, 64
Hall, Capt W. R., RN (later Adml Sir Reginald), 64, 68–9, 76, 78–9, 85–90, 93–5, 96–103, 105, 110–17, 122, 127, 129–31, 133, 136, 146, 162, 277
Hampshire, HMS, 105–6, 137
Harling, Lt Robert, RNVR, 186, 280
Henty-Creer, Lt, RN, 197
Hillgarth, Cdr Alan, RN, 160
Holland, John Philip, 40–1
Holtwick, Lt Jack S., Jr, USN, 169
Hood, HMS, 191
Hoover, President Herbert, 136
Horton, Adml Sir Max, 194
Hoy, Hugh Cleland, 83–4, 86, 93–4, 99, 111, 112
Hughes, Howard, 255–6
Hunt, William H., 43–4

'Incidents at Sea' Agreement, 1972, 231

James, Adml Sir William, 42, 86, 94, 105–6, 116, 276
Japanese Defence Agency, 252
Jefferson, President Thos., 24
Jellicoe, Adml Sir John (later Adml of the Fleet Lord), 104, 127, 168
Johnson, President Lyndon B., 179
Jutland, Battle of, 105–6, 111

Kenworthy, Cdr Joseph, RN, 101–2
Keyes, Adml Sir Roger (later Adml of the Fleet), 184
Kimmel, Adml, USN, 178
Kirk, Capt Alan, USN (later Admiral), 166–7, 176
Kitchener, Fld-Marshal Lord, 96, 105–6, 110
Knox, Capt Dudley W., USN, 134
Korean War, 203
Kroger, Helen and Peter, 207

Laird, Melvin, 246–7
Lanphier, Lt Tom, USN, 177
Lansing, Robert M., 101
Lee, Arthur, 14, 20, 24–6, 276
Liberty, USS, 225–6, 231, 235
Lincoln, Trebitsch, 92–5, 278
Lody, Lt Carl Hans, 77–8
Longley-Cook, Vice-Adml E. W., RN, 201
Lusitania, SS, 99–102, 114

MacDougall, Capt W. D., USN, 134
Madison, USS, 234
Magdeburg, 74–5, 79, 84, 103, 122
Magnetic Anomaly Detector (MAD), 270

Maine, USS, 53–5, 62
Mallet, Sir Victor, 181
March, Juan, 139–40
Martin, Daniel B., USN Eng-in-chief, 38
Marshall, General George, 178
Marryat, Capt F., 33
Mason, A. E. W., 92
Mason, Lt-Cdr Michael, RNVR, 163
Mason, Lt T. B. Myers, USN, 44–5, 66
Matchekhine, Alexandre, 253
Matsuo, Vice-Adml, 66
Midway Island, Battle of, 175–8, 203
Miller, Shipwright E. C., RN, 128
Minshall, Lt-Cdr Merlin, RNVR 151–2, 279
Minto, Lord, 30
Mitchell, Capt John, USN, 177
Mitoya, Lt-Cdr Sesu, 176
Mitsui Bussan Kaisha, 66
Montagu, Lt-Cdr Ewen, RNVR, 160
Morismura, Tadasi, *see also* Yoshi-kawa, 171
Morrison, Cdr R. J., RN, 47–8
Mountbatten of Burma, Adml of the Fleet Lord, 183, 185, 209–10

Nelson, Adml Lord, 30–1, 33, 276
Nelson, Senator Gaylord, 213
Niblack, Rear-Adml A. P., USN, 134
Nicholas, Sir Harris, 9, 275
NID (British Naval Intelligence Division):
  birth of, 44
  early history, 48–53, 59–61, 62–5, 68–73
  World War I, 74–6, 78–81, 105, 124, 128–32, 148–50
  World War II, 145, 153–64, 180–2, 184–96, 198, 201
  decline of, 205–6, 209–11, 215–16
NID 10, 161
Nimitz, Adml Chester W., USN, 176–8
NOBSKA summer study school, 208
North Pole, 22, 209
Norwegian campaign, 1940, 154–5

Oberkommando de Kriegsmarine (OKM), 138
Oertel, Albert, *see* Wehring, 148–50, 152
Oliver, Capt (later Rear-Admiral Sir Henry) RN, 67–9, 71–2
ONI (US Office of Naval Intelligence):
  birth of, 43–5
  early history, 51–2
  in Spanish-American War, 52–6, 60
  growth of, 60–1, 65–6, 83
  World War I, 117, 123, 129–30, 133–4
  World War II, 165, 168–9, 173, 176, 178, 180, 182
  post-war years, 202–3, 206–8, 211–13, 230, 234, 254, 258, 271

Operation Holy Stone, 235–6
Operation Hornbeam, 267
Operation Magic, 175, 177
Operation Mincemeat, 159
Operation Rubble, 180
Operation Torch, 183
Oswald, Richard, 22

Page Dr Walter, 88, 99, 278
Palmerston, Lord, 38
Papen, Franz von, 78, 81
Pearl Harbor, Japanese attack on, 165, 168–79
Pendulum Institute of Berlin, 190
Perry, Capt Matthew C., USN, 37
Perry, Capt Oliver Hazard, USN, 33
Philby, H. A. R. ('Kim'), 192, 205–7
Pitt, William (Earl of Chatham), 276
Pitt, William (The Younger), 31–2
Playfair, Lyon, 50
Pollock, Oliver, 13
Pound, Adml of the Fleet Sir Dudley, RN, 196
Preston, Capt (later Adml Sir Lionel), RN, 105, 109, 110, 278
Prien, Lt Gunther, 148–9, 150
Primorye, Soviet spy ship, 232
Project Caesar, 270
Project Jennifer, 254–8
Project Sanguine, 213, 248–9
Project Seafarer, 248
Project Sea Spider, 270
Proxmire, Senator William, 234
Pueblo, US spy ship, 225, 234–5
Pulteney, William, 22
Purple Machine, 137, 169, 171

Q-boats, 120

Reed, Joseph, 25
Regnart, Capt, RN, 65
Richardson, Leon Burr, 44
Riheldaffer, Cdr J. L., USN, 165
Riley, Lt-Cdr Quentin, RN, 186
Rintelen, Capt Franz von Kleist, 80–7
Robertson, James, 30, 276
Rochefort, Capt Joseph, USN, 170, 174–5, 178
Rodgers, Commodore C. R. P., USN, 43
Rodgers, Lt R. P., USN (later Capt), 52, 58, 66
Rodgers, William, 259
Roeder, Kapitan Hans, 189–90
Room 39, 166
Room 40, 74, 83, 103–4, 111–14, 122, 137, 138, 166
Room 1649, 137
Room 2646, 137
Roosevelt, President Franklin D., 177–8, 193
Rose, Ober-Leutnant Hans, 120
Rowlett, Frank B., 179
Royal Oak, HMS, 147–50, 152

Rushbrooke, Rear-Adml E. G. N., RN (later Vice-Adml), 162, 186
Russo-Japanese War, 61–2

SACLANT, 204
Safford, Cdr Laurence F., USN, 134
St Vincent, Adml Lord, 32
Sakata, Michita, 252
SALT Talks, 236, 241–2, 244, 255, 261, 264
Santa Cruz, Marquis of, 10
Scharnhorst, 195
Scheer, Adml von, 124
Schellenberg, Walter, 149–50
Schroeder, Capt Seaton, USN, 66
Shelburne, Lord, 20, 22
Sidmouth, Lord, 31
Sigsbee, Capt Chas D., USN, 52, 62
Silber, Jules Crawford, 118–20, 278
Simpson, Cdr Edward, USN, 43
Sims, Lt (later Adml W. S.) USN, 52–3, 55, 99, 116–17, 122–3, 129
Slessor, Marshal of the RAF, Sir John, 156
Smith, W. H., 45
Southard, Secretary of the US Navy, 34
Spanish-American War, 51–6, 62
Spy ships, 212–37, 262–3, 267–9
Stammer, Capt Karl, 77
Stanhope, Lord, 140
Steinhauer, Gustav, 62–3, 70, 151
Stimson, Henry, US Secretary of State, 136
Stormont, Lord, 20, 275
Szek, Alexander, 111

Talmadge, Major Benjamin, 11
Teneriffe, Marquis of, 51
Thomson, Sir Basil, 115
Tirpitz, 195–7
Townsend, Robert, 11–12
Trench, Capt, RM, 64–5
Trench, Capt Wilfrid, RN, 131
Troup, Rear-Adml, RN (later Vice-Adml Sir James), 146
Tryon, Adml Sir George, RN, 46
Turner, Adml Richmond K., USN, 176

Under-Sea Long Range Missile Systems, 241, 269

Ultra cipher-breaking project, 155–6
US Naval Mission in London, 1940–5, 166–7

Vassall, John, 206–8
Vigenère, Blaize de, 46, 50
Villeneuve, Adml, 30–1

Waldheim, Kurt, 257
Walker, Commodore John G., USN, 51
Walsingham, Sir Francis, 9–10, 76, 275
Ward, Ensign Henry H., USN, 58
Washington, General George, 14, 27, 275n
Wehring, Kapitan Alfred, *see* Oertel, 148–9
Welles, Rear-Adml Roger, USN, 116, 123, 130, 278
Wentworth, Paul, 21–2, 26, 275n
Weymouth, Lord, 21
Wharton, Thomas, 20
Wilbraham, Sir Philip Baker, 76
Wilkinson, Rear-Adml T. S., USN, 176
Wilkins, John, Bishop of Chester, 10–11
Williams, John, 20
Wilson, President Woodrow, 88, 113–14
Winn, Cdr Charles Rodger (later Rt Hon Lord Justice) RNVR, 182, 195
Winterbotham, Group-Capt F. W., 156, 279
Woodhull, Abraham, 12
Wright, M. Fisher, 44

Yamamoto, Adml Koroku, 170, 174, 176–7
Yardley, Herbert, 133–5, 168, 278
Yoshikawa, Takeo, *see also* Morismura, 173–5
Young, Filson, 103

Zacharias, Lt Ellis M., USN, 137, 211, 279
Zaharoff, Sir Basil, 52–3, 65–8, 277
Zeppelins, intelligence from, 121
Zimmermann Telegram, 111–13, 130, 278
Zumwalt, Adml Elmo R., USN, 254

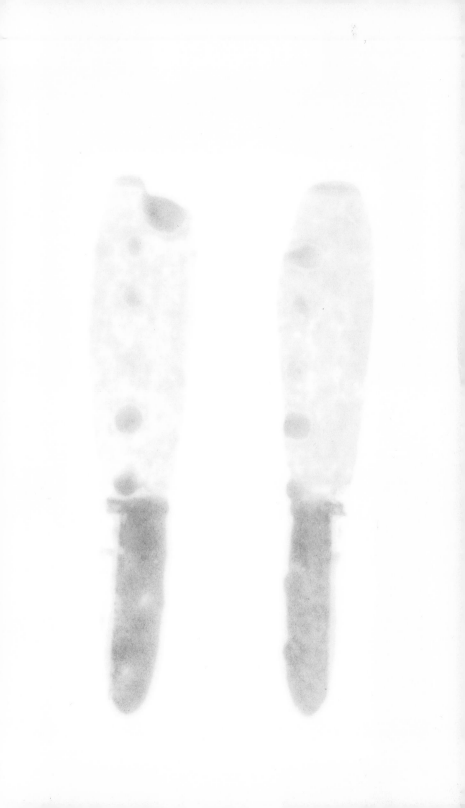